"Hamilton and Curran's concept of 'just green enough' has become a rallying cry for academics and activists trying to decouple environmental clean-up from high-end residential and commercial development. The cases in this timely and excellent book illuminate this goal, offering us hope for a transition toward more just sustainabilities."
– **Julian Agyeman,** *Professor of Urban and Environmental Policy and Planning,*
Tufts University, USA

"This is an essential book demonstrating the need for a new ecological, political, and social imagination to place interactional, reparative, distributional, and participative justice at the center of green city planning. Only through transformative green planning and creative lasting alliances will green interventions be public goods rather than environmental privileges."
– **Isabelle Anguelovski,** *ICREA Research Professor and Director,*
Barcelona Lab for Urban Environmental Justice and Sustainability,
Universitat Autònoma de Barcelona, Spain

"In 2012, Curran and Hamilton came up with 'just green enough,' a welcome vision for environmentally-minded urban development that foregrounded social justice and equity. Six years later, the concept's originators bring us this provocative look at the pitfalls and promises of JGE strategies, offering both sobering assessments and hopeful ways forward."
– **Melissa Checker,** *Associate Professor of Anthropology and Environmental*
Psychology, the CUNY Graduate Center, USA

"As cities across the world are 'going green' through revitalization projects geared toward resilience and sustainability, they struggle with a major challenge: avoiding displacement and disenfranchisement associated with gentrification. This refreshing, provocative volume brings together leading scholars who dare to move beyond critique, by exploring and proposing strategies and solutions."
– **Ryan Holifield,** *Associate Professor of Geography, University of*
Wisconsin-Milwaukee, USA

"*Just Green Enough* brings passion, imagination, along with some redemption to the sustainable development paradox. With a global reach, the book's contributors eruditely reveal important insights and examples of diverse social relations that engender positive urban environmental change. A must read for students concerned with progressive social change." ·
– **Robert Krueger,** *Director, Environmental and Sustainability Studies,*
Worcester Polytechnic Institute, USA

JUST GREEN ENOUGH

While global urban development increasingly takes on the mantle of sustainability and "green urbanism," both the ecological and equity impacts of these developments are often overlooked. One result is what has been called environmental gentrification, a process in which environmental improvements lead to increased property values and the displacement of long-term residents. The specter of environmental gentrification is now at the forefront of urban debates about how to accomplish environmental improvements without massive displacement.

In this context, the editors of this volume identified a strategy called "just green enough" based on field work in Greenpoint, Brooklyn, that uncouples environmental cleanup from high-end residential and commercial development. A "just green enough" strategy focuses explicitly on social justice and environmental goals as defined by local communities, those people who have been most negatively affected by environmental disamenities, with the goal of keeping them in place to enjoy any environmental improvements. It is not about short-changing communities, but about challenging the veneer of green that accompanies many projects with questionable ecological and social justice impacts, and looking for alternative, sometimes surprising, forms of greening such as creating green spaces and ecological regeneration within protected industrial zones.

Just Green Enough is a theoretically rigorous, practical, global, and accessible volume exploring, through varied case studies, the complexities of environmental improvement in an era of gentrification as global urban policy. It is ideal for use as a textbook at both undergraduate and graduate levels in urban planning, urban studies, urban geography, and sustainability programs.

Winifred Curran is an Associate Professor of Geography at DePaul University, USA.

Trina Hamilton is an Associate Professor of Geography at the State University of New York at Buffalo (UB), USA.

ROUTLEDGE EQUITY, JUSTICE AND THE SUSTAINABLE CITY SERIES

Series editors: Julian Agyeman, Zarina Patel, AbdouMaliq Simone and Stephen Zavestoski

This series positions equity and justice as central elements of the transition toward sustainable cities. The series introduces critical perspectives and new approaches to the practice and theory of urban planning and policy that ask how the world's cities can become "greener" while becoming more fair, equitable and just.

Routledge Equity Justice and the Sustainable City series addresses sustainable city trends in the global North and South and investigates them for their potential to ensure a transition to urban sustainability that is equitable and just for all. These trends include municipal climate action plans; resource scarcity as tipping points into a vortex of urban dysfunction; inclusive urbanization; "complete streets" as a tool for realizing more "livable cities"; the use of information and analytics toward the creation of "smart cities".

The series welcomes submissions for high-level, cutting-edge research books that push thinking about sustainability, cities, justice and equity in new directions by challenging current conceptualizations and developing new ones. The series offers theoretical, methodological, and empirical advances that can be used by professionals and as supplementary reading in courses in urban geography, urban sociology, urban policy, environment and sustainability, development studies, planning, and a wide range of academic disciplines.

Pragmatic Justifications for the Sustainable City
Action in the Common Place
Meg Holden

Sustainability Policy, Planning and Gentrification in Cities
Susannah Bunce

Housing Sustainability in Low Carbon Cities
Ralph Horne

Just Green Enough
Urban Development and Environmental Gentrification
Edited by Winifred Curran and Trina Hamilton

JUST GREEN ENOUGH

Urban Development and Environmental Gentrification

Edited by Winifred Curran and Trina Hamilton

Routledge
Taylor & Francis Group

LONDON AND NEW YORK

from Routledge

First published 2018
by Routledge
2 Park Square, Milton Park, Abingdon, Oxon OX14 4RN

and by Routledge
711 Third Avenue, New York, NY 10017

Routledge is an imprint of the Taylor & Francis Group, an informa business

British Library Cataloguing in Publication Data
A catalogue record for this book is available from the British Library

Library of Congress Cataloging in Publication Data
Names: Curran, Winifred, editor. | Hamilton, Trina, editor.
Title: Just green enough : urban development and environmental gentrification / edited by Winifred Curran and Trina Hamilton.
Description: Abingdon, Oxon ; New York, NY : Routledge, 2018. | Series: Routledge equity, justice and the sustainable city series | Includes bibliographical references and index.
Identifiers: LCCN 2017033211 | ISBN 9781138713796 (hardback) | ISBN 9781138713826 (pbk.) | ISBN 9781315229515 (ebook)
Subjects: LCSH: Sustainable urban development--United States. | Gentrification--Environmental aspects--United States. | Urban policy--United States. | Social justice--United States.
Classification: LCC HT243.U6 J87 2018 | DDC 307.1/4160973--dc23
LC record available at https://lccn.loc.gov/2017033211

ISBN: 978-1-138-71379-6 (hbk)
ISBN: 978-1-138-71382-6 (pbk)
ISBN: 978-1-315-22951-5 (ebk)

Typeset in Bembo
by Taylor & Francis Books

CONTENTS

ILLUSTRATIONS

Figures

Tables

CONTRIBUTORS

Fernando J. Bosco is Professor of Geography at San Diego State University. His research interests include the geographic dimensions of social movements and collective action, geography and human rights, social and political geographies of children, young people and their families, food geographies in urban contexts, emotional geographies, geographic thought, and qualitative research methods.

Jay E. Bowen is a PhD candidate in the Department of Geography, University of Kentucky. He studies agriculture in Seoul's greenbelt within the context of the region's rapid socioeconomic transformation. He researches how recent sustainability initiatives and economic restructuring interweave with the many different types of agriculture across one of the world's most populated urban areas. In paying particular attention to the individuals who perform this work, whether for pleasure, politics, tradition, to supplement their diet, or to earn a living, he also desires to unravel some of the complexities of the political economic changes underway in the region.

Jason A. Byrne is an internationally recognized Associate Professor of Urban and Environmental Planning in Griffith University's School of Environment (Gold Coast, Australia). A geographer and planner, Jason's research addresses urban political ecologies of green space, climate change adaptation, and environmental justice. He has over 100 scholarly publications, including a multiple-award-winning co-edited book, *Australian Environmental Planning: Challenges and Future Prospects* (Routledge). Jason has collaborated on international research projects investigating obesogenic urban environments (USA) and park ecosystem services (China), among others. Jason previously worked as a planning officer, environmental officer, and policy writer with the Western Australian government.

Winifred Curran is an Associate Professor of Geography at DePaul University. Her research focuses on understanding the effects of gentrification on the urban landscape, looking at labor, policing, education, environmental gentrification, and the gendering of urban policy. She is the author of *Gender and Gentrification* (2018).

Sarah Dooling is an independent researcher and consultant to city agencies and non-profits involved in green infrastructure, vulnerability assessments, and climate resilience planning. She is an expert on the social justice and equity dimensions of ecological design projects, and pays particular attention to the economic impacts on low-income and politically marginalized communities. She developed the idea of *ecological gentrification*, which describes the economic hardships for low-income households created by greening-up low-income neighborhoods in growing cities.

Peter V. Hall is Professor of Urban Studies at Simon Fraser University in Vancouver, Canada. His research examines the connections between port cities, seaports, and logistics, as well as community, local economic, and employment development. His publications include the co-edited *Integrating Seaports and Trade Corridors* (Ashgate, 2011) and *Cities, Regions and Flow* (Routledge, 2013), and the co-authored *Proposal Economy* (UBC, 2015). He is an Associate Editor of the *Journal of Transport Geography*. Between 2012 and 2015 he directed the Reclaiming the New Westminster Waterfront Research Partnership which included museum, education, labour, community, and academic partners.

Trina Hamilton is an Associate Professor of Geography at the State University of New York at Buffalo (UB). Her work focuses on how government regulation, social and environmental justice activism, and market mechanisms such as ethical consumerism drive corporate change and sustainable development. In addition to her work on the urban environment, Trina is currently working on a National Science Foundation-funded research project on the ethical diamond trade. She is co-director of the UB Center for Trade, Environment and Development and is actively involved with UB's Baldy Center for Law and Social Policy.

Pascale Joassart-Marcelli is Professor of Geography and Chair of the Urban Studies Program at San Diego State University. She holds a PhD in Political Economy and Public Policy from the University of Southern California. Her research focuses on the relationships between food, ethnicity, and place. She is interested in the role of food in structuring everyday life in immigrant and low-income urban neighborhoods and has received funding from the National Science Foundation to pursue research on this topic (with F.J. Bosco). She teaches Geography of Food, Food Justice, and Geography of Cities, among other courses.

Leslie Kern is an Associate Professor in the Department of Geography and Environment at Mount Allison University. Her research areas include gentrification, gender, embodiment, and urban environmental justice, as well as feminist methodologies. Her work appears in *Gender, Place, and Culture, Environment and Planning D*, as well as in a monograph from UBC Press titled *Sex and the Revitalized City* (2010).

Esther G. Kim is a PhD student in the Department of Environmental Science, Policy, and Management at the University of California, Berkeley. Her dissertation research involved investigating the environmental justice implications of the restoration and sustainable management of the Los Angeles River watershed. She is interested in the cultural politics of urban environmental issues, including the ways in which discourses and practices of urban sustainability intersect with racialized landscapes, place-based identities, and evolving conceptualizations of "urban nature".

Jessica Ty Miller is an Assistant Professor in the Earth and Environmental Studies Department at Montclair State University. She focuses on human-environment interaction through environmental perception and policy, identity, and planning. Her work in the past focused on the impacts of environmental policy and the production of urban space through greening policies, environmental perception of polluted spaces, and environmental justice. Her interests include environmental justice and environmental restoration, and how this process is shifting as a result of changing social and political landscapes. She has held planning positions in the past including environmental, sustainability, and transportation planning positions.

Priti Narayan is an activist-researcher, studying slum policy and practice in Chennai, India. She is associated with Pennurimai Iyakkam, a 38-year-old women's rights movement, and was earlier a researcher at Transparent Chennai, an action research group studying issues concerning the urban poor. Her current research as a PhD candidate in Geography at Rutgers University ethnographically examines how urban poor groups access land and basic services in the absence of legal land ownership. She has a Master's degree in Sociology from Columbia University.

Joshua Newell is an Assistant Professor in the School of Environment and Sustainability at the University of Michigan. He is a broadly trained human-environment geographer whose research focuses on questions related to urban sustainability, resource consumption, and environmental and social justice. His research approach is often multi-scalar and integrative and, in addition to theory and method found in geography and urban planning, he draws upon principles and tools of industrial ecology and spatial analysis. His work is supported by the U.S. National Science Foundation, NASA, and the U.S. Department of Agriculture, among others.

Hamil Pearsall is an Assistant Professor in the Geography and Urban Studies Department at Temple University. Her research bridges several themes in human environment and human geography: the social dimension of sustainability;

environmental justice and health; and community resilience to environmental and economic stressors. Her recent work has focused on environmental gentrification, the role of vacant land in urban greening efforts, and the impact of environmental justice on urban sustainability planning.

Noah Quastel is a Postdoctoral Fellow in the Geography Department of Simon Fraser University in Burnaby, Canada. With a background as both a lawyer and a geographer, he has conducted academic research on market regulation across diverse economic sectors, including electricity, mining, and housing industries. With research rooted in Western Canada but scaling outward to encompass national and global scales and networks, he seeks to understand the role of law and the state in mediating and transforming nature-society relations.

Christoph D. D. Rupprecht is a geographer working on green space, food, agriculture, and degrowth in Asia. He is a project researcher in the FEAST project at the Research Institute for Humanity and Nature in Kyoto (Japan) and an adjunct lecturer at the University of Tokyo, Kyoto University, and Doshisha University. He holds a PhD in urban geography, planning and ecology from Griffith University (Australia), and a Magister Artium in Japanese studies, biology and philosophy from Ludwig-Maximilians-Universität München (Germany).

Pamela Stern is Assistant Professor of Anthropology at Simon Fraser University. Her work focuses on the ways in which citizenship is enacted in the diverse communities in Canada. She has published in *Anthropologica*, *Critique of Anthropology*, *American Anthropologist*, *The Canadian Geographer*, and other journals. She is co-author (with Peter V. Hall) of *The Proposal Economy: Neoliberal Citizenship in 'Ontario's Most Historic Town'* (UBC Press, 2015) about contemporary life in the historic silver mining town of Cobalt, Ontario. She is also the editor of *Reading Cultural Anthropology: An Ethnographic Introduction* (Oxford Canada, 2015).

Julie Sze is Professor and the Founding Chair of American Studies at the University of California at Davis. She was also the founding director of the Environmental Justice Project for John Muir Institute of the Environment. She has published two books, numerous articles, and is the editor of a forthcoming edited collection on sustainability and social justice. Her research is on environmental inequalities, the relationship between social movements and policy implementation and in the areas of public and environmental humanities. Her commitments are to crossing boundaries: between campus-community, disciplinary fields, in collaborations with graduate students and in her undergraduate teaching.

Dan Trudeau is a Professor of Geography at Macalester College. His research interests include the political economy of public–private partnerships, the cultural politics of landscape production, and the social equity implications of urban design initiatives such as the New Urbanism. His scholarship has been published in journals including *Cultural Geographies, Environment and Planning, GeoForum, Journal of Planning Education and Research, Political Geography, Urban Geography,* and *Urban Studies.*

Jennifer Wolch is the William W. Wurster Dean of the UC Berkeley College of Environmental Design, where she is Professor of City and Planning. Her work has focused on urban homelessness, affordable housing, and human service delivery; the urban voluntary sector; urban sprawl and alternative approaches to city-building; human-animal relations in cities; physical activity and public health; and improving access to urban parks and recreational resources. Wolch has published several books and over 140 articles and book chapters. She received the Guggenheim Foundation Fellowship and Honors for Research from the American Association of Geographers.

Elizabeth Yeampierre is Executive Director of UPROSE, Brooklyn's oldest Latino community-based organization. She is a long-time advocate and trailblazer for community organizing around just, sustainable development, environmental justice and community-led climate adaptation and community resiliency in Sunset Park. Prior to assuming the Executive Director position at UPROSE, Ms. Yeampierre was the Director of Legal Education and Training at the Puerto Rican Legal Defense Fund, Director of Legal Services for the American Indian Law Alliance and Dean of Puerto Rican Student Affairs at Yale University. She holds a BA from Fordham University and a law degree from Northeastern University.

ACKNOWLEDGMENTS

We dedicate this book to the activists in Greenpoint and beyond who have committed themselves to realizing more just and green urban futures.

We thank all of our contributors for their valuable work and for moving the conversation forward.

We also thank Julian Agyeman for helping us find a home for this book project, and Rebecca Brennan, Leila Walker, and Naomi Hill for shepherding it through.

Finally, we would like to thank the Baldy Center for Law and Social Policy and the Geography Department at the State University of New York at Buffalo (UB), as well as DePaul's University Research Council for providing research funds for our work in Greenpoint.

FOREWORD

Why do so many images of future green cities appear to be populated with slick architecture, expansive lawns, and ostensibly wealthy White people? On first inspection one could be forgiven for thinking that the vectors of urban greening coalesce around race, class, privilege, and green politics. And often this has been the case. Indeed, a substantial literature shows that verdant streets and suburbs are typically hallmarks of social status and often, White privilege. But is this always the case? Does green have to be a proxy for wealthy? Or are there other modalities of green existence?

Back in the early 2000s, two of us had a conversation in a car travelling along the 110 Freeway in Los Angeles. As we approached downtown, we began talking about the Los Angeles River restoration project and the effects that the Cornfields and Taylor Yards park projects might have on marginalized and vulnerable communities. Neighbourhoods like Los Feliz were not yet gentrified, but early signs were visible (Chapter 12 in this book picks up that story). We began talking about what might, if anything, be done to counteract the effects of greening on property values. And how might the displacement of park-deprived residents be avoided in the process of ecological restoration and park provision? As the river was naturalized and partially restored, and fish, frogs, birds, and other animals began to return to that part of the city, would some people be forced out? Could this be stopped? Were options like rent control feasible? We didn't have suitable answers at that time. Looking back, almost two decades later, the gentrifying effect of greening is very evident along some stretches of the river. Was this inevitable?

These ecological restoration projects have their equivalents around the globe. The Cheonggyecheon Restoration in Seoul, for example, resulted in a more than 600% increase in biodiversity in the area. It also saw a marked drop in particulate pollution, a substantial reduction in urban temperatures along the corridor, and up to a 50% increase in property values, amounting to billions of dollars of returns on the initial investment (Byrne 2017). But we know little of the displacement effects of greening on residents in this part of the city. The abandoned Tempelhof Airport in Berlin, which was converted to a park in 2008, has similarly acted as a driver of investment as East Berlin's grey infrastructure became a greensward in the heart of a heavily urbanized and lower-income part of that city. That park has attracted hipster cafés, a creative class, and increases in rent. Much has been written about the Highline Park in New York as well, which has similarly driven investment and displaced lower-income populations. And the development of a large sustainability park on the site of a former meatworks and warehousing area in Barcelona similarly increased surrounding property values, with predictable effects (Sauri et al. 2009). Few examples of these urban "revitalization" projects have included measures to provide affordable housing, contain rent escalation, or preserve the social fabric of surrounding neighbourhoods. But does it have to be this way?

The chapters in this important book are instructive. They can be traced back to a formative study by Winifred Curren and Trina Hamilton (2012), which posed this exact question. Is it possible for lower-income communities to resist and manage the displacement effects of urban greening? These effects are not just due to property value increases. Greening takes investments in time and money. If those costs are transferred to private property owners and/or tenants, they can be substantial. And despite the rhetoric of biophyllic cities, greening can bring other costs too. If the wrong species are introduced, they can increase levels of asthma, result in weed invasion, overshadow and shade dwellings, and even damage urban infrastructure such as sewerage and water pipes and powerlines. This can be worsened by the impacts of climate change. In cities like Brisbane, Australia – where around 80% of the urban forest cover is on private land – these effects might not be as noticeable as in cities like Hangzhou, China, where substantial public investment is needed to increase green canopy coverage.

As towns and cities internationally rush to capture the biogenic services of "green infrastructure", such as cooling, stormwater reduction, and mental restoration, they may unintentionally be increasing the risk of windthrow during severe storm events, could see increases in mosquito and tick-borne diseases, or might promote wildfires – depending on local conditions. Large-scale greening projects could also amplify human–wildlife conflicts, for instance bringing predators like coyotes back into urban cores or providing roosts for bat colonies (with associated nuisance issues such as noise or odour). For these and other reasons, urban greening might reasonably be considered to be one of the most vexatious and challenging urban planning issues of the twenty-first century. So what lessons can we learn from cities and towns where experiments in all sorts of urban greening – from community gardens to tactical urbanist interventions like "parklets" – are underway?

The chapters in this book offer guidance. They document a wide range of experiences of different kinds of greening initiatives, in diverse neighbourhoods, across different kinds of cities and by different collectives of urban residents. Many expand on examples in cities already mentioned (e.g. New York and Seoul). Many chapters also report the now all-too-familiar displacement effects of greening. Even initiatives such as urban agriculture can have unintended and sometimes pernicious impacts (McClintock et al. 2016). This is a fine collection of examples of where the problems can occur, how they can be identified, and in some instances how they might be ameliorated. Informal and liminal green spaces, for example, can be an alternative model of greening.

The book also prompts questions only just beginning to be asked in the literature on urban greening. For instance, are there other axes of difference, such as gender, disability, sexual orientation, and age, which should be considered in the displacement effects of greening? Will greening initiatives today make our cities better or worse tomorrow? Can we broaden greening projects to encompass metropolitan areas rather than isolated projects? Might interventions such as verge gardening or urban forestry offer livelihood returns as well as improved aesthetics, walkability, and climate resilience? What is the role of emotional geographies when devising greening strategies? How do they affect residents' sense of place? Is affordable housing incompatible with greening objectives? What is the role of blue infrastructure as a component of "just green enough" interventions (e.g. Meerow and Newell 2017)? And how can we factor in the rights of non-human species into our decision making?

This book opens up important lines of inquiry and its contributors provide valuable additions to the rapidly expanding "just green enough" literature. We recommend it to all those interested in a socially just and ecologically resilient future of our cities.

Jason Byrne
Griffith University, Australia
Joshua Newell
University of Michigan
Jennifer Wolch
University of California, Berkeley

References

Byrne, J., 2017. From freeways to greenways, in J. Dodson, N. Sipe, and A. Nelson (eds), *Planning After Petroleum: Preparing Cities for the Age Beyond Oil*, Routledge, New York, pp. 157–166.

Curran, W. and Hamilton, T., 2012. Just green enough: Contesting environmental gentrification in Greenpoint, Brooklyn. *Local Environment*, 17(9), pp. 1027–1042.

McClintock, N., Mahmoudi, D., Simpson, M. and Santos, J.P., 2016. Socio-spatial differentiation in the sustainable city: A mixed-methods assessment of residential gardens in metropolitan Portland, Oregon, USA. *Landscape and Urban Planning*, 148, pp. 1–16.

Meerow, S. and Newell, J.P., 2017. Spatial planning for multifunctional green infrastructure: Growing resilience in Detroit. *Landscape and Urban Planning*, 159, pp. 62–75.

Sauri, D., Parés, M. and Domene, E., 2009. Changing conceptions of sustainability in Barcelona's public parks. *Geographical Review*, pp. 23–36.

INTRODUCTION

Winifred Curran and Trina Hamilton

In 2007, we started a conversation about environmental cleanup efforts along Newtown Creek, the industrial waterway that separates the New York City boroughs of Brooklyn and Queens. Our initial reaction to the news that then-New York State Attorney General (now Governor) Andrew Cuomo was suing ExxonMobil and four other companies over their toxic legacies in Greenpoint, Brooklyn and the adjacent Newtown Creek (Confessore 2007) was one of both incredulity and certainty – incredulity that an oil plume larger than the Exxon Valdez spill could be stretched out underneath this Brooklyn neighborhood without us ever having heard about it, and certainty that the State's long-delayed action must be the result of gentrification pressures, of either developer- or City-led efforts to ready the area for high-end residential and commercial development. This certainty was based on years of research in neighboring Williamsburg, where a massive rezoning of industrial land led to high-rise luxury residential developments (see Curran 2004, 2007) and the construction of new green space along the East River (though not as much green space as originally promised), in a neighborhood that had previously had no formal access to the water.

The equity deficit

Beyond Brooklyn, global urban development is increasingly taking on the mantle of sustainability and "green urbanism." This has often manifest as landscape urbanism, a design culture which "promises to clean sites of the formerly industrial economy while integrating ecological function into the spatial and social order of the contemporary city" (Waldheim 2016, 5). Yet the equity impacts of these developments are often overlooked, resulting in what has been called ecological gentrification (Dooling 2009; Quastel 2009), environmental gentrification (Checker 2011), or green gentrification (Gould and Lewis 2017). Gentrification has matured from

Ruth Glass' original definition, in which historic working class housing was slowly upgraded by the middle classes until a neighborhood's character had changed (Glass 1964). At this stage of late capitalism, the stock of neighborhoods available for the realization of the rent gap will almost invariably require some sort of environmental remediation. As manufacturing has moved or been forced out of the urban core (Curran 2004, 2007; Curran and Hanson 2005), industrial land has been rezoned to allow for the construction of luxury housing on the urban waterfront, and disused rail lines have been turned into parks (Lindner and Rosa 2017). The façade of environmental improvement, whether substantive or superficial, attracts investment to areas of the city that had previously been considered off limits. And the people who suffered the negative effects of environmental hazards and unequal access to environmental goods are the first to be displaced when environmental improvements are made. This has led some to question whether parks and other green amenities are the new LULUs – locally undesirable land uses – because of the threat of displacement that they bring (Anguelovski 2016; Checker 2011).

Sarah Dooling (2009) describes ecological gentrification as the process through which genuine ecological improvements, such as improved wildlife habitat, result in the displacement of vulnerable human populations, in her case study, the homeless in a local park. In this instance, the environmental improvement is real even as the equity part of the equation falls far short of what could be considered true sustainability. Environmental gentrification is often more pernicious, however. Following Checker (2011), we understand environmental gentrification as the "convergence of urban redevelopment, ecologically minded initiatives and environmental activism in an era of advanced capitalism. Operating under the seemingly apolitical rubric of sustainability, environmental gentrification builds on the material and discursive successes of the urban environmental justice movement and appropriates them to serve high-end redevelopment that displaces low income residents." In this conception, environmental concerns are co-opted in order to facilitate high-end development, resulting in the displacement of lower-income residents. Relatedly, Gould and Lewis (2017, 2) coined the term "green gentrification" to describe "how green initiatives cause and/or enhance gentrification," with displacement an often intentional outcome. They explain that the goal of such greening initiatives is "to improve the environmental quality of neighborhoods and turn economically 'wasted' spaces into productive spaces," but that "they do not do so equitably" (Gould and Lewis 2017, 2). The greening initiatives come from outside investors ("the green growth coalition") who appropriate an un-revitalized environmental resource; "it is the *appropriation of the economic values of* an environmental resource *by one class from another*" (ibid., 24). Gould and Lewis (2017, 11) explain that they use the term green gentrification "to align with what the agents of these urban processes claim to be doing for cities: 'greening'." The term adds an important element to the scholarship on this topic because it explicitly recognizes that the actual "greenness" of the initiatives in question is up for debate, but that the marketing of green is often the critical factor that leads to gentrification. We most often use the term environmental gentrification in reference to our case study as the gentrification of Greenpoint was in force before cleanup became government policy, and the movement for cleanup came not from outside investors but from a decades-long fight by local activists, namely the "five angry women" (Hamilton and Curran 2013) who led the cleanup effort from the 1970s to the present day.

Whether focused on aesthetic changes or true ecological improvements, on outsider or community-led greening, the literature on environmental gentrification is unified in its focus on the "equity deficit" (Agyeman 2013, 4) that often accompanies urban greening initiatives. This equity deficit may be the result of intentional displacement in the name of "higher and best" uses, or unintentional displacement resulting from the re-valuation of neighborhoods by various interests after greening efforts are initiated. Beyond the analysis of what drives environmental gentrification and how it plays out in different places, we draw from and hope to contribute to broader debates about creating and assessing social and ecological change in cities. For instance, within urban political ecology (UPE), which has traditionally focused on the production of urban natures and the role of nature in capital accumulation, there have been recent calls "to pay closer attention to the specific forces, discourses, practices, and actors that participate in the constitution of urban environments," and "to explore the differentiating forces that produce urban nature as well as those that seem to dominate it" (Gabriel 2014, 46). Indeed, Heynen (2014, 600) situates the "second wave" of UPE scholarship within a tradition of striving to "make legible the ever-changing interplay between people, cities, and things" in a way that "helps to imagine where political points for intervention exist."

Becoming just green enough

In this context, we identified a community vision and organizing strategy based on our field work in Greenpoint, Brooklyn, that we labeled "just green enough" (JGE) (Curran and Hamilton 2012). Just green enough was meant to describe a plan for remediation and revitalization that uncouples environmental cleanup from high-end residential and commercial development, to describe the surprising and somewhat hidden greening that we found on the industrial waterfront of Greenpoint along Newtown Creek. In contrast to our expectation that we would simply document another case of environmental gentrification, the activism that gave rise to the just-green-enough approach was focused explicitly on social justice and environmental goals as defined by the local community, those people who have been most negatively affected by environmental disamenities, with the goal of keeping them in place to enjoy any environmental improvements. In a place like Greenpoint, where cleanup of long-contaminated water and land is no mere amenity, but rather an environmental emergency, we explored how environmental and anti-gentrification activists were working to accomplish cleanup without displacement.

In 2015, we brought together a group of scholars working on similar issues for a series of sessions at the Annual Meeting of the American Association of Geographers in Chicago. Many of the chapters in this collection originated with presentations at that conference. These case studies situate processes of environmental gentrification and contestation within broader urban planning, urban theory, and other related frameworks, and help us to think about the political and ecological possibilities of just green enough and the ways these might be operationalized, as well as other strategies to accomplish "just sustainabilities" (Agyeman 2013).

Aiming for justice

Within the sustainability policy and planning literature, Agyeman (2013) and others have been at the forefront of dialogues that attempt to bridge environmental justice traditions focused on marginalized communities' disproportionate toxic burdens and unequal access to green space, with sustainable development planning that has too often marginalized social justice considerations (see also Agyeman et al. 2016). As Gould and Lewis (2017, 152) explain, "There is now a global urban green growth machine, which profits from urban environmental problems and their solutions," and is focused almost exclusively on economic growth and environmental improvement. While these "post-political" (Swyngedow 2007) planning processes and development coalitions are fixated on win-win projects, the following chapters illustrate why the solution is not just about integrating the social into projects planned around economic and environmental outcomes, or about promoting win-win-win projects that meet some "triple bottom line" (i.e. social, environmental, and financial returns) threshold. Rather, we should aim for justice (Agyeman 2013; Quastel et al. 2012; Sze et al. 2009). While there are certainly important environmental criteria that should be part of any adjudication of environmental initiatives, including decontamination, climate change mitigation, and wildlife habitat restoration, aiming for justice is messy. Agyeman (2013, 38) proposes "recognition, process, procedure, and outcome" as essential elements of a "just sustainabilities" approach. Our own work and the work of other researchers on environmental gentrification also points to the need to consider reparative justice for historical toxic legacies from the perspective of the ability to remain in place as neighborhoods are cleaned up.

The need for new assessment criteria is also found in the literature on socio-natures – unique assemblages of social and natural processes, where Mansfield et al. (2015, 292) have called for scholars "to push beyond merely recognizing and describing socioecological dynamics (in all their complexity) toward evaluating them." They argue that "it is time to rally not around the tired environmentalisms of 'protecting nature' but around protecting and fostering the social natures that lead to the most just outcomes for humans and nonhumans alike" (ibid.). We cannot assume or read the equity impacts of green spaces based on a simple typology of socio-natures, however. As Domene and Saurí (2007, 297) explain, "different social groups create different landscapes with different visual and symbolic characteristics" and "discrepancies in how they are seen, experienced and consumed." For instance, while urban gardens and urban agriculture have come under increasing scrutiny for their connections to gentrification in a variety of cities, from Vancouver (Quastel 2009) to San Diego (Joassart-Marcelli and Bosco, Chapter 6, this volume), and Seoul (Bowen, Chapter 8, this volume), in some contexts, such as Barcelona, urban gardens are the preserve of marginalized populations, a social and self-provisioning strategy threatened by more aspirational greening agendas (Domene and Saurí 2007). In addition to local outcomes, we might also think of protecting endangered spaces within the city in the same way that we think of endangered species preservation, in terms of maintaining the viability and diversity of a larger-scale ecosystem, requiring us to understand the role that different neighborhoods and urban spaces play within the broader urban region (see Goodling et al. 2015).

Finally, there is a need for more scholarship on how to combat gentrification, including environmental gentrification, even within neighborhoods that are already gentrifying. Labeling a neighborhood as gentrified often masks micro-scale heterogeneity and thus overlooks opportunities to contest gentrification and begin to create alternative models even within already-gentrifying neighborhoods. In their review of strategies for ensuring equitable outcomes from urban greening, Faber and McDonough Kimelberg (2014) differentiate market-based, institutional, activist, and contractual approaches. In their typology, market-based and institutional approaches focus on access to housing in greening neighborhoods, activist approaches (such as the JGE strategy in Greenpoint) focus on challenging narratives of what green should look like or how it should be achieved, and contractual approaches focus on community benefits guarantees around jobs, affordable housing, and community input (ibid. 85–88). Reviews such as the 2002 issue of the journal *Race, Poverty and the Environment* titled "Fixin' to Stay: Anti-Displacement Policy Options and Community Responses" (Vol. IX, No. 1, Summer 2002) and the Urban Institute's guide on housing strategies to preserve affordability (Levy et al. 2006) advocate policies such as inclusionary zoning, rent control, and community land trusts to keep some property out of speculative land markets. We have tools to do this. What has been lacking is the political will and the imagination to think about how cities could work differently. In New York City, Mayor Bill De Blasio's Department of Housing, Preservation and Development (HPD) recently "released a Request for Expressions of Interest (RFEI) for groups interested in forming community land trusts using city-owned property" (Savitch-Lew 2017). Yet, in the current political climate, many of these strategies are untenable, particularly in already-gentrifying neighborhoods where land is expensive and the inventory of city-owned land is negligible. Rather than trying to alleviate the negative effects of gentrification after they occur, we need to think about how to bake equity into the equation from the very beginning. In both detailing cases in which a concern for equity has been completely absent as well as exploring strategies for developing alternative, just futures, the chapters in this volume think through ways to do this.

Working toward justice necessarily results in context-specific "highest and best uses" that are not always tied to current market (especially speculative) values. It is not about short-changing disadvantaged communities or simply accepting the status quo either. Some have misconstrued the just green enough concept as a strategy that sacrifices or limits environmental cleanup and amenities in order to combat gentrification, a kind of "polluted protection" wherein toxicity protects communities from displacement (see Miller 2015); that is not at all what we envision. Just green enough is about cleanup and community service provision, not real estate development. It is clean water, not a waterfront café; equal access to green space, not tourist-oriented parks; democratic process, not privatized planning. It is about making space for different visions of green, visions that promote greater access and livelihoods, not about taking over space that is stigmatized as wasteland or under-utilized without understanding its history and alternative possibilities (see Safransky 2014). It is a call to rethink what we mean by "green" and to offer an alternative vision of what a remediated neighborhood can look like. It is about aggressive remediation, but also being sensitive to the need for livelihoods and places to call home. Planning for this will need to be creative and responsive, with genuinely community-driven processes that centralize a racial justice perspective (Sze and Yeampierre, Chapter 4), explicitly promote social justice by design, and actively contest gentrifications.

Beyond Greenpoint

We maintain that it is possible, and indeed necessary, to preserve and revitalize industrial spaces that contribute both economically and environmentally to working-class neighborhoods. Rather than displace these sorts of land uses as part of the cleanup process, they can instead be essential partners in a "just transition" (Newell and Mulvaney 2013) to a more sustainable economy, key actors in accomplishing the economic, environmental, and equity pillars of genuine sustainability while contesting, and limiting the potential for, environmental gentrification. We maintain that much of the redevelopment happening under the guise of urban sustainability is what Gould and Lewis (2017, 115) call "light green growth" that uses "a thin veneer of environmental consideration to keep the ecologically unsustainable game of limitless economic growth alive, while deepening social inequality." We are clearly not the only ones attempting to think through the challenges of environmental gentrification. In addition to the academic scholarship on the topic, it is making its way into policy debates. Indeed, the 2016 United Cities and Local Governments (UCLG) World Summit in Bogota included a session on "the right to the sustainable city" that advanced a "caring city" model of green urbanism in contrast to the neoliberal one that has taken hold in many places (UCLG 2016).

We offer just green enough as one iteration of a necessarily heterogenous set of just sustainabilities (Agyeman 2013). It is by no means a one-size-fits-all approach. While our case study in Greenpoint provided us with an example of a neighborhood united in an alternative vision of green, one that preserves industrial use and the working class, rather than a textbook case of environmental gentrification as we had expected, many of the dynamics at play in the neighborhood are not applicable in other contexts. In our case study, a still vibrant industrial sector allows for an alternative vision of economic vitality to challenge what is the "highest and best use" of the industrial waterway of Newtown Creek, and provides a physical barrier to where luxury residential development can occur. Clearly, not every urban neighborhood will have the option to maintain and grow an industrial sector. Industrial users are not safe from displacement, whether through rezonings (Curran 2004, 2007) or industrial gentrification (Checker 2015, 2017), in which initiatives that support local artisanal food and clothing producers, as well as tech and other "clean" industries, displace more traditional manufacturers. Indeed, our own case study neighborhood is itself vulnerable to these trends (see Curran and Hamilton, Chapter 2, this volume). And not all industrial operators are good community partners, or provide good-paying, working class jobs. But we want to highlight the multiple and varied ways there are to be green, in order to contest environmental gentrification as the only path to environmental improvement.

Secondly, we recognize that the relative racial cohesion of the neighborhood also sets it apart. In this working class immigrant neighborhood, Polish immigrants have been the most visible group, though the neighborhood saw an increase in the Latinx population with Puerto Rican immigration starting in the 1950s. The influx of white gentrifiers was actually welcomed by some residents as a way to counteract any racial transition (DeSena 2009). This may also explain why it was easier to make connections between the old-timers and the in-movers. Shared racial identities removed many of the negative preconceptions that typically accompany the influx of gentrifiers into working class, immigrant, or minority communities. Gentrifiers were more open to their neighbors, while long-time residents were more likely to look favorably upon in-movers (though residents were displaced and the neighborhood character changed regardless). While it is too often the case that, as Gould and Lewis (2017, 1) argue, "greening whitens," in this case, the benefits of clean-up will accrue largely to white communities regardless of gentrification. A sense of shared community is not the norm in many urban neighborhoods, where long-term residents struggle to maintain their neighborhoods' racial and ethnic identities as part of their vision for what a sustainable neighborhood should be (see Kern, Chapter 11, Kim, Chapter 12, and Pearsall, Chapter 13, this volume), and gentrifiers do not make an effort to support existing community causes.

Organization of the book

The chapters in this volume (as described below) push us to think through time (both backward to toxic legacies and the need for reparative justice and forward toward more comprehensive transitions), to anticipate the potential co-option of the JGE vision, and to shift from thinking about "fixes" to rights- and justice-based approaches. And that is exactly the point of this collection: not to extol the virtues of JGE, but rather to use it as an entry point into conversations about rethinking urban development and environmental change. For planners, the conversations are about checking their assumptions about what makes an ideal green space and how to engage communities in sustainability planning (Wolch et al. 2014). For politicians, the conversations are about the policy tools available and necessary to combat environmental gentrification in different places. In both cases, there is a need to move beyond spectacular green urbanism (Gould and Lewis 2017; Lindner and Rosa 2017). For community activists, the conversations are about effectively advocating for and creating change within different social, economic, historical, and policy contexts. And for scholars, the conversations are about how to document structural drivers of environmental gentrification, but also to open ourselves up to possibilities for change and to translate opportunities across contexts.

The first section of the collection is titled "Just green enough in transition." We start with our original article (Chapter 1) that defines the JGE concept and describes how it is being operationalized on the ground and in planning documents in Greenpoint. Elsewhere we have described the political opportunity structures and activist strategies that allowed this vision to prevail (Hamilton and Curran 2013), and in this volume we go back to Greenpoint and Newtown Creek to see how the community consensus around JGE is faring (Chapter 2). What we find is a resilient community vision pairing industrial revitalization and environmental clean-up, and actively challenging environmental gentrification. That said, the pressures of managing the Superfund process on the one hand, and protecting industrial activities from encroachment on the other, have led environmental and industrial advocates to pursue parallel projects and sometimes come to a head over specific spaces and planning priorities. In this same section, we introduce thoughtful critiques of the JGE concept from Sarah Dooling (Chapter 3), and Julie Sze and Elizabeth Yeampierre (Chapter 4). Dooling pushes us to think beyond JGE, to see JGE as a strategic interim vision and to imagine and enact more extensive economic and ecological changes on the path toward low-carbon futures. She concludes her chapter with a series of provocations meant to push scholars, communities, and planners to incorporate new definitions of labor and economy into efforts to transform our cities. Sze and Yeampierre take up this challenge with their case study of the environmental justice organization UPROSE's work in the Sunset Park neighborhood of Brooklyn. Their chapter calls on us not just to think of strategies to preserve existing industrial neighborhoods, but to transition the economy to one that is resilient in the face of climate change in partnership with existing business owners and residents, and to do so in a way that recognizes how structural racism has created existing inequalities. For UPROSE, climate adaptation is not just a technical and economic project, but a community-based economic development strategy. They centralize a racial justice perspective in order to insure that climate adaptation and economic development initiatives do not reenact policy violence by accelerating the displacement of the working class and communities of color.

The second section, "Green displacements and community identity," focuses on losses of community identity resulting from urban greening. Pamela Stern and Peter V. Hall (Chapter 5) examine new green spaces and residential developments along a previously industrial waterfront in New Westminister (a suburb of Vancouver, Canada), focusing in particular on the erasure of waterfront workers' knowledge and experience from the new spaces. Their excavation of workers' experiences highlights a lack of attention to representational justice in many urban greening initatives, and their documentation of shifting perceptions of risk and appropriate use along the waterfront identifies significant barriers to alternative sustainability imaginaries, ones that might revalue water-borne industrial transport over roadway expansion and its associated health impacts, for instance. Pascale Joassart-Marcelli and Fernando Bosco (Chapter 6) turn their attention to alternative food initiatives in San Diego. They show how, in this context, farmers' markets and community gardens are associated with physical displacement and cultural marginalization through their incorporation into neighborhood rebranding efforts serving investment and real estate interests, but they also identify policy tools for challenging this trajectory. Jessica Ty Miller (Chapter 7), in her case study of the Gowanus neighborhood in Brooklyn, demonstrates how the green gentrification of the area has completely ignored social concerns, leading to both physical and social displacement for residents who are not part of the new upscale vision for the Gowanus Canal area. While substantive greening is planned, rampant speculation has occurred even without major environmental improvements.

The third section of this collection, "State-led environmental gentrification," focuses attention on the role of the state (at multiple scales) in driving environmental gentrification. In his case study of greenbelt deregulation and residential development on the outskirts of Seoul, Jay E. Bowen (Chapter 8) situates the displacement of small-scale commercial farmers by a luxury green housing development within shifting state priorities and ideas about the deserving versus undeserving poor. In this case, the state, acting through zoning regulations, eminent domain, and affordable housing provisions, privileged self-provisioning (private gardens) and amenity and housing provision for the creative class over continued commercial farming and other low-income residents' needs. Turning to Chennai, India, Priti Narayan (Chapter 9) documents the state removal and relocation of hundreds of slums following the 2015 floods. She argues that while the relocations were rationalized by eco-restoration and disaster prevention discourses, they were actually an extension of a broader development project that continues to permit middle class and corporate developments in similarly, if not more, ecologically sensitive areas of the city, and even adjacent to the cleared slums themselves. Noah Quastel's discussion of the "sustainability fix" in Vancouver, Canada (Chapter 10), takes a multi-scalar view, and presents a different set of state contradictions. While Vancouver has received international acclaim for its green credentials, there is now widespread recognition that this greening has been accompanied by an epic affordable housing crisis, and Quastels' analysis illustrates the difficulties of curbing environmental gentrification in such contexts, even when a progressive administration is in power at the local level.

Our final section, "Mobilizing and planning for just, green futures," explores the variety of ways in which communities have tried to contest environmental gentrification with variations of just green enough strategies. Leslie Kern (Chapter 11), in her study of environmental gentrification in the Pilsen and Little Village neighborhoods of Chicago, offers place identity as a way to construct alternative visions of the just and sustainable city, arguing that in this working class immigrant neighborhood, any version of just green enough will have to be just Latinx enough. Establishing and preserving a strong community identity is key to exposing the history of environmental racism in the area and insuring some measure of reparation. Esther Kim (Chapter 12) develops a similar narrative in her study of the Frogtown neighborhood of Los Angeles which is facing environmental gentrification from redevelopment along the Los Angeles River. Here, activists have employed a politics of place that invokes narratives of past spatial injustices and challenges recent patterns of environmental gentrification, as well their ongoing exposure to air pollution from nearby facilities. This place-based identity brings together older and newer residents in the continued effort to resist environmental gentrification. In her study of the Reading Viaduct rails to trails project in Philadelphia, Hamil Pearsall (Chapter 13) finds that an environmental initiative that pays minimal attention to its social and economic impacts is likely to create strife, particularly in a neighborhood with diverse resident interests. In this case, just green enough was as much about process and inclusion as it was about differing visions for the community. A successful campaign against new property taxes to pay for the maintenance of the park gave voice to community opposition to park development devoid of social benefits for long-term residents, and the conflict highlights the need for comprehensive neighborhood planning processes rather than atomized projects. Christoph D. D. Rupprecht and Jason A. Byrne (Chapter 14) examine informal urban greenspaces (IGS) in Japan and Australia, arguing that, in contrast to traditional parks, they do not seem to trigger environmental gentrification, yet they often engage community residents in creative planning and management strategies. Their chapter posits an interesting question about when and under what conditions less planning (i.e. professional urban planning) might mean more access, particularly for marginalized populations. Finally, Dan Trudeau (Chapter 15), in his comparison of New Urbanist projects across the U.S., finds that the projects that are most successful in achieving a measure of social justice are those which intentionally plan to do so from the earliest stages. He argues that regulatory imperatives, patient capital, and institutional support for social equity are necessary for accomplishing just green enough strategies on the ground. Environmentally just neighborhoods do not happen accidentally; they have to be planned as such from the beginning.

Together, these chapters demonstrate the importance of intentionality in achieving neighborhood visions that are some variation of just green enough. History and context matter and should be considered in any redesign of urban space. An inclusive, democratic process is essential. All of these require that we start to fundamentally rethink how economic development and environmental protection in the context of a changing climate allow us to make reparations for the existing inequalities of cities. We reiterate calls to shift "from current reformist strategies toward policy, planning, and practice for transformational change" (Agyeman 2013, 165). We see JGE and related strategies as necessary interim measures, as buffers in both space and time so to speak – they provide a material buffer against a totalizing gentrification, and they buy additional time to create alternative futures.

References

Agyeman, J. 2013. *Introducing Just Sustainabilities: Policy, Planning, and Practice*. London and New York: Zed Books.

Agyeman, J., Schlosberg, D., Craven, L. and Matthews, C. 2016. Trends and directions in environmental justice: From inequity to everyday life, community, and just sustainabilities. *Annual Review of Environment and Resources* 41(1): 321.

Anguelovski, I. 2016. From toxic sites to parks as (green) LULUs? New challenges of inequity, privilege, gentrification, and exclusion for urban environmental justice. *Journal of Planning Literature* 31(1): 23–36.

Checker, M. 2011. Wiped out by the "Greenwave": Environmental gentrification and the paradoxical politics of urban sustainability. *City & Society* 23(2): 210–229.

Checker, M. 2015. Green is the new brown: "old school toxics" and environmental gentrification on a New York City waterfront. In Isenhour, C., McDonogh, G. and Checker, M. eds. *Sustainability in the Global City: Myth and Practice*. New York: Cambridge University Press.

Checker, M. 2017. A bridge too far: Industrial gentrification and the dynamics of sacrifice in New York City. In Lewis, P. and Greenberg, M. eds. *The City is the Factory*. Ithaca, NY: Cornell University Press.

Confessore, Nicholas. 2007. Cuomo to sue Exxon over pollution in Brooklyn. *The New York Times*, 8 February. http://www.nytimes.com/2007/02/08/nyregion/08cnd-brooklyn.html

Curran, W. 2004. Gentrification and the changing nature of work: Exploring the links in Williamsburg, Brooklyn. *Environment and Planning A* 36(7): 1243–1260.

Curran, W. 2007. "From the frying pan to the oven": Gentrification and the experience of industrial displacement in Williamsburg, Brooklyn. *Urban Studies* 44(8): 1427–1440.

Curran, W. and Hanson, S. 2005. Getting globalized: City policy and industrial displacement in Williamsburg, Brooklyn. *Urban Geography* 26(6): 461–482.

Curran, W. and Hamilton, T. 2012. Just green enough: Contesting environmental gentrification in Greenpoint, Brooklyn. *Local Environment: The International Journal of Justice and Sustainability* 17(9): 1027–1042.

DeSena, Judith. 2009. *Gentrification and Inequality in Brooklyn: The New Kids on the Block*. Lanham, MD: Lexington Books.

Domene, E. and Saurí, D. 2007. Urbanization and class-produced natures: Vegetable gardens in the Barcelona Metropolitan Region. *Geoforum* 38(2): 287–298.

Dooling, Sarah. 2009. Ecological gentrification: A research agenda exploring justice in the city. *International Journal of Urban and Regional Research* 33(3): 621–639.

Faber, D. and McDonough Kimelberg, S. 2014. Sustainable urban development and environmental gentrification: The paradox confronting the U.S. environmental justice movement. In Hall, Horace R., Cole Robinson, Cynthia and Amor Kohli, Amor, eds. *Uprooting Urban America: Multidisciplinary Perspectives on Race, Class & Gentrification*. New York: Peter Lang Publishers, pp. 77–92.

Gabriel, N. 2014. Urban political ecology: Environmental imaginary, governance, and the non-human. *Geography Compass* 8(1): 38–48.

Glass, R. 1964. Introduction: Aspects of change. In Centre for Urban Studies, ed. *London: Aspects of Change*. London: MacKibbon and Kee.

Goodling, E., Green, J. and McClintock, N. 2015. Uneven development of the sustainable city: Shifting capital in Portland, Oregon. *Urban Geography* 36(4): 504–527.

Gould, K.A. and Lewis, T.L. 2017. *Green Gentrification: Urban Sustainability and the Struggle for Environmental Justice*. New York and London: Routledge.

Hamilton, T. and Curran, W. 2013. From "five angry women" to "kick-ass community": Gentrification and environmental activism in Brooklyn and beyond. *Urban Studies* 50(8): 1557–1574.

Heynen, N. 2014. Urban political ecology I: The urban century. *Progress in Human Geography* 38(4): 598–604.

Levy, D.K., Comey, J. and Padilla, S. 2006. *Keeping the Neighborhood Affordable: A Handbook of Housing Strategies for Gentrifying Areas*. Washington, DC: Urban Institute. http://www.urban.org/sites/default/files/publication/50796/411295-Keeping-the-Neighborhood-Affordable.PDF

Lindner, C. and Rosa, B. eds. 2017. *Deconstructing the High Line: Postindustrial Urbanism and the Rise of the Elevated Park*. New Brunswick: Rutgers University Press.

Mansfield, B., Biermann, C., McSweeney, K., Law, J., Gallemore, C., Horner, L. and Munroe, D.K. 2015. Environmental politics after nature: Conflicting socioecological futures. *Annals of the Association of American Geographers* 105(2): 284–293.

Miller, Jessica Ty. 2015. Super fun superfund: Polluted protection along the Gowanus Canal. CUNY Academic Works. http://academicworks.cuny.edu/gc_etds/1055

Newell, P. and Mulvaney, D. 2013. The political economy of the "just transition". *The Geographical Journal* 179(2): 132–140.

Quastel, N. 2009. Political ecologies of gentrification. *Urban Geography* 30(7): 694–725.

Quastel, N., Moos, M. and Lynch, N. 2012. Sustainability-as-density and the return of the social: The case of Vancouver, British Columbia. *Urban Geography* 33(7): 1055–1084.

Safransky, S. 2014. Greening the urban frontier: Race, property, and resettlement in Detroit. *Geoforum* 56: 237–248.

Savitch-Lew, Abigail. 2017. De Blasio admin. opens door to community land trusts. *City Limits*, 10 January. http://citylimits.org/2017/01/10/de-blasio-admin-opens-door-to-community-land-trusts/

Sze, J., London, J., Shilling, F., Gambirazzio, G., Filan, T. and Cadenasso, M. 2009. Defining and contesting environmental justice: Socio-natures and the politics of scale in the Delta. *Antipode* 41(4): 807–843.

UCLG. 2016. *Permanent Working Platform: Co-Creating the City – Right to the Sustainable City*. https://www.bogota2016.uclg.org/en/sessions/permanent-working-platform-co-creating-city-1210

Waldheim, C. 2016. *Landscape as Urbanism: A General Theory*. Princeton and Oxford: Princeton University Press.

Wolch, J.R., Byrne, J. and Newell, J.P. 2014. Urban green space, public health, and environmental justice: The challenge of making cities "just green enough." *Landscape and Urban Planning* 125: 234–244.

PART I
Just green enough in transition

1

JUST GREEN ENOUGH: CONTESTING ENVIRONMENTAL GENTRIFICATION IN GREENPOINT, BROOKLYN

Winifred Curran and Trina Hamilton

Introduction

This case study is an examination of the ways in which "actually existing sustainabilities" (Krueger and Agyeman 2005) are constructed in a gentrifying neighborhood. While, as Syngedouw (2007, 20) notes, he has not been able to find anyone against "sustainability," the process through which urban environments are being remade under the rubric of sustainability are highly contested. As Dale and Newman (2009, 671) conclude, there is an important "differentiation between livability and equity." A major concern is environmental gentrification, in which environmental improvements result in the displacement of working class residents as cleanup and reuse of undesirable land uses make a neighborhood more attractive and drive up real estate prices (Banzhaf and McCormick 2007; Bunce 2009; Checker 2011; Cowell and Thomas 2002; Dale and Newman 2009; Dooling 2009; Quastel 2009). This concern is heightened in brownfield areas, where environmental cleanup may allow for the realization of the rent gap (Smith 1996), the difference between actual and potential ground rent that makes gentrification so profitable.

The surge in environmental awareness in cities has not been matched with concern for social equity (Quastel 2009). Instead, "sustainability is often conflated with environment or ecology, thereby obscuring the social dimension" (Jonas and While 2007, 125). And yet, sustainable development can potentially provide communities with alternative ways of thinking about economic development, resource use, and social justice (Raco 2005; see also Agyeman et al. 2002). As Raco (2005, 330) argues, "The enhanced focus on the impacts and externalities generated by economic development can challenge neoliberal inspired growth agendas and modes of regulations." This is especially true when these growth agendas and modes of regulation fail spectacularly, as they did in 2008. The Great Recession has had everyone rethinking how the global economy works and the role governments should play in urban economies. Evans et al. (2009) make the case that the recent financial crisis makes it possible to challenge the dominant political narratives of market-led regeneration.

Such is our hope for the Greenpoint neighborhood in Brooklyn, home of a massive, decades-old underground oil plume that was the subject of a recent settlement between the New York State Attorney General and ExxonMobil, and Newtown Creek, one of the most polluted industrial waterways in the United States and a recently declared Superfund site. Decades of environmental activism by long-term residents and collaboration with more recent in-movers, many of whom are gentrifiers, has resulted in a cleanup process that actively contests the assumed outcome of environmental gentrification. Our goal here is not in any way to depoliticize the process of gentrification, minimize the effect of displacement, or search for positives associated with gentrification (see Slater's 2006 critique of the literature that does this). We are not concerned with proving how gentrified Greenpoint is or is not. Rather, following Jonas and While (2007, 152), we are looking at the potential for new spaces of politics for sustainability, broadly conceived with social justice as a central tenet, opening up around new strategic territorial and class alliances and divisions. We argue that the conjoined struggle of long-term residents and gentrifiers around environmental cleanup has provided a space for a politics of sustainability that makes room for the working class and industrial uses in the neighborhood (at least in the near term). As an example of the fluidity and hybridity of approaches to sustainability and the contestation of neoliberalism, the Greenpoint example points to the importance of new forms of direct democratic involvement and individual citizenship as well as a demand for an increased role for the state in achieving cleanup (see Raco 2005, 2007).

Overall, we argue that a "just green enough" strategy is emerging in Greenpoint that makes room for continued industrial use and blue-collar work, where cleanup does not automatically or exclusively lead to the "parks, cafes, and a riverwalk" model of a green city. Too often, the cleanup of industrial urban neighborhoods and creation of new green space quite literally "naturalizes" the disappearance of working class communities, as more attractive neighborhoods become ripe for development. The "just green enough" strategy organizes for cleanup and green space aimed at the existing working class population and industrial land users, not at new development. Activists in Greenpoint want to achieve the cleanup of Newtown Creek while maintaining its industrial base, a strategy designed to put a stop to speculative development attracted to a neighborhood experiencing environmental improvements. So ideally, cleanup of the Newtown Creek will be just green enough to improve the health and quality of life of existing residents, but not so literally green as to attract upscale "sustainable" LEED-certified residential developments that drive out working class residents and industrial businesses. The Greenpoint case challenges the perceived inevitability of environmental gentrification and opens an already gentrifying neighborhood to active intervention.

The context

Greenpoint is the northernmost neighborhood in Brooklyn, bounded by Newtown Creek to the north and east, and the East River on the west. While Greenpoint was once referred to as the "garden spot" of the world because of its green pastures and isolation (DeSena 2009), Greenpoint's waterfront location helped to shape the neighborhood as an industrial powerhouse, a center for shipbuilding and the "five black arts: printing, pottery, petroleum and gas refining, glassmaking, and iron making" (Jackson and Manbeck 1998, 145) in addition to businesses like fat-rendering plants. By 1870, Greenpoint was home to more than 50 oil refining companies. By 1892, the majority of these were consolidated into Standard Oil Trust (later Mobil Oil) (NYS DEC 2011). This industrial history left a toxic legacy for the area's working class residents, historically Irish and Italian, now overwhelmingly Polish immigrants with a significant Latinx population.

As early as 1887, the *New York Times* said about the Creek, "On warm or sunny days, a quivering envelope of nauseous fog hangs above the place like a pall of death" (quoted in Newman 2007, B3). In 1894, residents complained to the governor that the Creek was a "public nuisance... whereby the health and comfort of the people of the community are jeopardized and endangered." A report commissioned by the governor found:

> The water of this creek for almost its entire length is dark-colored and offensive, by reason of sewage it contains in suspension and in solutions... A very considerable factor in the present condition of the creek's bottom has been the discharge for years of the refuse products from the oil works.
>
> *(New York Times 1894)*

During the 1950s, an estimated 17 to 30 million gallons of oil seeped into the Creek and 55 acres of surrounding land, predominantly from facilities owned by what is now ExxonMobil (EPA 2007). The spill was not discovered until 1978 by the Coast Guard on routine helicopter patrol. While cleanup officially began then, and a consent decree was signed with the state in 1990, very little had actually been done when Riverkeeper, an environmental organization, rediscovered the spill while on a boat patrol in 2002. They subsequently filed a federal lawsuit against ExxonMobil in 2004, followed by a lawsuit by the State Attorney General Andrew Cuomo (now governor) in 2007. While there has yet to be a comprehensive study of the health effects of the underground oil plume, soil tests reveal that the spill has released toxic vapors into the neighborhood (Walker 2007b). Combined sewage outflows (CSOs) also remain a problem, with the city itself remaining one of the largest polluters of the creek. From the late 1950s to today, public policies have led Greenpoint's eastern sector to become a "dumping ground" for burdensome facilities (NYC DCP 2002). The neighborhood houses both a waste water treatment plant and various waster transfer stations.

Despite this collection of disamenities, Greenpoint has long been a target of gentrification. As early as 1986, the *New York Times* described Greenpoint, "one of the city's best-preserved working class areas," as "feeling the exponential rent increases, housing turnover and influx of young professionals that have characterized gentrification in New York City" (Freedman 1986). DeSena (2009, 35) describes gentrification as having "gone rather smoothly" in Greenpoint, at least in part because of the racial similarities between Polish residents and white gentrifiers.

In part, it was gentrification that exposed the extent of environmental contamination in Greenpoint. Neighborhood residents and activists reported being able to see and smell oil as sites were dug up for new developments. This unpleasant reminder of the Creek's toxic past led to the politicization of many new residents.

The 2010 declaration of Newtown Creek as a Superfund site and settlement of the lawsuits against ExxonMobil raised hope in the neighborhood that cleanup might actually happen, at the same time that it has increased fears of environmental gentrification. Of particular concern to the broad variety of residents active in the cleanup efforts is the ability of manufacturing and the industrial working class to remain in Greenpoint. Across the spectrum of long-term residents, gentrifiers, business owners, environmental organizations, and local politicians, our interviews and observations at community meetings (conducted from 2008 to 2012) revealed a remarkably cohesive community vision of Greenpoint as just green enough to achieve cleanup, while maintaining working class residents and industrial land uses. We present this case study as an example of how sustainable development processes can foster visions of economic diversity, social justice, and democracy that directly complicate and contest gentrification and neoliberalization.

Methods

Our primary methodology was conducting semi-structured interviews with 24 informants from December 2008 to February 2012, both in person and by phone, if face-to-face interviews were not possible. Informants were drawn from newspaper reports of the events in Greenpoint as well as from the primary author's experience with community groups and activists in the area. Our informants ranged from long-term resident activists who had lived in the area for decades, to more recent arrivals who were in the area for as little as two years. We also interviewed non-resident environmental activists from groups like Riverkeeper, in addition to elected officials and city policy makers. Some informants were interviewed multiple times as events developed. Since much of this research was conducted as the lawsuits were ongoing, we were unable to get interviews with the Attorney General's office. State agencies like the Department of Environmental Conservation similarly did not respond to interview requests.

In addition to our interviews, we attended community meetings (such as the Newtown Creek Alliance and Community Board 1) from which we recorded our field notes. We consulted policy documents from the city, state, and federal government related to the spill, cleanup, and environmental and industrial policy. Finally, we conducted extended searches of both traditional and web-based journalism as well as other web-based forums such as blogs.

This paper is entirely shaped by the results of the research. We went into this expecting a classic case of environmental gentrification, but what we found led us to a more nuanced understanding of the vision and spaces for sustainability being constructed in Greenpoint, one that had remarkable consensus among a wide range of constituencies – long-term residents, more recent in-movers, local politicians, business owners, and environmental activists.

Environmental gentrification

Environmental gentrification and displacement are the result of urban environmental policies that have become inextricably linked to economic development and growth. Following Checker (2011, 212), we understand environmental gentrification as:

> the convergence of urban redevelopment, ecologically minded initiatives and environmental activism in an era of advanced capitalism. Operating under the seemingly a-political rubric of sustainability, environmental gentrification builds on the material and discursive successes of the urban environmental justice movement and appropriates them to serve high-end redevelopment that displaces low income residents.

This definition refers to the provision of new environmental amenities, as in Checker's (2011) study of Harlem, where selective sustainability policies threaten to displace low-income residents, as well as to the cleanup of disamenities. Brownfield sites may be particularly vulnerable, for, as While et al. (2004, 565) argue, "the transition to a post-industrial city presupposes a series of 'light green' policy actions, quite literally, to clean up the spaces of industrial capitalism." Desfor, Keil and Ross (2004, 170) describe the evolution of Toronto's soil pollution policies "as deeply embedded in processes of capital accumulation," wherein a new wave of redevelopment and investment (likely residential and commercial) is seen as the solution to historical legacies of industrial pollution. The profit potential from environmental improvements, however superficial, has led to the partial "greening" of capital (While et al. 2004), yet this environmental agenda is used to displace and exclude economically vulnerable populations (Checker 2011, Dooling 2009, Jonas and While 2007).

Cleanup makes a neighborhood more attractive and may drive up real estate prices, forcing up rents, and thus displacing the populations who suffered the consequences of industrial development, while richer homeowners capture the gains in their property assets (Banzhaf and McCormick 2007). Essoka (2010) finds a distinct racial aspect to environmental gentrification, concluding that brownfield revitalization leads to a decrease in Black and Latinx populations. Pearsall's (2009, 2010) work in New York City finds brownfield redevelopment exacerbating the vulnerabilities of certain populations to stressors like geographic displacement. Dale and Newman (2009) argue in their case studies in Vancouver and Toronto that there is an inverse relationship between the "greening" of neighborhoods and affordability in those neighborhoods. While some recent research challenges the direct connection between brownfield redevelopment and gentrification (Eckerd 2011), these concerns present low-income residents and environmental justice activists with what Checker (2011, 211) terms a "pernicious paradox- must they reject environmental amenities in their neighborhood in order to resist gentrification that tends to follow from such amenities?"

In Greenpoint, "a constellation of toxicity" (interview, June 2009) makes cleanup widely considered necessary. One informant, himself a gentrifier now heavily involved in local politics, put it this way: "There are environmental projects and plans and then there are environmental emergencies. This is an emergency" (phone interview, December 2008). Another informant, involved in public heath activism, acknowledged: "A lot of people who have suffered through this scar, this industrial past... they probably won't be around to see this clean new area, but at the same time I don't think that means that we shouldn't clean it up." She adds, "Across the board people want access, more parks, more green space... to be connected to nature" (interview, June 2009). So while cleanup is widely advocated, gentrification is a recognized danger, even within an already gentrifying neighborhood. The way in which residents and activists in Greenpoint are envisioning cleanup is in part to contest the narrative that gentrification is the inevitable result of "greening" the city that, once established, will consume the entire neighborhood.

Gentrification in crisis?

In a 2011 commentary, Davidson explores a series of crises facing gentrification research, both ontological, in the form of arguments over gentrification's constitutive properties, and financial, in terms of the Great Recession. He argues that there is an outstanding question in the research of how to think about the status of gentrified neighborhoods. The focus in the gentrification research on finding the next frontier, deciding what is or what is not gentrification, or developing a new terminology of gentrification, leaves the status of neighborhoods experiencing gentrification depoliticized (Davidson 2011). We agree with his contention that "simply to leave naturalized the disappearance of working-class communities... elevates market-based and class-based processes of social change to a problematic status of inevitability" (Davidson 2011, 1994).

The transformation of a gentrified neighborhood is rarely complete. Just because a neighborhood has been or is being gentrified does not mean that it is politically homogeneous. Our concern here is not with the literature on the liberal/ preservationist political views of many gentrifiers (e.g. Brown-Saracino 2009, Caulfield 1994, Ley 1996), but rather to a political identity forged in place through the everyday lived experience of a neighborhood. This is particularly important in a place like Greenpoint, where many gentrifiers were attracted to the obvious advantages of the area's proximity to Manhattan, waterfront views, and historic architecture, but were entirely ignorant of the area's environmental history and the history of struggle surrounding those environmental issues. Thus, the fight to clean up Newtown Creek has created a newly organized constituency, perhaps originally motivated by self-interest, but now more rooted in environmental justice. Many of the current activists, who are clearly gentrifiers, locate their concern in achieving justice for long-term residents who have suffered the ill effects of living in a toxic neighborhood. As one political activist argued in relationship to Superfund designation, "There absolutely has to be protection and funding for the people that are going to be displaced, or are going to lose the value of their homes" (phone interview, December 2009). Another environmental activist put it this way:

> you have real crimes being committed, environmental crimes, within the lives of these people who are just, in some cases, making ends meet... your goal is to make their lives better and somehow protect them... so we're not just coming in and fixing the problem and then all the developers come in and kind of benefit from it, but that the people are benefitting from it.
>
> *(interview, June 2009)*

The activism in Greenpoint is an attempt to battle the false choice of cleanup and reinvestment versus decay, and to recognize the injustice that gentrification (and previous decades of malign neglect from the city and state) represents.

This concern with environmental justice is also a partly self-interested recognition of the risk at which the gentrifiers of Greenpoint have been placed by real estate capital and a city, state, and federal policy that ignored the spill for decades and actively fought community efforts to achieve cleanup. As Coleman et al. (2005, 2525) recognize, neoliberal regeneration strategies have created "fertile conditions for the production of corporate crimes and harms." So the story in Greenpoint, as explained by one of our informants is:

> You have a lot of young, out of college, I'd say... who are moving into the area and have no idea, absolutely no idea [about the oil spill], which, I was one of those people... but, they're moving into these luxury condos... these glass towers are going up, and no one's really learning about it.... Then a subset of those individuals learn something about it and are really active and are really angry about the situation and then want to get something done.
>
> *(interview, June 2009)*

These gentrifiers have the skill sets to get the issue more attention. Indeed, several of our informants commented on their contributions of graphic design, multimedia, and communications skills, in addition to their general political influence as members of the sought-after "creative class." Overall, the coalition of old-timers and newcomers in Greenpoint demonstrates the possibility of new positionalities and potentialities for communities engaged in the work of environmental re-visioning. The fact of gentrification doesn't have to be the end of the story.

"Greening" Greenpoint

The greening of Greenpoint has taken many forms, from the recent declaration of Newtown Creek as a Superfund site, to historical battles against a waste incinerator and a new power plant, to more superficial interventions such as the construction of a local nature trail. In each case, local, long-term activists have been at the forefront of these environmental battles, and crucial to the construction of an environmental vision that both greens the neighborhood while also maintaining its working class character and allowing room for community residents to participate in the process. These processes, at a variety of scales, have, as Raco (2005) argued, allowed for alternative visions of economic development, social justice, and resource use. While the vision for the cleanup efforts is still being actively negotiated through community planning meetings, activist organizations, etc., we detail three examples of community attempts to contest what "green" looks like.

Newtown Creek Nature Walk

While at first glance, the construction of a nature walk on the shore of Newtown Creek may seem an attempt to gentrify the waterfront, the reality of this nature walk is quite different. Located in the shadow of the sewage treatment plant, this is, as an article in the *New York Times* (Ruen 2009) described it, "the ironic nature walk." As Ruen (2009) explains:

> When we think of nature, we imagine ourselves alone, surrounded by untouched beauty, connecting with our collective memories of the world as it was at the dawn of humanity. But "nature" is also defined as a characteristic or state of things, and this alternative meaning carries its own weight.

The Newtown Creek Nature Walk carries this weight, sitting as an example of the community's fight for access to the waterfront, more green space, and the recognition of the role the area's industrial past and present has played in the formation of New York City. The nature walk is the result of the community's fight with the city's Department of Environmental Protection (which operates the plant) for some amenities to counter the negative effect of the location of the sewage treatment plant in the neighborhood. It took nine years (and $3.2 million), but the Newtown Creek Nature Walk opened to great fanfare in 2007, and the city recently pledged an additional $14 million to expand the trail (Short 2011). As one informant, a lifelong resident of the area told us, "If you know this neighborhood, there's a great desire to be close to the water… I'd like to swim in the Creek. I used to swim in it as a kid. Probably got a mouth full of oil" (interview, June 2009).

The fight for the nature walk was part of the community's attempt to get more open space for the neighborhood, the lack of which has been reflective of the way in which Greenpoint has long been a dumping ground for undesirable land uses. Maintaining Greenpoint as a working class neighborhood does not mean continuing to deprive the area's residents of green space. On average, 26% of the land in New York City is preserved as open space. In Williamsburg-Greenpoint, the percentage is 4.3 (Weiss and Heimbinder 2011). The nature trail represents a significant victory of long-term residents' battles for amenities independent of entrepreneurial redevelopment processes.

There is no reason why residents of Greenpoint should have to choose between staying in their homes, having access to jobs, and having access to green space. The vision for the creek shared by the majority of stakeholders we interviewed incorporates all three. And the Nature Walk, in its ironic way, reflects that vision. One informant explains:

> They want to be connected to nature, even if that nature is a little dirty… so much of the industrial neighborhoods around the Creek have kind of closed off so people don't actually have to see it… but people would just like to have the walls knocked down a little bit and have access to the waterfront…. This is, I mean it's history too. It's the industrial history of the city and its skeleton is all there along the Creek.
>
> *(interview, June 2009)*

Ruen (2009) argues:

> As much as we have created the grand cultural playgrounds of Manhattan, we have also created the wretchedness of Newtown Creek. The two worlds need each other and cannot be set apart, though much of our economic system takes great pains to encourage the illusion that this is not the case.

Brownfield Opportunity Area

The Brownfield Opportunity Area (BOA), a New York State program, gives grants to local governments and community groups to develop strategies for brownfield redevelopment. The Newtown Creek BOA is a partnership between the Newtown Creek Alliance, Riverkeeper, and the Greenpoint Manufacturing and Design Center, a non-profit industrial developer, started in 2008. As described by one informant involved in the BOA, the vision is to redevelop the Creek as "a 21st century industrial corridor" (interview, February 2012). This is both a recognition of the Creek's current importance as an industrial site, "the last real industrial beltway in the city" as one city official said (interview, July 2009), with an estimated 15,000 jobs as of 2008 (Newtown Creek Alliance n.d.), as well as a vision for the future of Greenpoint as a working class neighborhood. None of the people we interviewed looked for the removal of industrial uses from the Creek. As one environmental activist explained:

> the Newtown Creek industry is so integral to these neighborhoods that is has always been a focus of this. The whole cleanup activism is keeping a mixed

land use and having businesses and residences and commercial retail available all together.... I've never heard anyone be like "oh no, we just want to make it all parks and residential things." Nothing like that.

(interview, June 2009)

One long-time resident remembers oil seeping up to the surface of her backyard garden as a kid, yet she explains: "Do I think the manufacturers here currently that had nothing to do with it should be blamed for it? No" (interview, June 2009). Residents want to keep industrial uses, in part, because they don't want to see the gentrification of the waterfront (phone interview, August 2010).

The vision of the BOA includes not just the preservation of the jobs and businesses already there, but a re-envisioning of what an industrial corridor can and should look like, including introducing new sustainable businesses and improving the area's ecology and environmental conditions. One informant involved in the BOA commented:

We support the continued use of industry... we would be happy seeing [a lot of ship traffic or barge traffic]. We would like to see a functioning waterway, which means ecologically functioning. So if it could be cleaned up to the point where it would sustain some return of fish life, some return of aquatic vegetation... I think, you know, it would be great to have sections of ecologically functioning marshland and wetland. I think that's entirely possible.

(phone interview, June 2009)

According to the Newtown Creek Alliance's website, close to half the jobs currently on the Creek are in transportation, warehousing and wholesale trade, sectors that are increasingly truck dependent and thus not especially taking advantage of their waterfront location (Newtown Creek Alliance n.d.). Expanding opportunities for more water-dependent businesses is sustainable not just because it will improve the environmental conditions in the area as a result of deceased truck traffic, but additionally because the types of business the BOA is seeking to create are better paying manufacturing jobs that help lift people out of poverty (interview, February 2012).

The BOA is part of the construction of a green, sustainable vision for the city developed through democratic means with an active place for manufacturing and the working class. This stands in stark contrast with the official sustainable planning document for New York, PlaNYC 2030 (also known as PlaNYC: A Greener, Greater New York), which has an entire chapter devoted to public participation and yet was written mostly by an independent consulting firm with minimal public input (Checker 2011) and minimal concern for jobs (interview, February 2012). It is also an important counter-narrative to outsiders' perceptions of the creek as ripe for residential and commercial redevelopment. As one recent Newtown Creek boat tour participant proposed: "It looks ugly with all the scrap metal around, but think about what it could be with parks, cafés and a river walk" (Walker 2007a). By contrast, the vision that the BOA is helping to foster is not about the transformation of vacant toxic sites, but rather the cleaning up of a still-viable working class neighborhood in order to protect public health, initiate ecological regeneration, and maintain and increase sustainable industrial uses of the area. The literature suggests that projects that fit the existing character of a neighborhood are less likely to trigger gentrification (Banzhaf and McCormick 2007), and that the maintenance of working class jobs can also act as a gentrification buffer (Walks and August 2008). Curran (2010) demonstrates the ability of manufacturers to remain despite gentrification, with the potential for benefits for manufacturers as a result of new markets. One industrial retention advocate echoed this sentiment, arguing:

> So many of our small businesses are in the construction supply chain, they are making glass, they are making countertops, they are fabricating cabinets... It is in some ways, it's the upside of gentrification for these small businesses.... If you're doing, if you can call your product green, and there's an immense interest in green building supplies in new construction, you're in good shape. So a lot of our guys... could make that connection and take advantage, exploit that opportunity, for their benefit.
>
> *(interview, June 2009)*

Superfund/ Newtown Creek Lawsuits

Superfund in and of itself can act as a stop on gentrification because of the negative effect it has on public perception of an area, and therefore, real estate prices. Our informants place the EPA timeline for remediation of Newtown Creek in the 20 to 25 year range. For this reason, the city was initially less than enthusiastic about the federal government's interest in Newtown Creek. As one academic commented in reference to Gowanus Canal (another recent Superfund site in Brooklyn), "Of course I understand that the city doesn't want to hinder real estate investment in the short term with a more cumbersome (but effective) Superfund cleanup. The game is obvious to all" (quoted in Chaban 2009). Having had the Superfund site declared, however, the city must now publicly embrace cleanup in an attempt to protect long-term property values. The perception of environmental attributes can be as important as the actual conditions, and the responsiveness of local and federal officials to community concern can be an important factor (Hurd 2002).

The interest in Newtown Creek as a Superfund site, strongly advocated by community environmental activists, was linked to increasing public pressure and attention to the site as a result of a series of lawsuits brought against ExxonMobil for their failure to make any progress in the recovery of oil from the Creek and surrounding neighborhood (interview, July 2009). The most important of these, the State and Riverkeeper lawsuits again ExxonMobil, were settled in November 2010. The settlement includes a $19.5 million Environmental Benefits Projects (EBP) fund to be distributed to community projects, the largest single payment of its kind in New York State history (State of New York Attorney General 2010).

Together, the Superfund process and the Environmental Benefits Fund present the potential for genuine community input and alternative environmental visions of Newtown Creek. Central to the Superfund process is the designation of a Community Advisory Group (CAG). Similarly, the EBP has a Community Advisory Panel (CAP) who will help to determine what community needs are and how the money will be spent. As Holden (2011) notes, public participation has been a key aspect of sustainable development. While there is nothing inherently democratic in the formation of these two bodies, as they were chosen by an outside consultant in each case, the members of these panels in Greenpoint are those who are recognized as some of the most committed and longstanding activists in the community. One informant, a representative of a local politician, explained the environmental activist community in Greenpoint this way:

> There are some neighborhoods that have been particularly dumped upon, environmentally, by the city, and Greenpoint is one of them.... The more the city or whoever sees that there are problems there, they say, oh, ok we can throw our waste transfer station, oh we can do that there, that's already, they've already given up on the neighborhood, and it's basically up to the neighborhoods to fight for themselves and that's what we see a lot in Greenpoint and Williamsburg.... The neighborhood is pretty well taken care of in terms of the people on the ground there, and they are very lucky to have them.
>
> *(interview, June 2009)*

As one environmental activist put it, "These are environmental veterans" (interview, June 2009).

Contested, co-opted, or ignored?

The vision of a sustainable Greenpoint that contests the inevitability of environmental gentrification is not without its challenges. Signs of gentrification continue to arise. A new "industrial chic" hotel has opened, with prices as high as $4950 for a month-long stay in a two-bedroom suite. This in a location one blogger termed "a used condom's toss from the Newtown Creek Waste Water Treatment Facility" (quoted in Gray 2011).

There is plenty of potential for conflict in the way in which processes such as the EBP play out, as well as the potential for cleanup to attract a group of gentrifiers not nearly as committed to the preservation of the neighborhood as those we interviewed. There has been some disagreement over what to prioritize on the Creek – recreational use for kayakers or the facilitation of barge traffic. Moreover, the yet-to-be-determined environmental projects to be funded as part of the ExxonMobil settlement may well be the kind of green amenities that attract a higher-income gentrifier less willing to live side by side with industrial uses. And, a successful Superfund cleanup would radically alter public perceptions of an area about which one of our informants queried, "How much more stigma could possibly be attached to Newtown Creek?" (interview, June 2009). The current zoning for the area along the Creek remains industrial, and the city official we interviewed said the city had no plans to change that, but those intentions could change if the real estate market rebounded, fueled by the environmental improvements the very activism we have detailed may help to achieve.

Conversely, another area of concern is that Superfund could have a negative effect entirely opposite from gentrification, namely economic depression and even the abandonment of the site by industry. While Superfund designation was widely welcomed, it was not universally seen as an unquestioned good. One informant expressed concern that the Superfund designation would lead to a kind of redlining when it comes to financing the industrial businesses in the area (interview, February 2012). Another activist and long-term resident worried:

> Depending on what economic situation you are in, designating something Superfund leaves it really without money and leaves it really deteriorating even worse and nobody does anything until money comes in.... There's a lot of stuff that business won't do, they won't touch because of the designation of Superfund.... [It's] another level of bureaucracy that a regular person doesn't want to deal with. I'm very hesitant about getting that designation because it may actually hurt us as a community.
>
> *(interview, December 2008)*

The future of environmental remediation and economic development in Greenpoint is thus still very much in process, subject to a shifting constellation of actors at a variety of scales; it is neither easy nor predetermined. Greenpoint cannot necessarily serve as a model or go-to guide of how to achieve environmental remediation without displacement, but is rather a case study in the messy contextual politics of sustainability that offer the possibility, if not a guarantee, of the potential for a democratic and socially just way to rethink the green city.

Conclusion

As one of our informants put it, "There's a textbook approach to environmentalism and then there's reality, right? And reality is that for all the love of trees and nature and everything, people have to have jobs, they have to have a place to live" (interview, June 2009). We offer this case study as an example of how "actually existing sustainabilities" are constructed at the intersection of environmental and neoliberal urban policy in ways that contest the dominant narratives of inevitability surrounding environmental gentrification and open up new spaces for political activism.

Activists in Greenpoint challenge the notion of gentrification as a complete and total neighborhood transformation and the notion of gentrifiers as necessarily always antagonistic to long-term residents' interests. They have refused to accept their own displacement as an inevitable outcome of the real estate market of New

York City and contest the dominant narrative of the postindustrial city. Instead, they have found ways to make strategic alliances that help to both achieve cleanup of Newtown Creek while also highlighting the importance of industrial businesses to the neighborhood and the city.

The alternative vision for urban sustainability constructed in Greenpoint is one we understand as "just clean enough," in which as much of the environmental hazard as possible is removed in order to assure community health while still allowing for industrial uses on the waterfront for the explicit purpose of maintaining the area's working class population. This vision challenges the understanding of "green" as only that which looks pretty or is somehow "natural," as is evidenced in the Newtown Creek Nature Walk. Rather, the vision of green presented by activists in Greenpoint is one that is explicitly classed, recognizing the historical injustices that created a neighborhood so polluted in the first place and demanding that these be righted for the direct benefit of those who suffered through it.

Finally, the Greenpoint case is not simply about alternative visions, but also about rethinking state intervention. While there is no doubt that urban environmental policy has increasingly reflected neoliberal/market ideals, activists in Greenpoint have called upon the power of the state to facilitate their alternative vision. From industrial zoning to the brownfield opportunity area (BOA) study and the Attorney General's lawsuit, the state has been brought back into the business of environmental justice rather than just environmental gentrification.

It is not enough to simply bemoan the process of gentrification and displacement in Greenpoint. Those who remain have actively contested gentrification through the construction of this alternative vision, re-politicizing the process to show that environmental gentrification need not happen the same way everywhere. In contesting the narrative of inevitability surrounding environmental gentrification, activists have formed alliances at a variety of scales, constructing an alternative vision of the sustainable city, forcing a more democratic, diverse, and just view of what green looks like.

Acknowledgments

This chapter is a slightly modified version (edited for length) of the following article: Curran, W. and Hamilton, T. 2012. Just green enough: Contesting environmental gentrification in Greenpoint, Brooklyn. *Local Environment* 17(9): 1027–1042. The original article is available at Taylor & Francis Online: http://www.tandfonline.com.

References

Agyeman, J., Bullard, R. D., and Evans, B. 2002. Exploring the nexus: Bringing together sustainability, environmental justice and equity. *Space and Polity* 6: 77–90.
Banzhaf, H. S. and McCormick, E. 2007. Moving beyond cleanup: Identifying the crucibles of environmental gentrification. Andrew Young School of Policy Studies Research Paper Series, Working Paper 07–29, May.

Brown-Saracino, J. 2009. *A Neighborhood That Never Changes: Gentrification, Social Preservation, and the Search for Authenticity.* Chicago and London: University of Chicago Press.

Bunce, S. 2009. Developing sustainability: Sustainability policy and gentrification on Toronto's waterfront. *Local Environment* 14(7): 651–667.

Caulfield, J. 1994. *City Form and Everyday Life: Toronto's Gentrification and Critical Social Practice.* Toronto: University of Toronto Press.

Chaban, M. 2009. Twice as smelly: Mayor wants to scrub Gowanus, avoiding Superfund listing. *The Architects Newspaper*, November 9. http://archpaper.com/news/articles.asp?id=4014

Checker, M. 2011. Wiped out by the 'Greenwave': Environmental gentrification and the paradoxical politics of urban sustainability. *City & Society* 23: 210–229.

Coleman, R., Tombs, S., and Whyte, D. 2005. Capital, crime control and statecraft in the entrepreneurial city. *Urban Studies* 42(13): 2511–2530.

Cowell, R. and Thomas, H. 2002. Managing nature and narratives of dispossession: Reclaiming territory in Cardiff Bay. *Urban Studies* 39(7): 1241–1260.

Curran, W. 2010. In defense of old industrial spaces: Manufacturing, creativity, and innovation in Williamsburg, Brooklyn. *International Journal of Urban and Regional Research* 34(4): 871–885.

Dale, A. and Newman, L. L. 2009. Sustainable development for some: Green urban development and affordability. *Local Environment: The International Journal of Justice and Sustainability* 14(7): 669–681.

Davidson, M. 2011. Critical Commentary. Gentrification in crisis: Towards consensus or disagreement? *Urban Studies* 48(10): 1987–1996.

DeSena, J. 2009. *Gentrification and Inequality in Brooklyn: The New Kids on the Block.* Lanham, MD: Lexington Books.

Desfor, G., Keil, R., and Ross, K. M. 2004. Contested and polluted terrain: Soil remediation in Toronto. In Gene Desfor and Roger Keil, eds. *Nature and the City: Making Environmental Policy in Toronto and Los Angeles.* Tucson, AZ: The University of Arizona Press.

Dooling, S. 2009. Ecological gentrification: A research agenda exploring justice in the city. *International Journal of Urban and Regional Research* 33(3): 621–639.

Eckerd, A. 2011. Cleaning up without clearing out? A spatial assessment of environmental gentrification. *Urban Affairs Review* 47(1): 31–59.

Essoka, J. D. 2010. The gentrifying effects of brownfields redevelopment. *Western Journal of Black Studies* 34(3): 299–315.

EPA. 2007. Newtown Creek/Greenpoint Oil Spill Study Brooklyn New York. September 12. www.epa.gov/region2/.../newtowncreek/newtowncreek_review.pdf

Evans, J., Jones, P., and Kreuger, R. 2009. Organic regeneration and sustainability or can the credit crunch save our cities? *Local Environment* 14(7): 683–698.

Freedman, S. G. 1986. Signs of transformation in neighborly Greenpoint. *New York Times*, October 15.

Gray, R. 2011. Box House Hotel in Greenpoint as "industrial chic" as it gets. *Village Voice*, August 23. http://blogs.villagevoice.com/runninscared/2011/08/box_house_hotel.php

Holden, M. 2011. Public participation and local sustainability: Questioning a common agenda in urban governance. *International Journal of Urban and Regional Research* 35(2): 312–329.

Hurd, B. H. 2002. Valuing superfund site cleanup: Evidence of recovering stigmatized property values. *The Appraisal Journal* (October): 426–437.

Jackson, K. and Manbeck, J. 1998. *The Neighborhoods of Brooklyn.* New Haven: Yale University Press.

Jonas, A. E. G. and While, A. 2007. Greening the entrepreneurial city? Looking for spaces of sustainability politics in the competitive city. In R. Kreuger and D. Gibbs, eds. *The Sustainable Development Paradox: Urban Political Economy in the United States and Europe.* New York and London: Guilford Press.

Krueger, R. and Agyemen, J. 2005. Sustainability schizophrenia or actually existing sustainabilities? The politics and promise of a sustainability agenda in the US. *Geoforum* 36(4): 410–417.

Ley, D. 1996. *The New Middle Class and the Remaking of the Central City.* Oxford: Oxford University Press.

New York Times. 1894. The nuisances must go. *New York Times,* December 12.

Newman, A. 2007. Fouled creek's improvement inspires a site for respite. *New York Times,* September 27: B3.

Newtown Creek Alliance. n.d. Working Waterfront. http://www.newtowncreekalliance. org/working-waterfront/

NYC DCP (New York City Department of Planning). 2002. Greenpoint 197a Plan. New York: New York City Department of City Planning.

NYS DEC (New York State Department of Environmental Conservation). 2011. Greenpoint Petroleum Remediation Project: Project History. http://nysdecgreenpoint.com/ ProjectHistory.aspx

Pearsall, H. 2010. From brown to green? Assessing social vulnerability to environmental gentrification in New York City. *Environment and Planning C* 28: 872–886.

Pearsall, H. 2009. Linking the stressors and stressing the linkages: Human-environment vulnerability and brownfield redevelopment in New York City. *Environmental Hazards* 8: 117–132.

Quastel, N. 2009. Political ecologies of gentrification. *Urban Geography* 30(7): 694–725.

Raco, M. 2005. Sustainable development, rolled-out neoliberalism and sustainable communities. *Antipode:* 324–347.

Raco, M. 2007. Spatial policy, sustainability, and state restructuring: A reassessment of Sustainable Community building in England. In R. Kreuger and D. Gibbs, eds. *The Sustainable Development Paradox: Urban Political Economy in the United States and Europe.* New York and London: Guilford Press.

Ruen, C. 2009. The ironic nature walk. *New York Times,* May 8. http://www.nytimes. com/2009/05/10/nyregion/thecity/10boul.html?mcubz=0

Short, A. 2011. "Walk" this way! City to expand Newtown Creek nature path. *Brooklyn Paper,* January 20. http://www.brooklynpaper.com/stories/34/3/wb_naturewalk_2011_ 1_21_bk.html

Slater, T. 2006. The eviction of critical perspectives from gentrification research. *International Journal of Urban and Regional Research* 30: 737–757.

Smith, Neil. 1996. *The New Urban Frontier: Gentrification and the Revanchist City.* London: Routledge.

State of New York Attorney General. 2010. Cuomo announces settlement with ExxonMobil to provide for comprehensive cleanup of Greenpoint oil spill, 17 November. www.ag.ny.gov/media_center/2010/nov/nov17b_10.html

Swyngedouw, E. 2007. Impossible sustainability. In R. Kreuger and D. Gibbs, eds. *The Sustainable Development Paradox.* New York: Guilford.

Walker, D. 2007a. A creek cruise with sights rare, even to New Yorkers. *New York Times,* July 16. http://www.nytimes.com/2007/07/16/nyregion/16cruise.html

Walker, D. 2007b. Exxon Mobil cleanup effort continues on 1950 spill. *New York Times,* July 19: B2.

Walks, A. and August, M. 2008. The factors inhibiting gentrification in areas with little non-market housing: Policy lessons from the Toronto experience. *Urban Studies* 45: 2594–2625.

Weiss, R. and Heimbinder, M. 2011. Creek Speak: Voices from Newtown Creek. Newtown Creek Community Health and Harms Narrative Project: Final report for the Newtown Creek Alliance. http://www.newtowncreekalliance.org/community-health/creek-speak/

While, A., Jonas, A.E.G., and Gibbs, D. 2004. The environment and the entrepreneurial city: Searching for the urban "sustainability fix" in Manchester and Leeds. *International Journal of Urban and Regional Research* 28(3): 549–569.

2

A JUST ENOUGH GREEN? INDUSTRIAL GENTRIFICATION AND COMPETING SOCIO-NATURES IN GREENPOINT, BROOKLYN

Winifred Curran and Trina Hamilton

When we first started doing work in the Greenpoint neighborhood of Brooklyn following the launch of a lawsuit against ExxonMobil and other polluters over an extensive underground oil plume, we expected to find a classic case of environmental gentrification in which cleanup of a historically polluted site was engineered in order to serve the demands of gentrifiers and create the potential for further real estate development. What we found instead was a dedicated group of activists who had been organizing for remediation since the 1970s who were educating new residents in the environmental history of the neighborhood and, together with both environmental and industrial preservation organizations, growing the constituency of people who valued the adjacent Newtown Creek as an industrial waterway and sought to preserve working class jobs in the area. Our labeling of this strategy as "just green enough" (JGE) sought to highlight how the collective vision emerging in Greenpoint explicitly challenged the coupling of environmental cleanup with industrial conversion into luxury housing or "parks, cafés, and a riverwalk" (Curran and Hamilton 2012, 1028).

The neighborhood consensus about maintaining industrial jobs and a working waterway while also accomplishing extensive environmental cleanup, ecological restoration, and adding community green space still exists, but is under strain as development further encroaches upon the area. A massive new residential development, Greenpoint Landing, on land rezoned from industrial use, a project that had been in the planning stages for over a decade but that most of our informants thought would never come to fruition, is now under construction. But perhaps of even greater concern for the realization of a just green enough vision in the neighborhood is industrial gentrification. Due to anomalies in the zoning code, uses beyond traditional manufacturing are creeping into the area. The industrial users that were at the core of the just green enough strategy are not always a unified constituency, with some users willing and able to take advantage of the opportunities provided by the gentrification of the area, while others are existentially threatened by these changes. Moreover, while the city administration celebrates the manufacturers in the area, it is doing too little to protect them.

The threat to industry continues even as the long-term remediation of the neighborhood remains in flux. The Superfund cleanup process has been moving very slowly, and is still at the site study stage, which started in 2011 and includes physical, ecological, and human health risk assessments of the Creek (EPA n.d.). Given the new presidential administration, some even fear, despite Environmental Protection Agency (EPA) assurances, that Superfund may functionally cease to exist (Enman 2017). There have, however, been environmental victories, such as the 40 different projects across the neighborhood that were funded by the $19.5 million Greenpoint Community Environmental Fund (GCEF) resulting from the ExxonMobil lawsuit settlement. Environmental advocates have also documented an impressive array of new life in and along Newtown Creek, including ribbed mussels, eels, killifish, herons, egrets, and even the odd bottlenose dolphin (Newtown Creek Alliance n.d.c). Moreover, the underground oil plume is shrinking, with over 12 million gallons of product recovered so far, from an estimated 19-million-gallon plume (NYSDEC n.d.).

In terms of actual remediation of the Creek, however, one advocate clarifies: "Clean is nowhere near where we're at" (interview, October 2016). And, as the low-hanging fruit of sustainability projects are realized, the next steps become harder. Competing priorities for specific sites have emerged, resulting from difficulties in trying to align environmental, economic, and equity concerns, and the further gentrification of the neighborhood has weakened the constituency for the just green enough vision. Developers and speculators have adapted to the maintenance of industrial zoning and developed new strategies to sell the authenticity of this industrial enclave while working to displace its long-term users. The maintenance of industrial zoning, a central element to the just green enough strategy, is not, in and of itself, enough to prevent gentrification. Of the rapid pace of change in the neighborhood, one industrial retention advocate says, "It's hard to separate what is from cleanup and what from gentrification" which was well underway before Superfund or any other form of remediation (interview, October 2016). Neighborhood advocates recognize the danger and are pushing for city policy to respond.

In this chapter, we take up Holifield's (2009, 655) project for critical environmental justice research "that, instead of describing or explaining environmental inequalities, traces the emergence and resolution of controversies and uncertainties surrounding environmental injustices." As Gould and Lewis (2017) point out, a just green enough strategy can be difficult to maintain in hot property markets, especially in global cities. But as with all elements of sustainability and social justice, they do not happen if you do not actively engage in work to make them happen. While the pressure from real estate markets is intense, city policy can make a difference. The degree to which any city administration, in partnership with state and federal government, is genuinely committed to just sustainabilities is the degree to which just green enough futures are possible. And while government policy provides the opportunity structures for contesting environmental gentrification, we must also attend to the mobilization and interaction of a wide range of stakeholders – residents, activists, advocates, allies, and non-human natures – to understand the unique socio-natures and political strategies that develop in different urban spaces.

Since our original article on JGE was published in 2012 (Curran and Hamilton 2012, reproduced as Chapter 1 this volume), we have continued our engagement with Greenpoint and Newtown Creek through follow-up interviews with both new activists in the area as well as long-term activists involved in our earlier work. We have seen the changes in the neighborhood on Newtown Creek Alliance (NCA) boat and walking tours, and our own excursions in the neighborhood. We follow news and social media accounts of developments in Greenpoint and Newtown Creek, including policy changes, real estate developments, and planning processes. Finally, we follow the Superfund and other planning processes through community meeting minutes and reporting. In this chapter, we track how just green enough has evolved on the ground, uncovering both the resilience and vulnerabilities of the community's vision for greening and industrial revitalization, and emphasizing the importance of ongoing, active intervention.

Dubai on the East River

Even as the degree and nature of remediation under Superfund remains an open question, the greening of Greenpoint is still a selling point for the neighborhood. A 2005 rezoning of the Williamsburg-Greenpoint waterfront allowed for luxury high-rise development on land previously zoned for manufacturing. In exchange, community residents were promised new, public access green spaces (which have often failed to materialize on the Williamsburg waterfront; see Gould and Lewis 2017 on Bushwick Inlet Park). These developments were first focused on Williamsburg, but high-rise development is now under way on the Greenpoint waterfront. As one real estate executive put it, "'I jokingly call Greenpoint the Dubai of the East River' because the area has developed so rapidly, 'but fast-forward five or 10 years and you can see a waterfront area that's connected through parks, which is a positive change'" (quoted in Laterman 2016).

According to one long-term resident and activist, what the high-rises are doing is "creating a Manhattan-like community. But, the rest of us live in Greenpoint and still have to deal with the industrial" (interview, October 2016). She expressed concern that there would be increased truck traffic in the residential areas closer to the Industrial Business Zone (IBZ) to divert traffic from the luxury housing on the waterfront. Gentrification does not make polluting uses disappear; it simple displaces them to other, more disadvantaged areas (Checker 2015; in press). This is but one of the ways in which green gentrification can exacerbate environmental injustice, and reveals how the nature of the just green enough project is affected by changes outside the immediate area. For JGE advocates, the goal has always been to reduce environmental health risks, not to accept more.

The bifurcation of the neighborhood that the waterfront rezoning has accomplished makes the work of activists more difficult. This same activist commented,

"Newer people in the neighborhood are more aware [of the environmental issues in the neighborhood] because of our work, the websites. But they're not actively taking part. I see the same old people at these meetings. We haven't really been able to engage the new people, especially around the Superfund" (interview, October 2016). She hypothesizes that this may be because the timeline for Superfund is too long, and they do not necessarily plan to still be in the neighborhood by the time it is clean(er). Or it may simply be that they are too far from it geographically. Indeed, the waterfront area around Greenpoint Landing feels like an entirely different world from the working waterfront of Newtown Creek. As close as it is, the industrial present and toxic legacies of Newtown Creek are still often invisible to those in-movers whose interest in the waterfront is confined to their view of Manhattan. This tension is evident even on the NCA donor list that now includes a real estate firm "specializing in the development of underutilized or environmentally impacted properties" alongside the traditional scrap metal operations and other industrial supporters (Newtown Creek Alliance n.d.b).

While the size and scale of Greenpoint Landing make it a neighborhood-changing development, long-term activists learned from the experience elsewhere on the waterfront, in which promised community benefits have taken over a decade to materialize, if ever (see Gould and Lewis 2017). This time they demanded that community benefits, in this case affordable housing, be built in the first stages of development, before the luxury high-rises displace the working class residents of the neighborhood whom the affordable housing is designed to serve. Three buildings of affordable housing have been constructed and will be filled via lottery for those making 30 to 60 percent of area median income, with preference given to the residents of Community Board 1, comprised of Williamsburg and Greenpoint. These will provide over 1,000 affordable units of the more than 5,000 unit development (Plitt 2016). This is, at best, a partial victory, given that many in the community were opposed to the rezoning (see Curran 2004, 2007; Gould and Lewis 2017) and do not like the heights of the towers allowed as a result. But the fact that some people are already living in the affordable units shows that there is a community benefit. Informants told us that residents of the affordable units can use the amenities of the luxury towers as well.

Even with some community benefits, the scale of this development has ripple effects that extend even to the industrial property market. While much of the industrial waterfront remains safe from rezoning to residential use, that industrial designation has not been enough to forestall real estate speculation in an area dominated by long-term manufacturers who provide thousands of jobs.

Industrial gentrification

Central to the just green enough strategy was the maintenance of industrial zoning in order to provide for the continued existence of working class jobs and an alternative vision of what a green economy and city could look like. But as the real estate market in Greenpoint evolves in the context of a rapidly gentrifying neighborhood, we are seeing that even industrial zoning is not enough to provide an affordable landscape for manufacturers. The fact that industrial zoning and existing industrial uses no longer act as dampeners to speculator interest was made clear to us by one activist and member of the boat club who described encounters he has had with real estate speculators in the industrial zone, even at some of the sites that NCA has developed specifically for employees at nearby industrial operations:

> In terms of real estate, I run into people up the Creek who are speculators: "Oh, this would be a great place for yadda yadda…" I met somebody through the boat club who was wanting to see a property – it was like total back of the creek industrial area – and I was like, "Well, what kind of business do you run?" And she was like, "Well, it would be a really cool spot, maybe for some studios. What would you like to see out of it?" And I was like, "Well, we'd like to see industry there. I don't know, if you're not going to use the water you could do interesting things with the shoreline to make it better ecologically." But yeah, people are obviously looking at a lot of the land around here.
>
> *(interview, October 2016)*

Greenpoint is now in danger from what Checker (2015; in press) has called industrial gentrification, in which cities "incentivize and promote small-scale, boutique, clean and green-tech manufacturing businesses" specifically in areas adjacent to gentrifying neighborhoods. This process not only gentrifies the targeted industrial zones, but it serves to displace existing heavy manufacturing to other areas of the city she describes as sacrifice zones (Checker in press, 151). In Greenpoint, this has meant celebrating certain types of businesses, such as Broadway Stages, a television and film production company, over other long-term users like Wonton Food Inc. and Martin Greenfield Clothiers, which actually provide more jobs for neighborhood residents. This shift from more intensive manufacturing to more of a "maker space" mentality means an influx of uses into the industrial zone that are more commercial than they are manufacturing. Industrial retention advocates report that commercial encroachment, permissible under the current zoning code, is now just as bad as threats from residential rezoning.

This commercial encroachment can take many forms. One of the most concerning, related to how businesses are classified under the North American Industry Classification System (NAICS), is office use disguised as production, with, as one industrial retention advocate put it, "three architects and a 3-D printer being considered manufacturing" (interview, October 2016). These kinds of businesses inflate industrial real estate prices, with high-end office users competing with small-scale manufacturers in a battle those manufacturers cannot possibly win. As this advocate put it, "We're seeing crazy land prices… If they say $30 a square foot, I hear commercial. No woodworker can afford that…." By contrast, affordable rent for manufacturers in the New York market is $16 per square foot.

Commercial use is permitted as-of-right (i.e. without needing a variance) in the area, but developers want more. In an area with a large supply of single story industrial buildings, those who are going to invest in high-end commercial want greater height and density. Developers want to capitalize on the fact that it is now cool to be in Brooklyn. The city wants to capitalize on this as well, encouraging high-end commercial and tech users. Some fear an upzoning to commercial use that could threaten long-term industrial tenants that provide thousands of jobs in food and garment production, among other industries. According to industrial retention advocates, the city should, "shore up industry, build that wall, build in those restrictions. But they are leading with 'let's make a deal.' Everything is on the table" (interview, October 2016).

Other as-of-right uses in the IBZ that threaten industrial users are hotels and self-storage facilities. Hotels allow for luxury uses within the industrial zone and attract businesses like restaurants and nightclubs to the area, further pushing up real estate prices. Self-storage facilities, while hardly glamorous, are actually industry's biggest competition, according to another industrial retention advocate and developer. They are a profitable interim use while property owners figure out what the long-term market will look like, but they provide very few jobs. Industrial retention advocates have organized against these uses, enough so that Mayor De Blasio announced an ordinance to require a special permit in order to build hotels or self-storage facilities within the city's IBZs. Heralded as a move to protect and grow industry and create jobs (Goldenberg 2015), more than a year after its announcement, industrial advocates argue that the ordinance has gone nowhere and nothing has been done to actually protect industrial businesses.

Another use that allowing hotels in the IBZ has brought is homeless shelters. The city is converting an existing youth hostel into a homeless men's shelter. While some neighborhood residents have resisted the move, rightfully arguing that an industrial area does not provide the services the homeless need, one person admitted, "Between you and me, I'm not so sad to see the shelter. It acts as a barrier to gentrification" (interview, October 2016). It is, however, another example of how certain historically disadvantaged neighborhoods are targeted for "undesirable" land uses as homeless bodies are even further marginalized.

Despite these encroachments, industrial zoning and small manufacturers are the key to keeping Greenpoint just green enough, and New York a sustainable city. One non-profit industrial developer argues, "It's all about zoning. That will stop it. It can be fixed easily." The problem is that the current zoning is "porous." If this industrial gentrification is allowed to persist, "there will be less and less to protect. It's hard to be an advocate of the few." And yet, he remains optimistic that "The volume of industry on the Creek will help save it…. Every city needs a backwater. It has what is necessary to survive and live: park school buses, fix cabs and elevators, fill tankers, move garbage. It's what makes a big city work" (interview, October 2016).

The key is to maintain industry without that being an invitation to continue to concentrate undesirable uses in this neighborhood. One long-term resident and activist who has organized for cleanup says, "I think there will, I want industry to be there, to produce good jobs. But there is also the opportunity for greening near industry, a place for workers to take their lunch break and breathe clean air.... We want to go forward with industry without environmentally bad businesses." Of the many concerns facing activists in Greenpoint, including a National Grid plan to expand organics processing and then turn the methane from the wastewater treatment plant into usable energy, which would take potential green space away from the industrial area, she says simply, "We have to keep watching" (phone interview, October 2016).

Competing socio-natures

As explained in the Introduction to this collection, the JGE vision that has emerged for Newtown Creek and its surrounding area is an example of environmentalism "after nature" (Mansfield et al. 2015). This applies to cases that are not about protecting stands of old growth forest or other relatively pristine or intact wilderness. It is not about "nature versus jobs," but rather about what kind of "social natures" we want to support in different places. Mansfield and her colleagues argue that "socioecological environmental politics is not over naturalness but rather over what should be done, by whom, to bring about which social natures, with what benefits" (ibid., 287). Debate over how exactly to balance industrial use and environmental benefit have led to some cracks in the just green enough consensus, as it transitions from the unified fight to resolve the ExxonMobil lawsuit and get a Superfund site declared, to a more contentious determination of how clean the area can get and what green should look like. In this section, we detail a number of projects in the neighborhood that reveal different, if not always competing, visions of how to be just green enough.

For industrial advocates, doubling down on the preservation of industry can sometimes take precedence over environmental restoration. Evergreen, the industrial advocacy organization previously known as EWVIDCO (East Williamsburg Valley Industrial Development Corporation) is developing a new Brownfield Opportunity Area (BOA) plan for the North Brooklyn industrial corridor (though the state has significantly reduced resources and staffing for the BOA program). While Evergreen's current BOA planning process retains both industrial revitalization and environmental goals, early planning meeting presentations were largely oriented around identifying the unique opportunities and needs of different industrial submarkets and subareas, ranging from heavy industrial to wholesale and mixed arts and industrial uses, with particular concerns around both project financing and encroachment. They propose not-for profit (NFP) and cross-subsidy financing models[1] that could overcome the lack of for-profit developer interest in industrial development and generate industrial jobs even in a hot real estate market (Evergreen 2016). The previous BOA, coordinated by the Greenpoint Manufacturing and Design Center (GMDC), the Newtown Creek Alliance, and Riverkeeper, was one of the key planning documents to promote a just green enough vision for the Creek and its surrounds (BOA 2012; Curran and Hamilton 2012, 1035). Indeed, the BOA

Final Report was organized around the twin goals of reactivating industry and restoring the ecology of the Creek, complete with images of restored wetlands and wildlife alongside "high-functioning" (i.e. relatively low environmental impact) industrial activity, and increased water- and rail-borne transportation (BOA 2012). Where the first BOA plan was aspirational, aimed at solidifying a community consensus around the just green enough strategy, this current planning process is aimed squarely at the encroachment detailed above.

Meanwhile, environmental advocates are focused on the Superfund process. They have been frustrated by the data collection and communication process. While the Environmental Protection Agency (EPA) approves the contractors, "they're hired directly by the PRPs [Potentially Responsible Parties]" and "they collect the data and then interpret the data on behalf of their clients," leading to significant back and forth among parties over research scope, methods, and interpretation (interview, environmental activist, October 2016). One small example of the disputes was over the species included in the consultants' baseline fish and wildlife surveys. This activist explained that the contractors did not include oysters in the survey, yet NCA members have seen oysters in their regular explorations of the Creek (interview, October 2016). While this may seem like a minor quibble, he explains that the Superfund cleanup processes are very much focused on "this current time period, they're not looking at what was here 300 years ago or 50 years ago," so it's critical to set as high a baseline as possible. It has been the role of environmental advocates such as NCA, with university and non-profit partners, to conduct their own ecological surveys of the Creek and to make visible the ecological regeneration that has already occurred, creating counter-discourses and knowledge that has its own regulatory potential (Krueger 2002). The current time period represents a significant improvement over 20 or even 10 years ago, illustrating the positive legacy of the decades of environmental justice activism in the community. In this activist's words,

> It would have been really interesting if they did the Superfund cleanup 20 years ago when there wasn't as much life here, how that would have impacted it because I think it would have been easier to say, "Well, forget ecological restoration, we don't see anything."... It's good we see more stuff here, so we can say, "Look, things want to come back," so we can protect them.
>
> *(interview, October 2016)*

In other words, nature itself is an important actor in the Superfund cleanup process and, as others have shown in forest conservation and other environmental battles, the specificity of different natural environments creates unique barriers and opportunities for activism (e.g. Braun 2002; Barnes and Hayter 2005), and these will shape what just green enough looks like.

Along the waterfront, industrial advocates are pushing to preserve industrial rights, specifically shoreline property owners' right to marine transit in the future, even where it is not currently viable. Meanwhile, environmental advocates see sites

FIGURE 2.1 Barge traffic on Newtown Creek

FIGURE 2.2 Canoe on Newtown Creek

along some of the Creek's tributaries that are already experiencing shoaling[2] and are currently unnavigable as ripe for wetland and wildlife habitat redevelopment (interview, environmental advocate, October 2016). Where some industrial advocates question whether it is possible, or even desirable, to get Newtown Creek clean enough for swimming, longtime residents see it as the ultimate measure of remediation. Discussion within the Superfund Community Advisory Group (CAG) steering committee became so heated that EPA staff recommended hiring a neutral, third-party facilitator (CAG 2016). Disagreements have also emerged around how much to encourage recreational boating in the Creek, which has substantial barge traffic (see Figures 2.1 and 2.2). Despite these disputes, the goal of preserving a united front persists, as the same meeting minutes explain: "Committee members noted the importance of presenting a cohesive voice regarding Newtown Creek's restoration. If the community and area businesses support the same vision, it becomes more powerful" (CAG 2016).

The potential for co-existence is evident in current projects such as the North Henry Street planning process for new public green space, wildlife habitat, and green infrastructure on city-owned land adjacent to a recycling operation. In addition to public access and ecological restoration goals, the planning document explicitly sets out a plan for shared use with the site's industrial neighbor and project partner, Allocco Recycling, providing "added capacity for staging, loading and storage" and "using hard barriers and fencing, safely separating industrial operations upland from restoration efforts and access features along the shoreline" (Newtown Creek Alliance n.d.a, p. 48). From a reparations and representational justice perspective, those communities, both workers and residents, who suffered through decades of toxicity, are precisely the communities who should be served by new green spaces. In this vision, green and industry are compatible in certain areas, and industrial preservation is the primary means by which to achieve some measure of social justice in the right of neighborhood residents to working class jobs in the neighborhood.

Finally, there is the vision of green enacted through the Greenpoint Community Environmental Fund (GCEF), a product of the ExxonMobil settlement. The GCEF distributed $16.8 million to 40 projects and leveraged an additional $37.6 million in matching contributions from grantees, bringing GCEF's total investment in improving Greenpoint's environment to over $54 million (http://gcefund.org/). One long-term resident and activist saw it as a "very good program. It's what I always wanted. It was very open to the community; the decisions were made by the community. It was the way it should be done." For this activist, the legacy project was the rebuilding of the local library. As she saw it, "Educating the kids is the point of the whole thing. Projects get them to learn about birds, the water, this info reaches the teachers, the parents, then everyone" (phone interview, October 2016). GCEF projects range from the library rebuild and planning for the North Henry Street project mentioned earlier, to a living dock on the Creek, the upgrading of a local park, street tree planting, environmental education programs, water testing, a green roof feasibility study for a local church, and recycling program for local restaurants. The range of projects funded through GCEF insured that most area constituencies could participate and received some benefit from the settlement.

FIGURE 2.3 Kingsland wildflower roof, with wastewater treatment plant in the background

FIGURE 2.4 North Brooklyn Boat Club

For all the diversity of these local greening initiatives, there was some concern expressed by environmentalists as to exactly how much environmental benefit was created. Some felt that more ecological good – specifically, more ecological reparations for and remediation of the area's toxic legacies – could have been accomplished instead of distributing funds to make sure that every group got a piece of the pie (interview, October 2016). Meanwhile, industrial advocates worried that some of the projects would encourage industrial gentrification at the expense of long-term industrial users. One such example is the Kingsland Wildflowers green roof that was built on top of a Broadway Stages facility in the industrial zone, within view of the wastewater treatment plant (see Figure 2.3). In addition to the increased habitat for birds and other wildlife, the roof is designed to slow stormwater runoff. To date, the space has also been used for lectures and community visioning workshops run by NCA and other groups. One danger of this opening up of the industrial area, of course, is that such a space could add gentrification pressure if it becomes a destination space, or if the programming shifts from its educational mission and it becomes more of a "pop-up" event space (see Schaller and Guinand 2017). It also gives Broadway Stages the opportunity to appear as a good environmental citizen, even as other industrial users do not consider them an especially good industrial neighbor. Broadway Stages is the type of business the city "panders to" at the expense of other industrial users, and while they provide good-paying working class jobs, they often bring in those workers from farther out on Long Island (interview with industrial retention advocate, October 2016). Broadway Stages is also behind a plan to build a new boathouse for the North Brooklyn Boat Club. While the club's current interim location is a much-loved but slightly ramshackle space on a strip of land alongside an industrial operation (see Figure 2.4), there is a plan in place for a new boathouse in a multi-story building to be built by Broadway Stages. While Boat Club members are excited about finally getting a proper boathouse, some also worry about how it might change the culture of the Boat Club, particularly as new, wealthier residents from the Greenpoint Landing towers join the neighborhood (interview, North Brooklyn Boat Club member, October 2016).

Both cases – the rooftop wildflower garden and boathouse – represent the types of sustainability initiatives often associated with environmental gentrification or what some have termed "settler environmentalism" (Paperson 2014 as cited in Breyer 2017; Safransky 2014). In other words, they produce spaces and recreational opportunities that are attractive to gentrifiers, and the risk is that they overshadow the community's main priorities. The fact that one of the original "five angry women" sees the GCEF as a model of how community engagement and environmental care should be done (phone interview, October 2016) provides some evidence that it has served the community, both in terms of the actual projects funded and in the process through which they came about. Despite potential gentrification pressure from individual projects, then, the fact that long-term residents can see direct and distinct benefits from the GCEF accomplishes some measure of redistributive justice, however partial and imperfect.

Conclusion – Ongoing lessons from Greenpoint

It is clear that the JGE vision is a living concept, subject to continuous negotiation over specific site and policy proposals. Moreover, there seems to be a new sense of urgency driven by the twin pressures of IBZ encroachment and Superfund planning, leading industrial and environmental advocates to more aggressively and actively try to secure their respective interests, though these are multiple and multifaceted. That said, both seem to recognize that their activities can act as buffers for each other, with green spaces within the IBZ acting as buffers against conversion of industrial use (showing that they can coexist and that they actively choose to do so), and industrial uses acting as buffers against environmental gentrification by providing working class jobs and at least some minimal cooling of the real estate market.

One of our mistakes in our original conception of the just green enough strategy was thinking that industrial zoning would provide more absolute protection than, in fact, it has. Capital has adapted to the existing constraints in Greenpoint and has developed new ways to extract value from the industrial landscape in the form of industrial gentrification. But just as capital has adapted, so too have industrial retention advocates. Preserving industrial use as a cornerstone of the just green enough vision for Greenpoint is an ongoing process, not a simple planning solution. The continued mobilization of long-term activists, and the organizational infrastructure to support them, is essential to ensure that the JGE vision does not get translated into watered-down cleanup or externalized benefits. But cleanup is slow, while, after decades of laying the groundwork, gentrification in Greenpoint is moving fast. For just green enough to continue to be successful as a strategy for preservation and restoration, policy needs to support ways to accomplish a just transition in Greenpoint, preserving both industry and the working class, through proper zoning and affordable housing provision, as well as envisioning a more environmentally responsible and socially just working waterfront by, for example, properly funding the BOA program.

Just green enough goes beyond simply setting aside some space for industry, but should rather be about fundamentally rethinking green spaces and what a just green looks like (see Dooling, Chapter 3, Sze and Yeampierre, Chapter 4). With the North Henry Street site, for instance, it is potentially of greatest use to those who work on the Creek, as a space of respite and refuge during breaks, as well as a broader public resource. We do not often plan green spaces for industrial workers to use during the work day, nor do we generally work on ways to get industrial business to actively engage in remaking their environments. While some who do not read our full articles or public statements might take just green enough to mean that we should short-change communities and not invest in extensive remediation or green space projects in order to prevent gentrification, that is the exact opposite of our conception. Rather, we seek to decouple environmental improvement from luxury redevelopment, to change the urban redevelopment conversation so that no community is ever forced to choose between green space and the ability to stay put. And in the end, a truly just green would require even further transitions, so that the noxious uses deemed too heavy for a remediated and revitalized industrial zone in Greenpoint are not simply moved elsewhere (see Checker in press), so that no neighborhood is ever as burdened as Greenpoint has been.

Notes

1 In this case, cross-subsidization refers to office and industrial mixed-use, with office space subsidizing industrial uses. Such projects would require zoning adaptations.
2 Shoaling refers to areas where the water depth has become very shallow, making marine navigation impossible.

References

Barnes, T. and Hayter, R. 2005. No "Greek-Letter Writing": Local models of resource economies. *Growth and Change* 36(4): 453–470.

BOA. 2012. Newtown Creek Final Report. http://www.gmdconline.org/images/New town-Creek-Final-Report-and-Appendix-2012.pdf

Braun, B. 2002. *The Intemperate Rainforest: Nature, Culture, and Power on Canada's West Coast.* Minneapolis: University of Minnesota Press.

Breyer, B. 2017. Urban greening as settler environmentalism: Vacant land re-use, racialized conflict, and aesthetic dimensions of environmental racism in Cleveland, Ohio. Paper presented at the Annual Meeting of the Association of American Geographers, 5 April 2017, Boston, MA.

CAG. 2016. Steering Committee notes. October 12. https://newtowncreekcag.wordpress.com/steering-committee-meeting-notes/

Checker, M. 2015. Green is the new brown: "Old school toxics" and environmental gentrification on a New York City waterfront. In Isenhour, C., McDonogh, G., and Checker, M. eds. *Sustainability in the Global City: Myth and Practice.* New York: Cambridge University Press.

Checker, M. In press. A Bridge Too Far: Industrial Gentrification and the Dynamics of Sacrifice in New York City. In Lewis, P. and Greenberg, M. eds. *The City is the Factory.* Ithaca, NY: Cornell University Press

Curran, W. 2004. Gentrification and the changing nature of work: Exploring the links in Williamsburg, Brooklyn. *Environment and Planning A* 36(7): 1243–1260.

Curran, W. 2007. "From the frying pan to the oven": Gentrification and the experience of industrial displacement in Williamsburg, Brooklyn. *Urban Studies* 44(8): 1427–1440.

Curran, W. and Hamilton, T. 2012. Just green enough: Contesting environmental gentrification in Greenpoint, Brooklyn. *Local Environment: The International Journal of Justice and Sustainability* 17(9): 1027–1042.

Enman, S. 2017. EPA officials to Trump: Stay away from Newtown Creek. *Brooklyn Daily Eagle*, February 2. http://www.brooklyneagle.com/articles/2017/2/2/epa-officials-trump -stay-away-newtown-creek

EPA. n.d. Superfund site: Newtown Creek, Brooklyn, Queens, NY – site status. https://cumulis.epa.gov/supercpad/SiteProfiles/index.cfm?fuseaction=second.topics&id=0206282#Status

Evergreen. 2016. North Brooklyn Brownfield opportunity area plan: Study content. http://evergreenexchange.org/projects/brownfield-plan/study-content

Goldenberg, S. 2015. Mayor, City Council to ban housing in city's 21 industrial business zones. *Politico New York*, November 3. http://www.politico.com/states/new-york/

city-hall/story/2015/11/mayor-city-council-to-ban-housing-in-citys-21-industrial-business-zones-027511

Gould, K.A. and Lewis, T.L. 2017. *Green Gentrification: Urban Sustainability and the Struggle for Environmental Justice.* New York and London: Routledge.

Holifield, R. 2009. Actor-network theory as a critical approach to environmental justice: A case against synthesis with urban political ecology. *Antipode* 41(4): 637–658.

Krueger, R. 2002. Relocating regulation in Montana's gold mining industry. *Environment and Planning A* 34(5): 867–881.

Laterman, K. 2016. A changing waterfront in Greenpoint, Brooklyn. *New York Times*, October 14. https://www.nytimes.com/2016/10/16/realestate/a-changing-waterfront-in-greenpoint-brooklyn.html?_r=0

Mansfield, B., Biermann, C., McSweeney, K., Law, J., Gallemore, C., Horner, L. and Munroe, D.K. 2015. Environmental politics after nature: Conflicting socioecological futures. *Annals of the Association of American Geographers* 105(2): 284–293.

Newtown Creek Alliance. n.d.a. North Henry Street: A vision for ecological restoration and community access. https://drive.google.com/file/d/0B2ME8bjE-6R0elJOZ0dEX3R0c28/view

Newtown Creek Alliance. n.d.b. Supporters. http://www.newtowncreekalliance.org/supporters/

Newtown Creek Alliance. n.d.c. Wildlife. http://www.newtowncreekalliance.org/wildlife/

NYSDEC. n.d. Greenpoint Petroleum remediation project – Project status. http://nysdec greenpoint.com/ProjectStatus.aspx

Paperson, L. 2014. A ghetto land pedagogy: An antidote for settler environmentalism. *Environmental Education Research* 20(1): 115–130.

Plitt, A. 2016. New batch of affordable Greenpoint Landing apartments available from $393. *Curbed NY*, October 28. https://ny.curbed.com/2016/10/28/13460404/brooklyn-greenpoint-landing-affordable-housing-lottery

Safransky, S. 2014. Greening the urban frontier: Race, property, and resettlement in Detroit. *Geoforum* 56: 237–248.

Schaller, S. and Guinand, S. 2017. Pop-up landscapes: A new trigger to push up land value? *Urban Geography.* doi: 10.1080/02723638.2016.1276719

3

MAKING JUST GREEN ENOUGH ADVOCACY RESILIENT: DIVERSE ECONOMIES, ECOSYSTEM ENGINEERS AND LIVELIHOOD STRATEGIES FOR LOW-CARBON FUTURES

Sarah Dooling

Introduction

Ecological gentrification is one of the most pernicious issues in rapidly growing cities using environmental strategies to address public health, climate change and contaminated urban land. The process of ecological gentrification happens through development and planning efforts claiming to be social and environmental responses to underdeveloped urban landscapes. Environmentally sensitive development is frequently motivated by ethics that appeal to wealthy, environmentally conscious residents, while excluding the needs and interests of current residents (Dooling 2009; Checker 2011). The dialectics of ecological gentrification are one of the legacies of Cartesian dualism that prioritizes and segregates nouns (e.g., parks, buildings, housing) over relational dynamics when assigning value in interconnected urban systems.

For the industrial communities of Williamsburg and Greenpoint, NYC, ecological gentrification began with the rezoning of the waterfront on the East River, which attracted river development projects and developers interested in converting industrial sites into high-end lofts and recreation spaces (Curran and Hamilton 2012; Curran 2007). For underinvested communities struggling with homelessness, like the downtown east side of Vancouver, ecological gentrification was a concerted effort among real estate developers and advocates of urban densification, who joined in espousing an environmentally progressive agenda. These urban development projects translated into an effort to rid the area of homeless people from newly constructed green spaces (Quastel 2009). In this era of urban sustainability and resilience, the eviction of working class and low-income residents and the removal of industrial businesses coincide with newly created green spaces and improved environmental conditions for flora and fauna. In city neighborhoods ripe for re-investment, these parts of town where poor and working class people have historically been able to find housing, greening initiatives are often a bellwether for creating more attractive – and more expensive – places to live.

In this chapter, I identify and discuss contradictions that contribute to ecological gentrification as an urban problem from the perspective of urban sustainability and resilience. The concepts of value and labor are important for understanding why and how the social and ecological dimensions of urban neighborhoods have been, and continue to be, regulated in isolation from each other. I review frameworks and visions of integrated urban environments found in urban ecology and environmental histories. The translation of synthetic approaches to urban systems into policies and urban planning practice has been limited by siloed structures in government and the persistent societal narrative that externalizes nature just enough to dominate it for economic gains. For cities that want to invest in green infrastructure projects, greening up is suddenly equated with pricing up neighborhoods. In this chapter, I describe the *just green enough* community response, which embraces a political stance admirable for its commitment to the preservation of livelihood strategies and environmental improvements. However, I contend that while the preservation of industrial livelihoods is necessary for maintaining immediate neighborhood stability, the JGE advocates must now focus on promoting livelihood strategies with less environmental impact on local populations and regional ecologies. Deliberations over an economic vision that is ecologically and human-oriented are the next step in moving communities towards urban resilience. I conclude with a series of questions that can inform an urban resilience movement committed to creating community economies that benefit people and our biotic neighbors.

Ecological gentrification: Genealogy of an idea

The term gentrification, as coined by British sociologist Ruth Glass (1964), focused on the displacement of working class households by middle class homeowners. The process of gentrification completely altered the social classes of neighborhoods through displacing lower-income households and improving the quality of housing stock with the arrival of wealthier homeowners. Most of the earlier work on conceptualizing, describing, and documenting gentrification focused exclusively on processes of displacing working class and low-income people, and, secondarily, on the economic dynamics of housing markets (Hartman 1979; Marcuse 1986). Research documenting the changing social demographics was aligned with political efforts to preserve working class neighborhoods and livelihoods. A decade later, vacant, underused, and industrialized parcels were renovated for occupation by the middle class, especially in U.S. cities where industrial productivity was declining (Smith 1996; Zukin 1987). These urban development projects were often part of city efforts to revitalize downtown urban cores as many local industrial economies contracted with the proliferation of globalized networks of trade (Smith 1996).

In the late 1980s, some researchers began to rationalize gentrification as an urban re-development process that promoted economic revitalization and class mixing, a perspective that gained traction in urban policy and urban development discourse (Blomley 2004; Byrne 2003). Critics argued that equating gentrification with the creation of mixed-income communities revealed the influence of a depoliticized liberalism on ideas of neighborhood change that ignored the synergies among affordable housing, urban poverty, and racial politics within which these urban projects were developed (Slater 2006). Gentrification as a process that displaced the working class and eroded their economic opportunities was subsumed by, and conflated with, gentrification that promoted economic diversity at the scale of a single project designed to attract new, rather than retain existing, residents. The process of upending working class and low-income neighborhoods was perceived as the unavoidable outcome of the invisible hand underlying urbanization, a perspective that was cultivated and reinforced by Reagan-era government divestments from social welfare programs and Margaret Thatcher's belief in a society based on self-reliance with minimal government support.

Following the 2008 financial crisis, in which over 4 million people completed housing foreclosures and lost their homes, housing prices are once again on the rise, and gentrification pressures seem more urgent than ever. Affordable housing advocates have worked diligently to implement regulatory strategies for maintaining and preserving existing affordable housing – including inclusionary housing (Ohm and Sitkowski 2004), low-income tax credits (Baum-Snow and Marion 2009), housing vouchers (Sard 2001), homestead exception districts (Bowman 2006), housing trust funds (Larsen 2009), community land trusts (Moore and McKee 2012), and rent stabilization programs (Pearsall 2012). However, most cities have not created a vision for the preservation and production of affordable housing, an omission which can be equated to a collective failure to see urban development possibilities beyond gentrification. Instead, watchdog groups and affordable housing advocates generate accounting reports that document the number of units which are needed to fill various affordability gaps. In fast growing cities, affordable housing and anti-gentrification groups are largely on the defensive, as developers are often granted tax breaks and awarded other subsidies that city politicians justify by claiming the economic prosperity of the city is dependent upon tax revenue. Developers offer the complementary logic that the cost of investment in high risk areas requires the highest return in the shortest amount of time. Building affordable housing is too expensive for developers who want to maintain deep profit margins, and pursuing state or federal funds to lower construction costs adds costs by extending project review and permitting time (Kimura 2016). The dominant discourse today is that gentrification is inevitable and largely unstoppable in an era of rising land costs, an absence of rigorous proactive affordability public policies, and an affordable housing crisis that is maintained by the aggressive pursuit of economic growth measures.

It is not surprising that the impacts of environmental improvements were not part of the early gentrification discussions and debates. While Glass was writing about social displacement, natural and social scientists in the U.S. considered cities ecological sacrifice zones. Just as the natural sciences ignored urban environmental issues, social sciences – including sociology, social work, urban planning, and economics – focused on housing, employment and economic development, and poverty alleviation to the exclusion of urban environmental issues. For natural and social scientists, cities were human settlements with little to no ecological value. However, as urbanization (i.e., as a land-change process of densification and/or expansion) intensified through the 1950s into the 1960s, and as the North American environmental movement protested against environmental degradation and increasing rates of human resource consumption, ecologists began to consider the city as a legitimate site for ecological research (McDonnell 2011). Natural scientists in the early years of urban ecology perceived humans as agents of destruction, and human actions were understood as a particular form of disturbance that disrupted environmental conditions and processes (Vitousek et al. 1997), reduced diversity of native flora and fauna, particularly specialists (McKinney 2002), and fragmented habitat (Dickman 1987). In cities, ecological and social phenomena remained estranged by siloed disciplines through the 1980s.

A long and rich history in sociology and environmental theory has asserted the indivisibility of people in human settlements from their natural and built environments, and the social value of urban green spaces. The planner and botanist, Sir Patrick Geddes, writing in the late nineteenth century in Scotland, envisioned cities within regional ecological capacities that, when carefully designed and tended, created vibrant urban habitats that were beautiful, economically productive and able to sustain an urban society based on social cooperation in lieu of economic competition (Geddes [1915] 2015). During this same time, Frederick Law Olmsted, the landscape architect, understood urban green spaces as essential for social cohesion that was maintained through the co-mingling of high and lower economic classes in public, and as a critical form of infrastructure which cleansed urban environments using the ecological processes of filtration and purification (Fishman 1982). Olmsted understood how beautiful green spaces relieved stress for people living in cramped, poorly constructed tenement housing. He also knew that cities benefited from landscapes designed to treat urban environmental conditions. While Olmsted's ideas have been influential in urban planning and landscape architecture, Geddes' broader urban vision has been largely forgotten.

Alexander von Humbolt (1769–1859) was the most influential and visionary scientist of his time, bringing together natural history, ecology, anthropology, and political economy (Wulf 2015). Based on his extensive explorations of the globe where he encountered diverse cultures and environments, Humbolt rejected the human-centered perspective that believed human domination improved nature through clearing and cultivation (von Humbolt 2014). Nature was a global force, connected to society through flows of energy, and humans were wise to first understand natural systems dynamics in order to co-inhabit landscapes with minimal disturbances. Humbolt's emphasis on ecological diversity and relational webs established the vision of ecology that dominates natural science today. Similar to Geddes and Olmsted, Humbolt offered a cosmological view of people and their natural environments living in a seamless web. Similar to Geddes, Humbolt has been largely forgotten by people outside academia, despite his influence on ecological science and key thinkers in environmental thought and history.

The environmental histories of Chicago (Cronon 1991), Houston (Melosi and Pratt 2007), and New Orleans (Colten 2005) reject the exclusively economic interpretation of city development, and detail how cities were, and continue to be, built out of specific geologies, waterways, forests, and topographies, and how political decisions and economic structures transformed non-urban landscapes into human settlements. Colten's work (2005), in particular, documents the racial and economic attitudes among city boosters and politicians that created uneven patterns of infrastructure development, and the resulting environmental inequities, many of which persist today.

Research in social sciences has long acknowledged connections among social and environmental dynamics in urban settings (Lefebvre 1992; Harvey 1996). The concept of ecological gentrification (Dooling 2009) was originally intended to delineate a wider set of urban dynamics involved in displacing poor people than had been conventionally analyzed by social scientists. I detailed how the designation and management of urban green spaces displaced homeless people camping and sleeping in those spaces, and identified the logic of human displacement in the guise of protecting urban natural places and advancing an environmental ethic. More recent definitions are situated more broadly in the economic process of neighborhood development and urban governance. Checker's (2011) definition of eco-gentrification reads as "the convergence of urban re-development, ecologically minded initiatives and environmental justice activism in an era of advanced capitalism" (212). Both definitions emphasize the subordination of equity and social justice issues to rhetoric that values urban green spaces for a nature absent poor people (Dooling 2009) and to profit-driven development intended for future, often wealthier, residents (Checker 2011). Collectively, research on eco-gentrification (Pride 2016; Chatterton 2010; Quastel 2009) and green gentrification (Gould and Lewis 2017) provide incisive accounts of ecological gentrification progressing through urban development efforts that claim to be socially and environmentally progressive, seemingly motivated by ethics that appeal to environmentally conscious residents able to afford cleaned-up, greened-up, expensive communities.

Today, as cities embrace urban sustainability ideals and call for densifying inner neighborhoods, development projects are being justified in terms of environmental, as well as social, benefits. With the proliferation of urban climate resilience plans, green infrastructure projects are becoming a common strategy for combating urban heat island effects (Bowler et al. 2010), improving stormwater quality (Keeley et al. 2013), reducing flood risk (Lin Chen, and Peng 2014), and enhancing capacity for carbon sequestration (Lovell and Taylor 2013). The broader social and economic contexts of ecological gentrification, including persistent patterns of uneven development that are sustained by worsening income inequality and a nationwide affordable housing crisis, demand that environmental improvements and associated development projects be assessed synthetically and critically. The value of urban green spaces, including those newly acquired for environmental protection (Dooling 2009), recently remediated (Curran and Hamilton 2012), or newly vegetated (Quastel 2009), is aligned with economic valuations that monetizes environmental improvements and attracts capital investments. More recent scholarship equates the arrival of high-end retailers selling organic and sustainable food production as the signal of a completely ecologically gentrified neighborhood (Anguelovski 2015). The marketing of neighborhoods as places where organic food is within walking distance, complete with bike lanes and public transit options, targets the newly arrived and future residents able to afford higher rents and food prices. With increased importance placed on environmental health and landscape performance by urban planning and development professionals, gentrification is no longer confined exclusively to issues of housing affordability and social justice. Now, a cleaned-up, greened-up environment is a signal that gentrification is or will be happening very soon.

The paradox of ecological gentrification calls for a dialectical analysis of social displacement, environmental improvements, and infrastructural upgrades. Urban change and development occur as groups seek to impose a settlement that re-defines the community to their advantage. The historical connections across oppositional social interests force a temporary resolution of some, but never all, of the contradictory claims on community resources. The economic organization of ecological webs of life (referred to aptly as capitalism-in-nature; Moore 2015) and the concurrent re-structuring of social relations in response to environmental changes (humanity-in-nature; Moore 2015) reflect the dialectical dynamics involved in gentrifying urban environments. Focusing on the flows of "power and capital in nature, and the flows of nature in capital and power" (Moore 2015, 15) moves analyses beyond conventional impact models that maintain the blinding dualisms of people and nature, and of nature and economics. Dialectical analysis has a long history among social scientists and critical theorists as an intellectual and political project that makes intelligible how social inequities are perpetuated through converging political, economic, technological, and regulatory forces, and the efforts to resist and reverse these forces (Lefebvre 1992; Jameson 2009; Harvey 1996; Guatarri 2000). Gentrification, as a dialectical phenomenon, is a product of the struggle that social communities enter into as they seek to shape the ecological webs of life and exercise influence within dominant economic, cultural, and biophysical agencies of change.

Just green enough: A response rooted in contradictions and dualisms

In hindsight, the dynamics involved in ecological gentrification anticipated a just green enough response. The *just green enough* stance (Curran and Hamilton 2012) argues that industrial livelihood strategies also face eviction with arrival of real estate firms that re-purpose industrial buildings into higher-end lofts. As a particular kind of anti-gentrification strategy, *just green enough* (JGE) advocates attempt to stabilize neighborhoods where industrial businesses and affordable housing are threatened by urban redevelopment projects attracted to neighborhoods given a renewed aesthetic due to environmental improvements. Their strategy is about preserving jobs and housing alongside environmental remediation and improvement efforts, a strategy that comes directly from the history of social justice activism and urban sustainability ideals. However, the environmental reality is that industrial production brings with it the production of environmental harms and ecosystem disservices, even in the context of existing environmental regulations. The insidious conundrum JGE advocates face is one of time and an ecological understanding of labor. Preserving livelihood strategies in the near-term is needed to maintain stability and production in the now. Yet, questions arise about the viability of current livelihood strategies for a future marked by anticipated resource scarcities and unavoidable ecological constraints. JGE must work simultaneously in the present and for a future whose uncertainties demand an all-together different conception of livelihood strategies and economic prosperity. Expanded conceptions of labor, including ecological labor that powers and maintains the ecological webs upon which we all depend, could force a rethinking of land valuation and productive activities. Viable livelihood strategies depend on healthy and diverse ecological communities, out of which extracted resources are transformed into commodities and goods. Livelihood strategies for ecological communities must also be protected, a move that situates economics in nature, as well as nature in economics.

The JGE advocates are not quite embracing the holistic visions of urban ecology espoused by Geddes, Olmsted, and von Humbolt. By focusing on immediate and near-term economic stability, the JGE advocates root themselves in the dominant economic paradigm and inadvertently reinforce the prioritization of economic prosperity over environmental degradation. Ideas about urban sustainability and resilience call for the transformation of all aspects of society, including modes of production and economic practice (Hart and Milstein 1999; Rees 1995; Ahern 2011; Folke 2006). JGE advocates have an opportunity to address environmental harms associated with industrial production on local and regional ecosystems, and deliberate new forms of livelihood strategies that avoid the denigrating side effects of environmental improvements. Such deliberations are necessary to avoid trading the preservation of immediate stabilities for future scenarios that must have, by all scientific accounts, a significantly lower carbon footprint.

Competing and exclusionary definitions of value aggravate efforts to realize integrated conceptions of economics and ecology. For ecologists, an ecological community has value when it is able to retain essential functions (e.g., photosynthesis, water filtration), and value is improved as (functional and taxonomic) biodiversity increases because more niches convey increased stability in the face of disturbances and disasters (Elton 1958; Hooper et al. 2005). All too often, however, the intrinsic and use values assigned to ecological communities by scientists and urban sustainability scholars are consistently re-configured to fit within the logic and operations of economic rationality (Moore 2015). The monetization of ecological processes, as practiced by ecosystem services practitioners, represents this kind of system re-configuration and assigning of value. An ecosystem services approach simplifies complex ecological dynamics into discrete numeric units that are monetized and incorporated into cost-benefit assessments, and prioritizes only those landscape processes that directly benefit people (Gomez-Baggethun and Perez 2011; Schaffler and Swilling 2013). Many proponents of ecosystem services assert that monetization of the environment, and the establishment of markets, is the most efficient and effective way to instill and sustain value in landscapes that are relevant for policy-makers. Ecosystem service practitioners view the domination of markets and profits as the final arbiter of development and policy decisions. In the end, the language of ecosystem services only reinforces the contradictory logics of economics and ecology.

The displacement of intrinsic and use values of nature from public discussions and policy decisions has happened, in large part, because society cannot muster the political imagination to consider value as other than financial and economic goals, as other than profit generating. The idea that humanity exists within nature, and depends on environmental processes for existence, is obscured by the powerful market rationality that desensitizes people from seeing themselves as always in active relationship with the natural world, in the traditions of Geddes, Olmsted and von Humbolt. The separation of people from the biophysical and ecological is maintained by an economic logic that values monetary gains through production above all else – including environmental and human health. Just green enough advocates find themselves in a corner, where alternative and more progressive possibilities for urban development vanish under the weight of a dominating market mentality and a siloed urban governance structure, both of which contribute to depoliticizing public spaces of deliberation.

Our urban futures: Diverse economies and ecologies

The underlying question in deliberations over urban development efforts and neighborhood preservation efforts in the just green enough stance is: *how shall we live?* These are precarious times in which most people are struggling to secure prospects for a future marked by economic and environmental uncertainties. Urban sustainability and resilience concepts emphasize the transition to low-carbon futures as a critical component to living into an uncertain future (Bulkeley et al. 2012, 2014). The JGE advocates, in their focus on the immediate future, are seeking stability in the preservation of industrial-based businesses. In seeking to halt the displacement of jobs stemming from speculative urban development practice, the JGE advocates are attempting to push back on powerful logic that prioritizes economic growth over economic stabilization. Since the beginning of the modern era, scholars have questioned the compatibility of economic rationality with social cohesion and our long-term survival on a planet with finite resources (Moore 2015; Gorz 2012). In the short term, preservation of an industrial economic base for urban neighborhoods facing development pressures is laudable, even necessary. As a resilience strategy, however, it falls back on convenient, short-sighted measures that simply push off to the future hard decisions for economic and social transformation to sustain life on earth.

To re-make the politics of displacement (Hern 2016) and to reverse the dynamics of ecological gentrification requires bolder, more experimental strategies informed by a longer view of society's future. The ultimate challenge facing cities is the transformation of economic values and systems in order to enable stewardship and cooperation, as opposed to exploitation and competition. Ecological gentrification and the just green enough response are an outgrowth of the persistent dualism maintained by economic logic between people and nature, a dualism that obfuscates the material and ecological realities of humanity-in-nature dynamics. Any efforts to transcend capitalism by appealing to concepts of holism (as espoused in urban sustainability frameworks) or egalitarianism will be stymied by this binary that locks people and nature into false opposition (Moore 2015). Resisting and preventing displacement of job and residents, while ecological communities are improved, represent incremental victories that are beneficial in the short term but inadequate for building long-term community resilience.

Communities need to engage the more difficult task of creating a future built on a different vocabulary and language of economy that allows people to read the economy for difference (Gibson-Graham 2006). A diverse economic landscape contains a mixture of capitalist and non-capitalist forms of labor, production and ownership. Drawing from similar concepts in natural science ecology that assert biologically diverse communities are better to withstand external disturbances, some scholars contend that communities with a diverse mixture of economic approaches are also more likely to remain stable in the face of economic, and environmental, uncertainties because of the functional redundancies such diversity creates (Gibson-Graham 1996).

Transition towns are local communities that have been experimenting with diverse economies while exercising degrees of autonomy. Initially formed in response to concerns over climate change and peak oil (Aiken 2012; Flintoff 2013), transition towns work backwards from a future vision of *how shall we live?*, a vision that values self-sufficiency at the local scale primarily related to energy and food production. The Transition Town Network (TTN), established in 2005, includes 300 communities worldwide, and considers these experimental communities as "open source and development project[s]" (Flintoff 2013), as necessary spaces which allow the dialectical dynamics driving urban development and economic growth to inform experiments in low-carbon living. The concepts of resilience, transition and community that inspire and guide TTN communities are taken from the principles of permaculture and complex systems, where new models of governance and landscape design emerge from the acknowledged indivisibility of human and environmental well-being (Aiken 2012).

Transition towns have been critiqued for being small, self-selected groups that don't engage in direct political action (Aiken 2012). Participating in transition initiatives might be considered an exclusive enterprise that requires investment of capital and time. However, the U.S. Transition Network's REconomy Program, based on a 2010 model developed in the UK, has led to the establishment of various co-operatives in an effort to move away from an extractive and exploitative system

(Mommaerts n.d.). Five transition groups in England have developed their own currencies to ensure re-investment within their communities. Other groups have raised funds to build England's first community-owned power station in an urban neighborhood (http://www.transitiontownbrixton.org/). Efforts to experiment with small and larger changes in economic practices are not incongruous with the JGE strategy; indeed, these efforts could be the next evolution in JGE's approaches to promote long-term stability.

I contend that the JGE position must broaden its response to the question of *how shall we live?* While the JGE struggle has made the loss of livelihood strategies part of the fight against gentrification broadly, and ecological gentrification specifically, their insistence on preserving industrial jobs seems equivalent to fighting over an individual domino piece (jobs) as opposed to changing the (economic) game. The larger challenge is the cultivation of ethical ecological-economic sensibilities so that society's notions of ecology and economy allow cities and individuals to take responsibility for living in communities, for living as humanity-in-nature (Gibson-Graham and Miller 2015). Creating small spaces where different economic values are pursued inserts plausible counter-narratives that can crack open spaces for alternatives to the dominating system of exploitation, competition and inequities. The JGE position defends the economic security of residents in the face of aggressive speculative development with inadequate regulations, but simultaneously fails to offer a broader vision of urban development, a vision rooted in an ethics of interdependencies of all residents, including biota.

Conclusion

As society faces the daunting task of transitioning to a low-carbon future, critical thinkers need to place questions about ecological gentrification and the preservation of industrial jobs into larger frameworks that re-connect the present to the future. Urban resilience is one framework, and refers to the ability of people, biota and their networks to persist, adapt and transform systems that limit current or future adaptive capacity (Meerow, Newell, and Stults 2016). The emphasis on adaptation and transformation can complement and expand JGE's emphasis on short-term stability. The question for the urban resilience movement might be: *where do we transform our systems so we can live in integrated socio-ecological communities that ensure maximum survival of all species?*

Certitudes of modern economic domination must be ruptured by a more discerning and diverse concept of economy. Community groups, like the JGE advocates, are part of this rupturing. The history of social movements in this country provides evidence that political pressures, applied at many levels, can result in transformative policies (e.g., civil rights, women's rights). As climate change threatens economic and social stability, however, cultivating a broader and more inclusive vision of value and labor in urban communities is urgently needed. The dialectical contradictions inherent in ecological gentrification, and the inadvertent bind of the JGE response, can generate a social movement focused on transforming economics. An urban resilience movement can insist on co-joint human and environmental well-being that is attentive to the polluting externalities associated with industrial livelihood strategies. Rethinking the economy as diverse processes and interrelationships through which people and biota co-create livelihood strategies is a first step in moving towards urban resilience characterized by transformation, inclusion, and justice.

How might we dissolve the distinction between ecology and economy, and redefine economy as "ecology from the standpoint of actors constituting a community and producing livelihoods together" (Gibson-Graham and Miller 2015, 14)?

How might we expand the concept of labor to include ecosystem engineers that maintain the biophysical processes of photosynthesis which powers the ecological webs upon which we all depend? How might this expanded concept of labor transform current modes of industrial production?

How might society identify and regulate many forms of economic value, and create diverse economies better able to thrive in the face of increasingly uncertain futures? How might economically diverse cities and neighborhoods defy displacement (of people and biota) and invert contemporary urbanism out of which ecological gentrification is perpetuated?

How might labor be employed, investments be structured, and governance be made more responsive in a world committed to cities and neighborhoods as living, diverse urban ecologies?

These are questions that move communities beyond dualistic approaches into unchartered terrain, a frightening prospect that becomes bearable only when societies are clear about their values. The urban resilience movement proposed here builds on resistance to ecological gentrification and negotiating away community benefits to developers. One must ask communities to consider economies as ethical and political spaces of decision, where community is the outcome, not the ground (Gibson-Graham 1996). Ecological gentrification is a problem that points to the need to build diverse community economies in place, an effort that requires expansive vision and courage, and a refusal to endow capitalism with authority to resist change to its dominating place in society.

References

Ahern, J. 2011. From fail-safe to safe-to-fail: Sustainability and resilience in the new urban world. *Landscape and Urban Planning* 100(4): 341–343.

Aiken, G. 2012. Community transitions to low carbon futures in the transition towns network (TTN). *Geography Compass* 6(2): 89–99.

Anguelovski, I. 2015. Alternative food provision conflicts in cities; Contesting food privilege, injustice and whiteness in Jamaica Plain, Boston. *Geoforum* 58: 184–194.

Baum-Snow, N. and Marion, J. 2009. The effects of low income housing tax credit developments on neighborhoods. *Journal of Public Economics* 93(5–6): 654–666.

Blomley, N. 2004. *Unsettling the City: Urban Land and the Politics of Property*. New York: Routledge.

Bowler, D.E., Buyung-Ali, L., Knight, T. and Pullin, A. 2010. Urban greening to cool towns and cities: A systematic review of the empirical evidence. *Landscape and Urban Planning* 97(3): 147–155.

Bowman, J.H. 2006. Property tax policy responses to rapidly rising home values: District of Columbia, Maryland, and Virginia. *National Tax Journal* 59(3): 717–733.

Bulkeley, H., Broto, C. and Edwards, G. 2012. Bringing climate change to the city: Towards low carbon urbanism? *Local Environment* 17(5): 545–551.

Bulkeley, H., Broto, C. and Maassen, A. 2014. Low carbon transitions and the reconfiguration of urban infrastructure. *Urban Studies* 51(7): 1471–1486.

Byrne, J.P. 2003. Two cheers for gentrification. *Howard Law Journal* 46(3): 405–432.

Chatterton, P. 2010. The urban impossible: A eulogy for the unfinished city. *City* 14(3): 234–244.

Checker, M. 2011. Wiped out by the "greenwave": Environmental gentrification and the paradoxical politics of urban sustainability. *City and Society* 23(2): 210–229.

Colten, C.E. 2005. *Unnatural Metropolis: Wresting New Orleans from Nature*. Baton Rouge: Louisiana State University Press.

Cronon, W. 1991. *Nature's Metropolis: Chicago and the Great West*. New York: WW Norton and Company. 530 pp.

Curran, W. 2007. "From the frying pan to the oven": Gentrification and the experience of industrial displacement in Williamsburg, Brooklyn. *Urban Studies* 44(8): 1427–1440.

Curran, W. and Hamilton, T. 2012. Just green enough: Contesting environmental gentrification in Greenpoint, Brooklyn. *Local Environment* 17(9): 1027–1042.

Dickman, C.R. 1987. Habitat fragmentation and vertebrate species richness in an urban environment. *Journal of Applied Ecology* 24(2): 337–351.

Dooling, S. 2009. Ecological gentrification: A research agenda exploring justice in the city. *International Journal of Urban and Regional Research* 33(3): 621–639.

Elton, C. 1958. *The Ecology of Invasions by Animals and Plants*. London: Methuen. 181 pp.

Fishman, R. 1982 *Urban Utopias in the Twentieth Century: Ebenezer Howard, Frank Lloyd Wright, Le Corbusier*. London: MIT Press. 332 pp.

Flintoff, John-Paul. 2013. Local, self-sufficient, optimistic: Are transition towns the way forward? June 15. https://www.theguardian.com/environment/2013/jun/15/transition-towns-way-forward

Folke, C. 2006. Resilience: The emergence of a perspective for social-ecological systems analyses. *Global Environmental Change* 16(3): 253–267.

Geddes, P. 2015 [1915]. *Cities in Evolution: An Introduction to Town Planning Movement and to the Study of Civics*. Andesite Press. 440 pp.

Gibson-Graham, J.-K. 1996. *The End of Capitalism (As We Knew It): A Feminist Critique of Political Economy*. Minneapolis and London: University of Minnesota Press. 299 pp.

Gibson-Graham, J.K. 2006. *A Post Capitalist Politics*. Minneapolis: University of Minnesota Press.

Gibson-Graham, J.-K. and Miller, E. 2015. Chapter 2: Economy as ecological livelihood. In Gibson, K., Bird Rose, D., and Fincher, R. (eds.), *Manifesto for Living in the Anthropocene*. Brooklyn, New York: Punctum Books, pp. 7–16.

Glass, R. 1964. Introduction: Aspects of change. In Centre for Urban Studies and Glass, R. (eds.), *London: Aspects of Change*. London: MacKibbon and Kee, pp. xiii–xlii.

Gomez-Baggethun, E. and Perez, M. 2011. Economic valuation and the commodification of ecosystem services. *Progress in Physical Geography* 35(5): 1–16.

Gorz, A. 2012. *Capitalism, Socialism, Ecology*. Brooklyn, New York: Verso. 147 pp.

Gould, K. and Lewis, T.L. 2017. *Green Gentrification: Urban Sustainability and the Struggle for Environmental Justice*. New York: Routledge. 181 pp.

Guatarri, F. 2000. *The Three Ecologies*. London: Athlone Press. 174 pp.

Hart, S. and Milstein, M. 1999. Global sustainability and the creative destruction of industries. *Sloan Management Review* 41(4): 23–33.

Hartman, C. 1979. Comment on "Neighbourhood revitalization and displacement: A review of the evidence". *Journal of the American Planning Association* 45(4): 488–491.

Harvey, D. 1996. *Justice, Nature and the Geography of Difference.* Oxford, UK: Blackwell Publishers. 468 pp.

Hern, M. 2016. *What Is a City For: Remaking the Politics of Displacement.* Cambridge, MA: MIT Press. 254 pp.

Hooper, D.U., Chapin, F.S., Ewel, J.J., Hector, A., Inchausti, P., Larorel, S., Lawton, J.H., Lodge, D.M., Loraeu, M., Naeem, S., Schmid, B., Setala, H., Symstad, A.J., Vandermeer, J. and Wardle, D.A. 2005. Effects of biodiversity on ecosystem functioning: A consensus of current knowledge. *Ecological Monographs* 75(1): 3–35.

Jameson, F. 2009. *Valences of the Dialectic.* London, UK: Verso Books. 625 pp.

Keeley, M., Koburger, A., Dolowitz, D.P., Medearis, D., Nickel, D. and Shuster, W. (2013). Perspectives on the use of green infrastructure for stormwater management in Cleveland and Milwaukee. *Environmental Management* 51(6): 1093–1108. doi:10.1007/s00267-013-0032-x

Kimura, D. 2016. Why is affordable housing so expensive? Affordable Housing Finance. August 16. http://www.housingfinance.com/news/why-is-affordable-housing-so-expensive_o.

Larsen, K. 2009. Reassessing state housing trust funds: Results of a Florida survey. *Housing Studies* 24(2): 1173–1201.

Lefebvre, H. 1992. *The Production of Space.* Oxford, UK: Wiley-Blackwell. 464 pp.

Lin, W., Chen, W. and Peng, C. 2014. Assessing the effectiveness of green infrastructure on urban flooding reduction: A community scale study. *Ecological Modeling* 291: 6–14.

Lovell, S. and Taylor, J. 2013. Supplying ecosystem services through multifunctional green infrastructure in the United States. *Landscape Ecology* 28: 1447–1463.

Marcuse, P. 1986. Abandonment, gentrification and displacement: The linkages in New York City. In Smith, N. and Williams, P. (eds.) *Gentrification of the City.* London: Unwin Hyman.

McDonnell, M.J. 2011. The history of urban ecology: An ecologlist's perspective. In Niemelä, J., Breusteb, J.H., Guntenspergen, G., McIntyre, N.E., Elmqvist, T., and James, P. (eds.), *Urban ecology: Patterns, Processes, and Applications.* New York: Oxford University Press, pp. 5–13.

McKinney, M.L. 2002. Urbanization, biodiversity, and conservation. *Bioscience* 52(10): 883–890.

Meerow, S., Newell, J. and Stults, M. 2016. Defining urban resilience: A review. *Landscape and Urban Planning* 147: 38–49.

Melosi, M. and Pratt, J. (eds). 2007. *Energy Metropolis: An Environmental History of Houston and the Gulf Coast.* Pittsburgh, PA: University of Pittsburgh Press. 352 pp.

Mommaerts, M. (n.d.). 25 Enterprises That Build Resilience. Transition US REconomy Project Report. http://www.transitionus.org/sites/default/files/25_Enterprises_that_Build-d_Resilience.pdf

Moore, J. 2015. *Capitalism in the Web of Life.* Brooklyn: Verso Books. 336 pp.

Moore, T. and McKee, K. 2012. Empowering local communities? An international overview of community land trusts. *Housing Studies* 24(2): 280–290.

Ohm, B.W. and Sitkowski, R.J. 2004. Integrating new urbanism and affordable housing tools. *Urban Lawyer* 36(4): 857–866.

Pearsall, H. 2012. Moving in or moving out? Resilience to environmental gentrification in New York City. *Local Environment* 17(9): 1012–1026.

Pride, T. 2016. Resident led urban agriculture and the hegemony of neoliberal community development: Eco-gentrification in a Detroit neighborhood. PhD dissertation. Wayne State University, Detroit, Michigan.

Quastel, N. 2009. Political ecologies of gentrification. *Urban Geography* 30(7): 694–725.

Rees, W. 1995. Achieving sustainability: Reform or transformation? *Journal of Planning Literature* 9(4): 343–361.

Sard, B. 2001. Housing vouchers should be a major component of future housing policy for the lowest income families. *Cityscape* 5(2): 89–110.

Schaffler, A. and Swilling, M. 2013. Valuing green infrastructure in an urban environment under pressure. *Ecological Economics* 86: 246–257.

Slater, T. 2006. The eviction of critical perspectives from gentrification research. *International Journal of Urban and Regional Research* 30(4): 303–325.

Smith, N. 1996. *The New Urban Frontier: Gentrification and the Revanchist City*. New York: Routledge. 267 pp.

Vitousek, P., Mooney, H., Lubchenco, J. and Melillo, J. 1997. Human domination of Earth's ecosystems. *Science* 277(5325): 494–499. doi:10.1126/science.277.5325.494

Von Humbolt, A. 2014. *Views of Nature*. Stephen T. Jackson, Laura Dassow Walls, and Mark W. Person (eds). Chicago: University of Chicago Press. 344 pp.

Wulf, A. 2015. *The Invention of Nature: Alexander von Humbolt's New World*. New York: Alfred A. Knopf. 473 pp.

Zukin, S. 1987. Gentrification: Culture and capital in the urban core. *Annual Review of Sociology* 13: 129–147.

4

JUST TRANSITION AND JUST GREEN ENOUGH: CLIMATE JUSTICE, ECONOMIC DEVELOPMENT AND COMMUNITY RESILIENCE

Julie Sze and Elizabeth Yeampierre

Introduction

In Kenneth Gould and Tammy Lewis' (2016) book, *Green Gentrification: Urban Sustainability and the Struggle for Environmental Justice*, they analyze how "greening" projects and politics trigger gentrification. By looking at empirical case studies from four different Brooklyn neighborhoods, they pose the question: how can cities "go green" without triggering gentrification in the context of rising rents and the (so-called) decline of manufacturing? Their analysis is mostly centered on how green gentrification has *already* happened, but they end on a cautiously optimistic note, by suggesting that Sunset Park represents the "last best hope" for achieving truly sustainable urban greening in Brooklyn. Sunset Park's unique situation is largely due to the efforts of United Puerto Rican Organization of Sunset Park (UPROSE), an environmental justice organization which advocates for a just transition in relationship to climate change.

With a just transition model, UPROSE is explicitly rejecting old economic development models centered on environmental pollution and fossil fuel extraction. Rather than accept the status quo in terms of environmental politics and climate policy, UPROSE foregrounds a climate justice strategy that incorporates a community revitalization strategy, political vision, and a racial justice analysis policy. In doing so, the organization actively rejects the symbolic/ spectacular symbols of sustainability and climate resiliency for the area that are being promoted by real estate developers and government actors (Hum 2014). Just transition is the move to a "lower carbon economy that recognizes the trade-offs between... competing needs and priorities (such as energy poverty in the developing world) and seeks to address them in an equitable manner" (Newell and Mulvaney 2013). The central idea of just transition is that a lower-carbon future takes politics and justice seriously, including (but not limited to) energy access, historical patterns of development, and violence.

This article, written by a scholar and an activist, picks up where the scholarly literature on green gentrification leaves off by asking: how does UPROSE connect the dots between industrial retention, climate adaptation policies, and centering their racial and social justice discourses? In many ways, although UPROSE does not use the just green enough concept to frame their work, there are conceptual overlaps with Curran and Hamilton's (2012) work on how environmental remediation can coexist with working class and industrial uses. In their research on Greenpoint, Curran and Hamilton suggest that green initiatives need not be tied to speculative real estate development. Instead, a *just green enough* framework foregrounds long-term residents' environmental goals and supports already-existing local activism. Similarly, by using *just transition*, UPROSE is focusing on the *justice* component of just green enough, an aligned approach which needs better articulation within this framework.

The potential alignment between *just transition* and *just green enough* illustrates how and why frames matter, as well the ways in which concepts and theories are actually generated out of existing social movements. UPROSE uses *just transition* as its frame in part because of the labor/environmental justice roots of the just transition concept, which has evolved in the last two decades in response to climate change. Initially, the concept came out of 1990s efforts to bridge the labor and environmental movements (Just Transition Alliance). This chapter focuses primarily on what a just transition might begin to look like at the local level. This piece analyzes UPROSE and their work in Sunset Park to better understand how addressing urban climate change through a just transition strategy centralizes a racial justice analysis in promoting climate justice action and policy. In short, climate adaption is not just a technical and economic project, but a community-based economic development strategy. Without centralizing a racial justice perspective, climate adaption and economic development initiatives are likely to reenact policy violence, specifically by reinforcing market fundamentalist approaches to space and accelerating the displacement of the working class and communities of color.

Ultimately, the question of whether UPROSE's approach is scalable or replicable is not the central point. Their experiences and their analytic are invaluable in terms of how just transition is conceptualized more broadly, and the particularities of their approach to climate justice and just transition offer some lessons for those interested in just green enough, climate change, and urban policy.

Beyond green gentrification

In 1966, Puerto Rican activists established the United Puerto Rican Organization of Sunset Park (UPROSE). The organization was formed to provide social services to a growing Puerto Rican community facing severe levels of discrimination and injustice. The organization has identified explicitly with the environmental justice movement since the 1990s, since civil rights lawyer Elizabeth Yeampierre took over as executive director (Sze 2007). Retaining its social justice foundation, the organization shifted from direct social services to organizing, advocacy, and the development of intergenerational indigenous leadership. In addition, given the growing diversity of Sunset Park, including significant Chinese and Arab populations, the organization shifted its demographic focus. The organization came to embrace a multi-ethnic model of community development and base-building. UPROSE is Brooklyn's oldest Latinx, and multi-ethnic community-based organization. UPROSE's recent work also dovetails with, and crucially alters and expands, existing activism and scholarship in three interrelated areas: just sustainability, green gentrification and climate justice.

In Agyeman, Bullard, and Evans' (2003) *Just Sustainabilities: Development in an Unequal World*, the editors and contributors to that ground-breaking volume outline a just sustainability framework. They outline "some of the key conceptual and practical challenges confronting both the ideas of sustainability and environmental justice in order to understand if and how we might see greater linkages between these ideas and their practical actions in the future." Just sustainability is defined as "the need to ensure a better quality of life for all, now and into the future, in a just and equitable manner, whilst living within the limits of supporting ecosystems" (Agyeman et al. 2003, 5). Scholars and activists working from the just sustainability framework have generally focused on the widespread "equity deficit" in mainstream urban sustainability policy and planning (Agyeman 2013).

Recent scholarship on *critical sustainabilities* seeks to complicate what critical approaches to sustainability mean, beyond the "equity deficit." Greenberg distinguishes between market, justice, vernacular, ecotopian, and eco-oriented sustainabilities (Critical Sustainabilities n.d.). For example, she describes how sustainability rhetoric dovetails with capitalism, in what she calls the "market-oriented" approach, or efforts "to sustain the environment for capital", and with it the quality of life required for a corporate-friendly metropolis, as well as the technologies that enable this quality of life, from hybrid tech buses to vertical gardens (Greenberg 2013, 64). Lindsey Dillon and Julie Sze have focused just sustainability away from making mainstream environmentalism more just or equitable, to conceptualizing anti-racist movements like Black Lives Matter *as* sustainability justice movements (Dillon and Sze forthcoming).

How sustainability is framed and operationalized has enormous consequences. Sustainability is a branding strategy in world city economic development (Greenberg 2015; Sze 2015). Scholars have argued that cities like San Francisco and New York are increasingly defined by "green gentrification" (Checker 2011; Gould and Lewis 2016). Checker (2011) describes how environmental upgrades and cleanup lead to gentrification. Economic inequality (i.e. the tech boom in the Bay Area) is a large factor in struggles over housing access and displacement, and gentrification/displacement is the overarching reality that structures contemporary sustainability and land-use struggles in highly economically stratified cities. Greenberg (under review) examines how a market-oriented sustainability project displaced a long-standing recycling center in San Francisco. In addition, access to nature is a key feature of high-end real estate development in the Mission Bay area of San Francisco (Wong 2016). The "revitalization" of the Los Angeles River similarly sees images of nature increasing land values in impacted communities, and thus counters a justice-oriented conception of the river where all communities (including working class and homeless peoples) have access to the river as a public, non-marketized space (Alcazar 2016; see also Kim, Chapter 12, this volume).

Parts of Brooklyn have become exemplar case studies of extreme displacement and gentrification in the last two decades, with select neighborhoods costing more to live in than high-end areas of Manhattan. Scholars have highlighted the negative social consequences of green growth coalition efforts to both "green" and "grow" the global city, and suggest policy choices to address their contradiction (Gould and Lewis 2016). One of the Brooklyn neighborhoods most at risk is Sunset Park, which Mayor Bloomberg declared a "sustainable urban industrial district" (Hum 2014). This phenomenon is not unique to the United States, but is part of a global urban spatial reconfiguration tipping the scales toward inequality (Anguelovski 2015).

More recently, Mayor Bill de Blasio ran on a platform of addressing "the tale of two cities," signaling a dramatic departure from neoliberal market-driven policy. However, in naming Alicia Glen, former director of the Goldman Sachs Urban Investment Group, to be Deputy Mayor for Housing and Economic Development, the administration has demonstrated an unwillingness to challenge the economic models and institutional structures driving hyper-gentrification and displacement. A case in point is the administration's proposed Brooklyn-Queens Connector, or BQX, a 16-mile streetcar line navigating the waterfront between Sunset Park and Astoria. Championed by Deputy Mayor Glen, the BQX is heralded as a marvel of sustainability and equity: emissions-free mass transit linking public housing to burgeoning job hubs. Omitted from these portraits is the fact that behind the BQX is a consortium of luxury real estate firms with major stakes in waterfront development. The project depends on tax increment financing, which captures value added to properties along the corridor. In working class communities like Sunset Park, where residents are struggling with soaring rents and small commercial and industrial businesses are treading water in a booming waterfront real estate market, the BQX is a prime example of green gentrification.

Although the scholarship on green gentrification and critical/just sustainabilities is both vibrant and central, what is less prominent in the key works in those fields is a focus on the voices and perspectives of the communities most impacted by gentrification and top-down sustainability initiatives. This centering of the voices most impacted is a central tenet of the environmental justice movement, exemplified by the movement truism: "we speak for ourselves." The environmental justice movement developed (in part) as an explicit reaction to the lack of adequate attention to race and class issues by mainstream environmental movement organizations. Up until then, the US environmental movement was focused more on saving pristine natural environments and their non-human inhabitants than protecting the lives and environments of diverse human communities. In a 1990 letter co-signed by 100 community-based activists to the heads of eight prominent national environmental organizations, Richard Moore of the Southwest Organizing Project highlighted not only the narrow focus, but also the lack of diversity of staff and of programs in the mainstream environmental movement, as well as its reliance on corporate funding (Sandler and Pezzullo 2007).

Environmental justice critiques of the mainstream environmental movement as top-down, technocratic, and elitist have been well documented. What is less well understood is how that critique has changed the broader environmental movement in the context of climate justice. This shift from the top-down mainstream environmental approach is best exemplified by an initiative titled "Building Equity and Alignment for Impact" (BEA). The BEA seeks to move resources away from the 2% of environmental groups, mainly the large national environmental organizations that receive 50% of philanthropic dollars, to focus on ground-up and local organizing, based on the belief that the grassroots must be at the heart of environmental change. The BEA is philosophically rooted in the Jemez Principles, developed at the Democratic Organizing Meeting hosted by the Southwest Network for Environmental and Economic Justice (SNEEJ), in Jemez, New Mexico, in December 1996. These principles are: Be Inclusive; Emphasis on Bottom-Up Organizing; Let People Speak for Themselves; Work Together in Solidarity and Mutuality; Build Just Relationships Among Ourselves; and Commitment to Self-Transformation (SNEEJ 1996). The BEA is focused on how funders can support what they define as the grassroots' capacity to expand and contribute "toward a base-building, bottom-up, collaborative approach, and away from a funder-driven, top-down approach" (equity), and "break down historic barriers between big green, grassroots and funding sectors, building authentic relationships toward greater alignment and solidarity" (alignment) (BEA n.d.). The BEA, in alliance with grassroots environmental and climate justice leaders, focuses on widening the number of people focusing on climate issues through marches and direct action, alongside traditional legal and policy approaches.

One such visible action was the People's Climate March in 2014, which coincided with United Nations (UN) climate talks. Over 400,000 people attended the march (People's Climate March 2014). UPROSE was a key organizer of the People's Climate March, and through the BEA is familiar with national and global approaches to climate action, in general, and just transition, in particular. In their policy and activism, UPROSE seeks to centralize the lived perspective of their community leaders, especially the young people, as those most impacted by gentrification and climate change. First, on the issue of gentrification in Brooklyn, UPROSE contests the notion of sustainability as a high-end life-style imperative that threatens the displacement of working class people and people of color, centering instead on climate resilience that takes working class and racial identities seriously. UPROSE rejects green gentrification as inevitable and natural. In New York City, protecting the industrial economy and a manufacturing identity is seen as central to rejecting the unfettered marketization of land use, the neoliberalism that leads to the displacement of working class peoples from a racially minoritized space. Because of the industrial character of the community (detailed below), the climate adaptation plans UPROSE advocates focus on creating local, and clean/ green jobs in the walk to work sector, rather than on promoting development projects that lead to the displacement of existing working class populations and communities of color.

Post-Sandy contexts – Industrial retention policy and spectacles of industry

Sunset Park is a predominantly working class immigrant community, what urban planning scholar Tarry Hum (2014) calls "a global immigrant neighborhood." In 2013, the median household income was just over $41,000 (vs. the city-wide average of $57,369). Between 2000 and 2010, the Asian population in the neighborhood surged by 57%. In 2010, the total population was 109,973, of which 48% was Latinx/ Hispanic, and 37% was Asian (Hum 2014, 55).

Sunset Park is in some ways "ground zero" for climate adaptation debates in New York City, because of the large expanse of waterfront real estate. In 2009, Mayor Bloomberg announced a plan to make Sunset Park a "sustainable urban industrial district." At this announcement, two community organizations of Asian and Latinx residents protested the rezoning of Sunset Park with signs and chanting "Sunset Park is not for sale" in multiple languages (Hum 2014), in part because of the Mayor's plans to transform the industrial working waterfront to support artisanal manufacturers for elite consumer markets. Sunset Park residents do not want a reprise of Williamsburg's transformation, a historically working class and mixed race and religiously diverse community that has thoroughly gentrified in the last two decades because of city policies that favor developers (see Curran 2004, 2007). In 2007, the National Trust for Historic Preservation named Brooklyn's industrial waterfront one of the nation's eleven most endangered places. In addition, Sunset Park is a designated "Significant Maritime Industrial Area" (Hum 2014). Despite these designations, Mayor Bloomberg and city agencies like the NYC Economic Development Corporation sought to shift the City's industrial retention policy away from the traditional uses (on the waterfront and beyond), to "modern" industries such as specialty foods, customized furniture, and craft-based and high "value-added" manufacturers, with a special emphasis on artisanal products (Hum 2014). To facilitate this transition, the city sought to open the floodgates through rezoning.

These plans for a "sustainable urban industrial district" were further challenged after Superstorm Sandy in 2012. Sandy devastated many waterfront neighborhoods; it flooded a large expanse of land, leading to over 47 deaths, caused 19 billion dollars of property damage, shut down the stock exchange, and took out the power grid and transportation infrastructure throughout the Northeast. In New York City, the damage was immense and is related to a central fact: waterfront trade is what built major cities historically, but that proximity to water makes the cities central to global finance particularly sensitive to sea-level rise and intensifying flooding related to climate change.

In Sunset Park, real state developers took over what was historically known as the Bush Terminal, seven massive buildings on the waterfront that composed an iconic site of Brooklyn industrial development. The development company, called Jamestown, partnered with other investors to buy a controlling interest in the site from the previous owners who defaulted in the wake of the massive damage of Superstorm Sandy (de Mause 2015).

Sandy's harm to Sunset Park was thus in stages. First were the actual threats related to the flooding and damage. Second is the financial fallout, on both micro- and neighborhood scales (e.g. Bush Terminal/ Industry City). These post-Sandy plans for climate resiliency use excessively muscular and "strong" language that seeks to "tame nature" (Lang 2016). The real estate developers are most well-known for Chelsea Market in what used to be a dilapidated meat-market district of Manhattan, but is now an extremely high-end residential area. The developers renamed the Bush Terminal site "Industry City" and sought to brand the area through artisanal food, "innovation economy" companies, and events like large DJ dance parties (Berger 2014). Innovation, like sustainability, is a word that obscures as much at is illuminates. Used by Jamestown, innovation evokes the cutting edge of technology and growth. The ironies, of course, abound.

First, the company's name, Jamestown, itself evokes the very first permanent English settlement in Virginia (1607). The main antagonists of the Jamestown developers recall this history in an image of settlers and Natives with the tagline "There's nothing innovative about displacement" (this line explicitly references the developer's call to nurture "innovation" and creative industries at the site; Hum 2014). UPROSE contests the Industry City plans for the community (Gonzalez

FIGURE 4.1 Protesting Jamestown's development plan
Image credit: UPROSE

2016). UPROSE focuses on six basic principles for industrial development and climate resilience: 1) ensuring community control over infrastructure for planning projects; 2) protecting the needs of long-time residents, workers and businesses; 3) expanding blue-collar union jobs; 4) promoting the development of maritime dependent industrial uses; 5) protecting manufacturing zoning; 6) incorporating climate adaptation and resiliency into waterfront development. These are the central principles through which UPROSE both responds to development and also promotes their own projects and initiatives (as seen below).

Operationalizing a just transition

Urban theorist Manuel Castells' concept of collective consumption politics is useful for understanding the contested policies embedded in markets, governments, and communities. Specifically, he writes that states (or governments) provide, or facilitate, the goods and services that sustain urban living (Aldana Cohen 2016). Thus, the allocation of goods and services is a *political question* and shapes why and how UPROSE is involved in climate resiliency policy.

UPROSE is focused on defining the terms and the questions, not just responding in the context of "community engagement and outreach," which they critique as offering dated approaches to communities. They focus on how to make things, preferably locally in Sunset Park, and generate good, high-paying local jobs in a lower-carbon world. They are also focused on "reclaiming narratives" about sustainability and where the vector of knowledge and expertise comes from, by centralizing the stories and experiences of elders, youth, the working class and communities of color.

UPROSE's participation in climate adaptive future workshops and funding for reinventing the waterfront with a community focus, combined with their past environmental justice organizing and policy development, converged to shape their climate justice agenda. UPROSE focuses on intersectional analysis in asking, "What do communities need to deal with climate change, what do we know now and what don't we know?" In framing this question with climate adaptation in mind, the organization seeks to use an asset, specifically local knowledge, in building resilience, rather than adopting a deficit view of their community and its members. As Hum (2014, 194) notes in her study of Sunset Park, UPROSE focuses on conjoining "sustainability and resilience through job retention, economic growth and environmental protection."

Here, the fusion of sustainability and resilience through job retention, economic growth and environmental protection, or just transition through other means, is similar to, but also deviates a bit from, the just green enough approach. Both focus on industrial and manufacturing jobs for local residents as their primary frame. Conceptually, however, the key pivot after the "just" is not a remediation that avoids gentrification, but an overall ideological shift in terms of carbon economies more broadly. The approach is arguably broader in just transition, and more fundamentally transformative.

UPROSE's fusion of sustainability and resilience is operationalized through the Climate Justice Center, what they call "NYC's first grassroots-led, bottom-up, climate adaptation and community resiliency planning project." Activities of the center include a number of distinct, yet interrelated projects: community-owned solar, and small business climate adaptation and resilience, education and outreach.

UPROSE has a number of distinct *community-owned solar* projects in development. First, they are working with the Metropolitan Transportation Authority (MTA) on a community-owned solar array. The community-owned array would use access at MTA property to produce renewable energy. Second, UPROSE is working with St. Michael's Church to install community-owned solar, in response to the Pope's encyclical on the environment, "Laudato Si" or "Be Praised" (or "Praised Be"), which calls for renewable fuel subsidies and energy efficiency. Lastly, UPROSE is working with an artists' cooperative that owns their own building to develop a solar project. Each of these projects has a different partner, model of cooperation, and owner/ ownership structure. But what they all share is the organization's commitment to finding spaces for solar in a community and land-use context where solar is not easy to install, and to work as equals in these efforts.

UPROSE's *small business climate adaptation and resilience* activities have been focused on organizing and educating local small businesses to be climate adaptable through a federal grant. The neighborhood is full of small auto finishing shops and other similar businesses; the focus is on how to improve their operations in an extreme weather event and train them, rather than criminalizing and closing shops. This curriculum has been implemented with community trainers along the 4th Ave Green Improvement District, asking, for example, how do you containerize the chemicals you work with? (Some owners were pouring anti-freeze down drains). Many of these local business owners and workers are residents. A climate justice and just transition agenda is not a displacement agenda, but one focused on protecting the health, local economy, and climate together. UPROSE's focus is on "adapting the community infrastructure to climate change" through a "block-by-block, building-by-building assessment, mapping and relationship–building process to create, implement and manage a truly grassroots-led climate adaptation and community resiliency plan" (UPROSE, n.d.). Yet another future pathway is to build industrial production for solar energy in their community. This plan is still nascent, but is part of their vision for just transition. Collectively, these activities are UPROSE's attempt to operationalize climate justice and just transition at the local level.

Central to this local knowledge is the global perspectives from the community members who come from all over the world. Rather than focusing on the working class and immigrant populations as a problem to be addressed, the organization focuses on their immigrant experiences as strengths. Examples include building and caring for community gardens and saving water through stormwater barrels. These acts are pragmatic but also symbolic of a different kind of sustainability than the spectacular approach. It honors the perspectives of elders and youth, and practices of making and saving, rather than high-end consumption. Part of these global and immigrant perspectives is the receptivity to ownership structures that do not prioritize individual ownership or growth models under capitalism. Sunset Park in general is a "hotspot" for workers cooperatives, in part because cultural familiarity with collective traditions and a focus on sustainability are "indigenous" to immigrant communities (Hum 2014, 201).

Lastly, UPROSE is focused on youth climate justice, and the activities of meaning making, building, art, direct action and education. UPROSE has organized large Climate Justice Youth Summits (the last in 2015 with over 400, mostly young, people of color), where information and networking across neighborhoods centralizes the voices of the youth. The main questions the summits address are: how do we learn across spaces, across the just transition, and how to build the future we want to live in? Part of this learning is to cross neighborhoods, and to connect their local struggles with national struggles for climate and environmental justice (e.g. solidarity actions and events supporting indigenous communities protesting extraction at Standing Rock in North Dakota as well as transnationally).

To summarize, their agenda is part pragmatic and yet is potentially transformative, based on system change. According to Yeampierre, UPROSE is moving the economic development corporation away from the status quo of what constitutes economic development. Their view of markets is complex. On the one hand, "markets don't save us." Capitalism is an extractive politics that got us into the current mess, and there are limits to what it can do. On the other hand, drawing on the organizing and theory-building of climate justice and just transition allies in the movement, UPROSE is committed to *shifting* markets to reflect values of community, lower carbon, and justice. They seek to shift markets based on their participation in national strategy contexts (such as the *Our Power Campaign: Communities United for a Just Transition*), and on theorizing just transition and praxis-oriented approaches.

In many ways, this critique is echoed in much previous environmental and climate justice activism. Market skepticism is a central worldview of the environmental justice and climate justice movements, in part because of how past policies and a focus on the bottom line negatively impact communities of color. Environmental justice activists work on environmental issues primarily in low-income communities of color, and often conceive of themselves as distinct from the broader environmental movement (Perkins and Soto-Karlin forthcoming). Their communities live with a disproportionate burden of pollution compared to wealthier areas. The link between poor people and pollution is due, in part, to market forces that result in both poor people and polluting industries locating in places with cheap land (Cole and Foster 2001). As a result, they have long critiqued market-based approaches to environmental governance, as they often see markets as part of the problem, rather than part of the solution.

On the other hand, shaping markets through their values is a key feature of UPROSE's Just Transition Strategy. Their approach is shaped by the Just Transition Framework, specifically, the idea that capital can be moved through a values framework. For UPROSE, their political values are against displacement of working class populations and green gentrification. One of their central values is that existing populations of the working class, immigrants, and people of color are assets to the community, and that development that ushers in their removal from the neighborhood destroys a collective good. Thus, rather than accept the high-end gentrification of Sunset Park in a reprise of Williamsburg, UPROSE focuses explicitly on manufacturing zones as a way to be both climate and community resilient.

Conclusion

Resilience is both a metaphoric term and an environmental one in the context of *just transition*, as exemplified by UPROSE. Renowned environmental justice scholar David Pellow (under contract) defines the concept of just resilience:

> I have urged scholars and activists to go beyond the boundaries of the state and capital to explore the ways that humans and more-than-humans can and do resist the current social order to bring new imaginings, visions, practices, relationships, and communities into being that are anti-authoritarian and sustainable, and that embody what I call *just resilience* – a resilience marked by social and environmental justice. *Just resilience* is an important concept for environmental studies scholars because, among many reasons, there are forms of resilience that are *unjust* and we should distinguish between them.

In this vein, UPROSE is focused on racial and social justice in its definition of climate resilience and just transition, and they have much to add to the just green enough framework in their vision and projects. In its insistence on their voices and their analytic in response to top-down spectacular sustainability, UPROSE is thereby a living example of Pellow's just resilience. In a context of extreme economic, racial and environmental inequality, UPROSE is proudly and consistently driven by its youth voices, its racial and social justice analytic, its focus on history and community, and on struggle. The organization embodies an anti-racist sustainability in their worldview and their praxis (Dillon and Sze forthcoming).

References

Agyeman, J., Bullard, R.D. and Evans, B., eds. 2003. *Just Sustainabilities: Development in an Unequal World*. Cambridge, MA: MIT Press.

Agyeman, J. 2013. *Introducing Just Sustainabilities: Policy, Planning, and Practice*. London and New York: Zed Books.

Alcazar, R. 2016. Sustainability Dreaming: How New Urbanism Narratives Inhibit Speculative Thinking. Unpublished Thesis, University of California, Davis.

Aldana Cohen, D. 2016. The Rationed City: The Politics of Water, Housing, and Land Use in Drought-Parched São Paulo. *Public Culture* 28(2): 261–289.

Anguelowski, I. 2015. From Toxic Sites to Parks as (Green) LULUs? New Challenges of Inequity, Privilege, Gentrification, and Exclusion for Urban Environmental Justice. *Journal of Planning Literature* 31(1): 23–36.

BEA, n.d. Our Goals. http://www.bea4impact.org/

Berger, E. 2014. *Gentrification Inc., Fast Company*, August 7. https://www.fastcompany.com/3033870/gentrification-inc

Checker, M. 2011. Wiped Out by the "Greenwave": Environmental Gentrification and the Paradoxical Politics of Urban Sustainability. *City & Society* 23(2): 210–229.

Cole, L.W. and Foster, S.R. 2001. *From the Ground Up: Environmental Racism and the Rise of the Environmental Justice Movement.* New York: NYU Press.

Critical Sustainabilities. 2016. https://critical-sustainabilities.ucsc.edu/sustainabilities-2/

Curran, W. 2004. Gentrification and the Nature of Work: Exploring the Links in Williamsburg, Brooklyn. *Environment and Planning A* 36(7): 1243–1258.

Curran, W. 2007. "From the Frying Pan to the Oven": Gentrification and the Experience of Industrial Displacement in Williamsburg, Brooklyn. *Urban Studies* 44(8): 1427–1440.

Curran, W. and Hamilton, T. 2012. Just Green Enough: Contesting Environmental Gentrification in Greenpoint, Brooklyn. *Local Environment* 17(9): 1027–1042.

de Mause, N. 2015. As Industry City Promises a New Sunset Park, Some Residents Fight to Maintain the Old One. *City Limits Magazine*, October 27.

Dillon, L. and Sze, J. Forthcoming. *Equality in the Air We Breathe: Police Violence, Pollution, and the Politics of Sustainability, Situating Sustainabilities through Interdisciplinary and Social Justice Perspectives.* NYU Press.

Gonzalez, D. 2016. In Sunset Park, a Call for "Innovation" Leads to Fears of Gentrification. *The New York Times*, March 6.

Gould, K. and Lewis, T. 2016. *Green Gentrification: Urban Sustainability and the Struggle for Environmental Justice.* New York: Routledge.

Greenberg, M. Under review. What Do We Mean by Green? Critical Approaches to Urban Sustainability in the Luxury City. In *Situating Sustainability*, edited by Julie Sze. New York: NYU Press.

Greenberg, M. 2015. "The Sustainability Edge": Crisis, Competition, and the Rise of Green City Branding. In *Sustainability in the Global City: Myth and Practice*, edited by Cynthia Isenhour, Gary McDonough, and Melissa Checker. Cambridge: Cambridge University Press, 105–130.

Greenberg, M. 2013. What on Earth is Sustainable? *Boom: Journal of California* 3(4): 54–66.

Hum, T. 2014. *Making a Global Immigrant Neighborhood: Brooklyn's Sunset Park.* Philadelphia: Temple University Press.

Lang, S. 2016. Promise or Peril: Incorporating Resilience into Sustainability Planning for the Post-Hurricane Sandy New York City Waterfront. Conference Presentation, Association for American Geographers, April 2016.

Newell, P. and Mulvaney, D. 2013. The Political Economy of the "Just Transition". *The Geographical Journal* 179: 132–140. doi:10.1111/geoj.12008

People's Climate March. 2014. Wrap-Up. http://2014.peoplesclimate.org/wrap-up/

Pereira, I. 2016. Williamsburg Leads NYC in Gentrification, Reports Says. *AM NY*, May 11. http://www.amny.com/real-estate/williamsburg-leads-nyc-in-gentrification-report-says-1.11786129

Pellow, D. Under contract. Afterword. In *Sustainability Now! Sustainability How?: Social Justice and Interdisciplinary Perspectives*, edited by J. Sze. New York: NYU Press.

Sandler, R. and Pezzullo, P. (eds.) 2007. *Environmental Justice and Environmentalism: The Social Justice Challenge to the Environmental Movement.* Cambridge, MA: MIT Press.

SNEEJ. 1996. Jemez Principles for Democratic Organizing. Meeting hosted by Southwest Network for Environmental and Economic Justice (SNEEJ), Jemez, New Mexico, December 1996. http://www.ejnet.org/ej/jemez.pdf

Sze, J. 2007. *Noxious New York: The Racial Politics of Urban Health and Environmental Justice*. Cambridge, MA: MIT Press.

Sze, J. 2015. *Fantasy Islands: Chinese Dreams and Ecological Fears in an Age of Climate Crisis*. California: University of California Press.

UPROSE. n.d. Climate Justice Center. https://www.uprose.org/climate-justice/

Wong, A. 2016. Reimagining the San Francisco Waterfront: Industrial Cargo Hub, Empty Plot or Thriving Community? The Nature of Land Use Development: A Case Study of San Francisco's Mission Bay. Unpublished Thesis, University of California, Davis. https://ams.ucdavis.edu/sites/ams.ucdavis.edu/files/attachments/wong_andrea_thesis_final_draft.pdf

PART II

Green displacements and community identity

5

GREENING THE WATERFRONT? SUBMERGING HISTORY, FINDING RISK

Pamela Stern and Peter V. Hall

In a collection of papers on urban regeneration (Leary and McCarthy 2013), Susan Brownill observed that city builders have come to regard post-industrial waterfront redevelopment as a necessary first step in the quest for urban competitiveness. Yet, despite the apparent universality of the redevelopment imperative, waterfront redevelopment projects unfold in different ways attributable to distinct local histories, urban governance arrangements, politics, and policies (Brownill 2013). While the redevelopment of industrial waterfronts is widely understood as a positive move that enhances the economic status of a neighbourhood, a city, or a region, any change of use necessarily entails a contingent re-evaluation (and revaluation) of industrial activities, workers, and lands. It is not news that environmental remediation of former industrial brownfields makes neighbourhoods that were disdained by the economically advantaged suddenly desirable to them with the common result that longtime poor and working class residents are excluded or displaced (Checker 2011; Dale and Newman 2009; Dooling 2009; Goodling, Green and McClintock 2015; Quastel 2009).

Curran and Hamilton (2012) argue that displacement can be avoided by pursuing redevelopment strategies that privilege the social needs and environmental priorities of poor and working class residents. Rather than appealing to the eco-consumptive preferences of urban elites and to the bottom lines of developers, Curran and Hamilton advocate for redevelopments that are "just green enough" to ensure that the poor and working class residents who endured the noise and pollution of industry benefit from and influence its cleanup. An assessment of risk as well as the allocation of cost-benefits attendant to redevelopment is also central to Curran and Hamilton's analysis. In comparison with iconic environmental gentrification of industrial spaces that seeks to reduce risk for investors, "just green enough" strategies aspire simultaneously to an equitable distribution of economic, environmental and health cost-benefits of industrial activity, and reduced risk of displacement for existing residents.

In this chapter we report on the way that waterfront redevelopment has been playing out in one small municipality, New Westminster, located on the Fraser River within metropolitan Vancouver, British Columbia. In particular, we consider where concerns about equity and social justice intersect with desires for what one city councillor described as investing the city with a "modern, rising hip image" (Jamie McEvoy, during City Council meeting, 22 April 2013). We explore the discursive and planning practices that have underpinned redevelopment of the city's once industrial waterfront. Some cities have viewed the departure of waterfront industry as an opportunity to remake the city as less working class (see Dudley 1994) or have actively pushed industrial users away in favour of seemingly more desirable activities. Beyond the downtown waterfront, the City of New Westminster has not actively pushed to convert industrial lands to recreation, retail, and housing. Conversion has occurred, nonetheless, through incremental rezoning applications.

As the city has rebuilt its industrial riverfront with condominiums, retail, and linear parks, it has contributed to the redefinition of the Fraser River as a space of non-work to be enjoyed as an environmental amenity. Through this process, however, it has so thoroughly erased most evidence of the recent industrial work done there by city residents that few current residents can identify former industrial sites. It has also symbolically erased the city's industrial heritage by devaluing and ignoring older working class residents' knowledge of the river and the waterfront as not relevant to that modern, rising hip image (Clarke 2011; High 2013). During the recent industrial past, residents worked and played in and alongside the water, but knowledge of this has been submerged. City officials frequently highlight the need "to connect our waterfront to our neighbourhoods" (Mayor Jonathan Cote quoted in Smith 2015). Simultaneously, however, residential developments contribute to hardening the barrier between the land and the water and encourage a perception of the river as risky, too dangerous for swimming or recreational boating. City makers in New Westminster and elsewhere are unable to imagine "just green enough" alternatives in which industry and recreation coexist, because they fail to hear the voices of those who both worked on and enjoyed the waterfront.

Redevelopment of the New Westminster waterfront occurs in the context of development practices in Metro Vancouver. Its 23 municipalities comprise a single housing, employment, and consumption market of 2.3 million people. Metro, as the governance structure is known, carries out region-wide land use planning, though each municipality retains authority to regulate local land use. Metro's regional plans (Metro Vancouver 2011b) have repeatedly identified the retention of industrial and agricultural lands as important to the health of the region. In urging retention of industrial land, Metro planners hope to prevent, or at least slow, abandonment of centrally located industrial facilities. In practice, however, Metro and its constituent municipal governments have, in the names of sustainability, liveability, and revitalization, allowed conversion of industrial land to non-industrial uses at the expense of significant industrial sprawl (Metro Vancouver 2011a). Historically, the region's industrial economy was organized around water-based transportation for moving raw materials and finished products, but few of the industries that remain on waterfront lands now use the water for transportation (Hall 2012). In particular, shipping containers that could move on barges (or local rail) are repositioned by truck, contributing to pollution from diesel particulates, road congestion, and demand for new roads (Hall 2015). Planners and city officials often frame waterfront redevelopment as sustainable; however, undercutting greenness, waterfront redevelopment is implicated in the movement of industrial work to sites away from the water and onto local roads.

Waterfront redevelopment has certainly played an important role in the recent economic growth of metropolitan Vancouver. Iconic and highly publicized redeveloped industrial waterfronts in the City of Vancouver (Kear 2007) have been recruited to Vancouver's campaign to be recognized as the world's "Greenest City" (City of Vancouver 2012). The green-chic ethic that has captured Vancouverites' imagination is buttressed by province-wide tourism branding that emphasizes British Columbia as a place of wild, often watery, nature. Other municipalities within Metro Vancouver have also recognized and tried to capture the symbolic and actual capital represented by waterfront land. One consequence is that area waterfronts are widely, if mistakenly, imagined as non-industrial spaces. For several redeveloped places, the knowledge that they were previously sites of industry has indeed faded from public memory.

New Westminster

The data presented here derive from the (Re)Claiming the New Westminster Waterfront research partnership, conducted between 2011 and 2015 by faculty and students from Simon Fraser University, the New Westminster Museum and Archives, retired longshoremen, and others with an interest in the city and its working waterfront. Data include ethnographic and oral history interviews with 94 current and retired waterfront workers, users, and residents. The research team also engaged with city officials, produced maps that show changes in waterfront land use activity, and reviewed news reports, planning documents, and other archival material. As residents of New Westminster, we (the authors) regularly take advantage of the amenities of the post-industrial waterfront. Yet, through the research partnership, we also became aware of just how thoroughly developers, city planners, and politicians have erased the physical and symbolic traces of industry, and more critically, of industrial workers.

New Westminster is a city of approximately 66,000 people, centrally located within the Vancouver metropolitan region. Situated on the north bank of the Fraser River approximately 25km east of downtown Vancouver, New Westminster was, until the 1970s, an important commercial centre for people in suburban and rural districts. From its earliest years, the city was also an important industrial and transportation centre. New Westminster has experienced the economic and social changes familiar to everyone interested in historically industrial urban waterfronts. Not surprisingly, many New Westminster residents, including working class residents, are pleased with the deindustrialized and ecologically gentrified (Dooling 2009) waterfront, seeing redevelopment as enhancing both the liveability and the sustain-ability of the city without making a distinction between the two (Hall and Stern 2014; Dale and Newman 2009). Although it sometimes struggles with conflicting development impulses, the current labour and green-oriented city council tries to meet resident needs and to overcome the city's longstanding reputation as industrial and gritty (and in the immediate post-industrial era, derelict and crime-ridden), without becoming merely a bedroom suburb to Vancouver.

To be sure, the municipal government does address equity issues. New West-minster was the first municipality in British Columbia with a municipal living wage ordinance. It also actively pursues policies that favour affordable and rental housing, transit use, supportive services for the homeless and those at risk of homelessness, as well as a wide variety of public amenities. But we argue that, in practice, redeve-lopment from industrial to residential and recreation brings localized benefits to particular sites while harming the overall sustainability of the city and the region. A "just green enough" strategy that promoted the use of the river for industrial activities (especially for goods movement) and explicitly included industrial areas in active transportation and public space improvements would be both more environmentally sustainable and more equitable.

Industrial New Westminster

A 1950s promotional film about New Westminster produced by the Province emphasized the city's industrial character by showing the interiors of several of the city's mills and factories as well as the busy shipping docks. Today, industry is rarely mentioned in recitations of the city's history. In telling the story of New West-minster, municipal officials and others usually emphasize the city's place as the oldest Canadian city west of the Rockies and its presumed Anglo-British heritage as British Columbia's colonial capital. Other tellings emphasize the attractive Victorian and Edwardian architecture and the scenic beauty of the Fraser River.

Largely ignored in official and lay recitations about the past are New Westminster's and the Fraser River's place in the development of industrial and transportation infrastructure. For a century until the mid-1980s, the city was heavily industrial and markedly blue collar and multi-ethnic. The first bridge across the Fraser River (built in 1904 and still in use for rail) is located at New Westminster. Port terminals, located downtown, were major sites for the export of Canadian wheat and wood products. Until fairly recently, the city's waterfront hosted commercial fishing docks, vegetable canneries, machine shops, lumber mills, and several shipbuilders. A large proportion of the workforce for these industries lived in New Westminster.

Industrial work and workers were part of the habitus of nearly all New Westminster residents. In the mid-1960s, lands zoned for industrial use constituted a little over 21% of the city's land mass (New Westminster 1990, 52 and 55). In the previous decade "roughly 60 percent of the [city's] employment was located in the industrial sector" (ibid., 21). These were, for the most part, unionized, well-paying jobs. Our oral histories confirm that most city residents had neighbours or family members who worked somewhere on or near the waterfront. The port terminals were especially prominent in older residents' mental picture of the city. In an interview, sisters, whose father was a longshoreman, noted that as children and teenagers in the 1950s and '60s, they also went to the waterfront.

> *Colleen:* Sometimes we would go down in the car with our older sister to pick up, 'cause her husband also worked, he worked for Pacific Coast Terminals. Sometimes we would go down and pick up my brother-in-law.
>
> *Kathleen:* [looking at a photograph] There! That's what we used to see. That would be like at the foot of 8th or 6th [Street] or something.
>
> *Colleen:* There were always big ships down there. You know what? It is still kind of weird to drive down there and not see any big ships because growing up that was just commonplace, there were always ships in there.
>
> *(interview 16 March 2014)*

The waterfront in New Westminster was among the first in Metro Vancouver to deindustrialize. The first physical movements of industry away from the New Westminster riverfront occurred in the early 1960s, but deindustrialization of the

FIGURE 5.1 Longshoremen loading flour, New Westminster, ca 1970. Used with permission, Pacific Coast Terminals

city only became apparent a decade later. Economic recession in the 1980s and globalization in the 1990s contributed to a drawn-out period of industrial, commercial, and population decline. The port terminals closed in 1980, while the last lumber mills closed in 2007 and 2008, leaving large portions of the working waterfront derelict for years. New Westminster is no longer a prime site for processing Canadian resources, now done at interior sites or overseas. Goods, however, continue to pass through the city, on the roads, rails, and to a much lesser extent, the river. Most current city residents' day-to-day experiences with industrial work or workers are with the approximately 6,000 tractor-trailers that pass through the city each day. Half of these marine- and domestic-container bearing trucks travel through the downtown along a roadway hugging the waterfront (Jerry Behl, Transportation Engineer City of New Westminster, pers. comm.). This roadway, along with a parallel century-old rail corridor, creates a physical barrier between the central waterfront and other parts of the city. Lands zoned for industrial purposes – just 12% of the city's landmass in 2010 (Metro Vancouver 2011a) – are currently confined to the edges of the city.

In the early 1980s, a right-wing provincial government pursued an urban renewal-like program to redevelop the abandoned port terminals and adjacent lands for condominiums, a hotel-office complex, and a festival marketplace. The First Capital City Development Company (FCC), the provincially created, but time-limited, redevelopment agency, was authorized to consolidate developable parcels in central New Westminster, arrange financing, and permit construction without interference from the city council or the statutory citizen-led advisory planning council. This is not to suggest that city officials opposed the broad contours of the FCC waterfront redevelopment program. In 1988, the city council enacted zoning changes necessary for similar redevelopment at another part of the waterfront. Both redevelopments have been financially and politically successful, though both projects proceeded slowly and were substantially modified.

The city's working class image probably contributed to delays in realizing the FCC redevelopment plan, and in fact, the plan to erect condominium towers along the full length of the former port lands was not completed. A developer of six waterfront condominium towers went bankrupt without breaking ground, and another, with approval for 5 towers, held its waterfront land for three decades and, in 2016, sold its interest. In this period, as home prices in Vancouver soared, New Westminster shed some of its gritty image, becoming one of the region's fastest growing cities with both immigrants and Canadians born elsewhere. The city council asserted its political and financial capital to create a beautiful waterfront park on the 4-hectare parcel previously held by the bankrupt developer, and to negotiate with the other developer for fewer (but taller) towers and more public waterfront space. While the adjacent downtown shopping district has not recovered from its original decline, New Westminster's post-industrial waterfront now hosts attractive, moderately priced (for Metro Vancouver) condominium housing, retail that serves local residents, and several well-used, mostly linear parks. Many observers consider the redeveloped waterfront in New Westminster an example to emulate.

FIGURE 5.2 Redeveloped downtown waterfront
Photo by Peter Hall

Disconnecting from history or connecting to the river?

City officials have repeatedly described connecting the city to the river as one of the primary aims of the ongoing downtown and waterfront redevelopment. Connection is treated as an unquestionable good. Yet, aside from finding a way to mitigate the barrier imposed by the rail and truck corridor, thus improving physical access to the riverfront, what officials mean by "connection" is never explicit. The current Downtown Community Plan (New Westminster 2012) makes references to protecting view corridors, creating places where people can interact with the river, enhancing the natural habitat for wildlife (ibid., 94), fostering stewardship, and providing opportunities to experience the tidal activity (ibid., 29). Similar to claims made about waterfront redevelopments in other Metro Vancouver municipalities, connection to the river appears to be primarily visual and aesthetic (Hall and Stern 2014). An important implication is that connection is not at all about waterfront work; indeed, the very idea of the waterfront as a place of work has been so discounted that it is no longer recognized as something lost.

The undervaluing of industrial work in the history of the city is made even clearer by comparing references to the local retail sector with the absence of reference to industry. The Downtown Community Plan makes multiple references to the architectural heritage of the neighbourhood and repeatedly singles out a downtown shopping street as a site of special heritage value, while simultaneously ignoring the history of the adjacent shipping wharves. The iconic art deco style shipping terminal building dating from 1929 was demolished to make way for waterfront condominiums. Acknowledgements of past industrial uses of the river barely make it into planning documents.

The city has also disconnected industry and industrial workers from the heritage interpretation it does at the various waterfront parks. Although recently installed photographic bands in the newest park include a few images of work and the former port terminals, these are buried amongst more than 80 images of buildings, festivals, cultural events, and historic individuals stretching back to the earliest days of the city. At another part of the downtown waterfront, the city and various partners installed 24 interpretive plaques along a one-kilometre stretch of the esplanade where ships once berthed. Of these, half describe some aspect of river ecology, seven reference historical events or activities along the river, and just five describe current activities on the river and riverfront. Depictions of river-based industry, where they are included, describe either activities in other Metro Vancouver municipalities or are incorrectly presented as something in the city's distant past.

The interpretive plaques are also notable for what is not mentioned: the terminal closures in 1980, the decision to redevelop the waterfront, the amalgamation of the port authority responsible for the Fraser River terminals with the Vancouver port in 2008, or anything at all about waterfront workers. For example, the plaque describing the Queensborough neighbourhood, originally established to be an industrial district of the city, gives the mistaken impression that the deindustrialization of that neighbourhood occurred in the distant past rather than in the 1990s. The caption on an aerial photo of Queensborough reads: "Industry used to crowd the waterfront as shown in this 1940s photograph." The reference to crowding encourages the wrong assumption that industry on the waterfront was a barrier to public access. In these ways, the official narratives produced by parks planners and other city officials about the water and the waterfront relegate industrial workers and work places "to a time and space outside the contemporary social world" (Clarke 2011, 446). Several people who contributed to the oral histories described their sense that the waterfront has been sanitized of industrial work and especially industrial workers.

> Yeah, we were talking about Pacific Coast Terminals earlier; it's all condos there now, high-rise condos. They would never know there were docks there, the amount of work and the type of works we've done, down right where they were living, they would never know.
>
> *(interview with retired longshoreman, 20 January 2014)*

> It's a pity you couldn't find a [small building], put it on the waterfront, and you know just put in the names of the boats that were built and the names of the guys who worked there and a few pictures, at least you could have something.
>
> *(interview with former employee of the Fraser River Port Authority,*
> *14 Apr 2014)*

That really hurt us when they tore our net sheds down. Those sheds were used by my grandfather, father, and me. Now it's a park.

(interview with semi-retired fisherman, 18 February 2014)

Is this, to borrow from historian Steven High (2013, 150), an instance of "postindustrial processes of forgetting" that treats the existence of blue-collar workers as an embarrassment to the city's ambitions to be hip and modern? New Westminster is not unique in severing ties to its recent industrial history or of treating industrial work as unconnected to the city's future or even to its current residents. Clarke (2011, 447), writing about industrial workers in France, notes that discourses that "consign factories and those who work in them (or used to work in them) to the past is itself one of the common mechanisms by which [a workforce] that does exist is conjured away before our very eyes."

By eliminating industry and industrial workers from local heritage sites, the city misses out on the knowledge held by the former workers at those sites in general, and their knowledge of the river in particular. Instead it substitutes "expert" knowledge about the industrial waterfront that produces discourses and perceptions of the river as dangerous and the industrial riverfront as necessarily inaccessible. These practices of post-industrial forgetting are implicated in the process of disconnecting the city from its industrial waterfront. Such a discursive construction also precludes the "just green enough" goal of serving extant, working class interests; instead, connection is to be made to an imagined, non-industrial, yet risk-filled nature. The language of danger and risk, however, are framed as ones that the city can (and does) manage through its redevelopment practices. Those decisions present opportunities for new forms of accumulation through real estate development, but these go unquestioned or are even celebrated as a way for the city to assert a competitive advantage over other places (McCann 2009; also Harvey 1989). Following this logic, connection is necessarily partial, incomplete, and exclusionary of workers' knowledge.

Working (class) knowledge of the river

The industrial riverfront did not contain playgrounds, bike paths, or places for a leisurely stroll, but it was far from closed to the public. As noted above, a substantial portion of the local jobs in the decades after World War II were in waterfront industries, so that many residents, both men and women, came to the waterfront to work. In the process, they came to learn about the river in a diversity of ways.

We worked year round, and I never worked in a building with heat in it. Your movement kept you warm, you know what I mean, the harder you worked the warmer you got.... We'd stand on ice when we were planking the boat, nailing the planks up underneath. The boat is right, actually, in the river itself.

(interview with retired master boat builder, 18 Feb 2014)

So you have to climb down [a rope ladder] to get to the [log] booms. I'm like, I'm like, [gulp] well, okay. "Well, I know who's gonna get wet first," the foreman goes, because apparently my colour just went poof. And he goes, "You don't have to go down." "What! Pardon me! I'm going down! It's my job to go down!" So I went down and there was this guy and he goes, "Shirley, do it this way." And I go, "No, don't do it that way. You're gonna fall in. Go this way, you're gonna fall in." Boom! Right down, and he got soaked. I was the driest person on that log!

(interview with a currently working longshoreman, 28 Jan 2015)

A lot of people seem to think that if you do it every day… it would be terribly boring. The river pilot thing is anything but boring. Even if it's the same ship you go in on every week, it's never the same river.

(interview with retired river pilot, 23 Jan 2013)

Even when the waterfront was primarily industrial, industry did not form an impermeable barrier to the waterfront for the non-working population. Many residents visited to purchase fish directly from boats, to collect packing materials for reuse, or to dine in a well-loved dockside seafood restaurant. And we heard from several men and women who had played in and on the river as children.

I thought I was a great explorer; I knew the river so well I could go anywhere. I wanted to go for a row… I thought I'd be really smart and go rowing. I checked the wharf and usually you can tell which way the current is going. Well, it looked like it was running in. See all this is tidal, and as the tide changes, the direction changes…. Anyway, it was foggy and I figured that the tide was running back so we're safe…. The water was actually going the opposite way; we went right by all the [log] booms… and we ended up at Port Mann [several km upstream]. Well, I wasn't going to phone my father…

(interview with a semi-retired fisherman, 18 February 2014)

This narrator grew up in a family of boat builders, tug boat operators and fishermen; his knowledge of the all too real dangers of the river came from direct experience, not from observations from the safety of the shoreline.

Risk and certainty

Redevelopment of industrial waterfronts introduces new uncertainties for a city, even as it provides new opportunities for property-based accumulation (Hagerman 2007; Stanley 2013). And, indeed, redevelopment of New Westminster's waterfront was accompanied by physical changes that transformed the liminal edge from a soft and permeable one suitable for launching boats, loading cargo and landing fish, but that was also vulnerable to flooding, shoreline change, intrusions of mosquitoes, and river-borne odours. In contrast, what real estate developers seek, and by statute and planning practice governments are encouraged to create, are rigid and impermeable barriers between land and water that afford residential and commercial owners protection against flooding and erosion. The redeveloped shoreline is understood to hold structures – residences and commercial buildings – that require protection from risk. In this sense, assertions of risk and danger to life and property mitigated through redevelopment are, in fact, the risks and dangers that are created by redevelopment.

Risks are not simply inherent in nature, but are built up out of knowledge practices that follow governance practices. According to the former head of the Fraser River Port Authority, himself a life-long New Westminster resident, the Fraser River became dangerous only after it became an insurance liability for the city.

> If you have ever walked down the waterfront, you will have noticed that there is a little node every 2–300 meters. The master plan was that for each of those nodes, there would be a gangway and a float to interact with the water. When the city planner and the city Chief Administrative Officer saw those gangways and floats, all they saw was their liability at risk and they cancelled them all.
>
> *(interview, 14 April 2014)*

Probabilistic assessments of risk do not necessarily match people's lived experiences. Much of the literature on divergent assessments of risk concern instances or events in which people experience harm as greater (or more uncertain) than attributed in official evaluations. But it can work the other way. Governments or other experts may assert risks that the public does not feel (for example, the security theatre that we all perform whenever we travel by airplane). According to Reno (2011, 516), how people assess and respond to assertions of danger determines whether they "are counted as expert or lay, wise or mystified, 'sanitary' or 'unsanitary'." It is easier to enforce elite knowledges of the river and the waterfront when fewer people have the intimate knowledge of a place obtained through work.

Assertions of risk work as technologies of governance that can allow for dispossession and uneven accumulation of wealth (Stanley 2013). Over time, official assertions of risk have become naturalized as truths framing the ongoing redevelopment of New Westminster's waterfront. According to a municipal parks planner, risk is one of the principal concerns informing the way the city redevelops the waterfront.

> [A]s you can see in this area you have a gorgeous view, up the river and down the river.... We are trying to open it up and make sure that people are understanding what happens on the river, with the tugboats, with the seals, you know, the salmon fishing, all the different things it offered us, the barges that go by with woodchips so there's an understanding of the river for goods movement, for the ecology as well.... So you want to bring them closer, the only thing with this river, [it] is a very fast moving river, and you

can't really go down to touch the water, it's too dangerous. It's not like a slow-moving river.

(interview, 28 April 2014)

Such certainty about the risks from the river obscures knowledge of other possible dangers. Instead, identifications of certain dangers, such as the fast-moving river, may allow people to avoid confronting other sites of discomfort or apparent disorder (Reno 2011, 520). And both play out in the micropolitics of day-to-day urban governance of rezoning, planning, and bylaw enforcement. City officials have presented the "fact" of a dangerous river to dismiss requests for a public boat wharf and swimming beach downtown, both of which would allow more opportunities to actually connect the city and citizens to the river. City officials are less willing to acknowledge that some condominium owners regard the waterfront as an extension of their private property and that they may fear that a public wharf, in particular, would be attractive to noisy youth and strangers.

They were going to build another dock, and we rose up cause we didn't want it in front of here. They might stay overnight, have parties on it.... They had a small dock in here when we first moved [in], in front of the hotel and office building. It just wasn't looked after.... We're keeping an eye on it, that they're not going to try [to build another one] here.

(interview with riverfront condominium owner, 22 February 2013)

We're your typical neighbourhood pub. One thing about New Westminster, these railroad tracks out here, it separates the quay where we are right now... from New Westminster.... [T]hese railroad tracks separate the good from the bad. Because there's lot more bad stuff going on that side of the tracks than this side of the tracks.... All these homeowners down here, they own condos... [T]his is their deck; this is where they feel safe; this is where they know everybody; this is where they meet their friends.

(interview with waterfront pub manager, 5 July 2016)

In informal conversations, planners and elected city officials have sometimes described the continued existence of waterfront industrial sites as an obstacle to their goals to provide more waterfront recreation trails. They have also described plans to link up the several waterfront parks, pushing walkways, and bicycle paths into lands designated for industrial use. Unlike a public wharf, more pedestrian and bicycle infrastructure would surely meet with the approval of many residents and make the waterfront even more symbolically and financially desirable. However, while this could offer alternative forms of transportation for the remaining industrial workers, it could also further the belief that waterfront land is too valuable for industrial uses.

There surely were and remain some important physical bases for regarding the river as dangerous, but this danger, we suggest, comes as much from the loss of

FIGURE 5.3 Waterfront container transloading facility, served only by road and fenced off from the river

Photo by Peter Hall

knowledge of the river as from its inherent nature. Indeed, if the physicality of the river is a source of danger, it has become more so because the physical transformation of the river's edge has made it both objectively more dangerous and subjectively more difficult to know.

As discussed above, many of the contemporary waterfront industries have stopped using the water for transportation. While this is mostly because of the way that road transportation is (under)priced, it is possible that knowledge of the river as dangerous also subtly discourages industrial use. The river is presented as a visible and well-understood risk that is a threat to property-based accumulation, but the trucks that carry cargo have not been understood this way (at least, not until recently). Assertions of risk may not end with waterfront industrial uses, but may move to encompass other sites of industrial work – precisely what "just green enough" strategies are meant to guard against. Several city officials have expressed to us their belief that the remaining industrial waterfront users are hostile to greening strategies that include river-based goods movement and/or public access to the waterfront in industrial zones. And, for their part, several industrial users feel threatened or ignored by the city.

The New Westminster case pushes us to consider the limits of "just green enough" strategies to arrest gentrification of industrial lands. The success of "just green enough" turns on the ability to construct and articulate an "alternative vision of the sustainable city" (Curran and Hamilton 2012: 1039) as one that includes industrial work. As we have shown in this chapter, even industrial waterfront redevelopments that make space for working class residents do not necessarily make space for knowledge about or from those residents. Instead, we argue that the exclusion of working class knowledge – in this case about the river, and work on the river – has permitted city officials to reframe industrial waterfronts as dangerous and risky rather than productive. This framing of industrial waterfront spaces as post-productive permits them to be discursively constructed as in need of cleanup. In the New Westminster case, the river is also reframed as source of risk, but in the sense that it is seen as part of wild nature rather than as a place of dirty, dangerous industrial work.

The threat to "just green enough" strategies, as we see it, comes from this reframing of the river as too wild to touch, unsuitable as a place of work. And, reframing the landward waterfront as safe, as Green, as a place of non-work, as a place of recreation, contributes to a perception of Greenness, but counterintuitively, has the effect of making the city less Green, less sustainable than it might be if the river and riverfront were recognized as places of work. This constitutes a reassignment of risk; as the waterfront is made safe for property-based accumulation, it is rendered less suitable for industrial use in general, and for water-based industry and transportation in particular. Instead, the redeveloped waterfront is tangible evidence of the city's and real estate developers' efforts to open up the waterfront to the (non-working) public and render it safe. The result is reduced regional ecological and human sustainability from roadway expansion for goods movement and increased airborne diesel particulate emissions.

References

Behl, J., Transportation Engineer, City of New Westminster. 2015. Personal communication, March 31 and April 1, 2015.

Brownill, S. 2013. Just add water: waterfront regeneration as a global phenomenon. In *The Routledge Companion to Urban Regeneration*, Michael E. Leary and John McCarthy, eds., London: Routledge, pp. 45–54.

Checker, M. 2011. Wiped out by the "Greenwave": environmental gentrification and the paradoxical politics of urban sustainability, *City & Society* 23(2): 210–229.

City of Vancouver 2012. *Greenest City Action Plan*, Vancouver, BC: City of Vancouver.

Clarke, J. 2011. Closing Moulinex: thoughts on the visibility and invisibility of industrial labour in contemporary France, *Modern & Contemporary France* 19(4): 443–458.

Curran, W. and T. Hamilton 2012. Just green enough: contesting environmental gentrification in Greenpoint, Brooklyn, *Local Environment* 17(9): 1027–1042.

Dale, A. and L. L. Newman 2009. Sustainable development for some: green urban development and sustainability, *Local Environment* 14(7): 669–681.

Dooling, S. 2009. Ecological gentrification: a research agenda exploring justice in the city, *International Journal of Urban and Regional Research* 33(3): 621–639.

Dudley, K. M. 1994. *The End of the Line: Lost Jobs, New Lives in Postindustrial America*, Chicago: University of Chicago Press.

Goodling, E., J. Green and N. McClintock 2015. Uneven development of the sustainable city: shifting capital in Portland, Oregon, *Urban Geography* 36(4): 504–527.

Hagerman, C. 2007. Shaping neighborhoods and nature: urban political ecologies of urban waterfront transformations in Portland, Oregon, *Cities* 24: 285–297.

Hall, P. V. 2012. Connecting, disconnecting and reconnecting: port-logistics and Vancouver's Fraser River, *L'Espace geographique* 41(3): 223–235.

Hall, P. V. 2015. The social life of truck routes. In *Transport, Mobility, and the Production of Urban Space*, J. Cidell and D. Prytherch, eds., Abingdon: Routledge, pp. 117–133.

Hall, P. V. and P. Stern 2014. Implicating waterfronts in regional sustainability, *Local Environment* 19(6): 591–604.

Harvey, D. 1989. From managerialism to entrepreneurialism: the transformation in urban governance in late capitalism, *Geografiska Annaler, series B Human Geography* 71(1): 3–17.

High, S. 2013. Beyond aesthetics: visibility and invisibility in the aftermath of deindustrialization, *International Labor and Working Class History* 84: 140–153.

Kear, M. 2007. Spaces of transition spaces of tomorrow: making a sustainable future in Southeast False Creek, Vancouver, *Cities* 24(4), 324–334.

Leary, M. E. and J. McCarthy, eds. 2013. *The Routledge Companion to Urban Regeneration*, London: Routledge.

McCann, E. J. 2009. City marketing. In *International Encyclopedia of Human Geography*, Vol. 2, R. Kitchin and N. Thrift, eds., Oxford: Elsevier, pp. 119–124.

Metro Vancouver 2011a. *Metro Vancouver 2010 Industrial Lands Inventory, Metro Vancouver Metropolitan Planning, Environment, and Parks Department*, http://www.metrovancouver. org/services/regional-planning/industrial-lands/resources/Pages/default.aspx

Metro Vancouver 2011b. *Metro Vancouver 2040: Shaping Our Future, BYLAW NO. 1136, 2010 of the Greater Vancouver Regional District*. http://www.metrovancouver.org/services/ regional-planning/PlanningPublications/RGSAdoptedbyGVRDBoard.pdf

New Westminster 1990. *A Report on Industrial Land in the City of New Westminster and Greater Vancouver Region*, New Westminster Planning Department.

New Westminster 2012. *Downtown Community Plan (Schedule "A" to Bylaw No. 7396, 2010 and Schedule B to Bylaw No. 6476, 1998)*, www.newwestcity.ca.

Quastel, N. 2009. Political ecologies of gentrification, *Urban Geography*, 30(7): 694–725.

Reno, J. 2011. Beyond risk: emplacement and the production of environmental evidence, *American Ethnologist* 38(3): 516–530.

Smith, C. 2015. New Westminster mayor Jonathan Cote hopes to connect more neighbourhoods to the downtown waterfront, *The Georgia Strait*, 7 June.

Stanley, A. 2013. Natures of risk: capital, rule, and the production of difference, *Geoforum* 45: 5–16.

6

ALTERNATIVE FOOD AND GENTRIFICATION: FARMERS' MARKETS, COMMUNITY GARDENS AND THE TRANSFORMATION OF URBAN NEIGHBORHOODS

Pascale Joassart-Marcelli and Fernando J. Bosco

Introduction

In the past decade, food has emerged as a central element of a cultural and symbolic economy centered on selling lifestyles and aestheticizing the ordinary as a way to brand urban places (Zukin 2008; Bridge and Dowling 2001). Food has become an important marker of identity, used as a "social weapon" to distinguish high culture from low culture (Bourdieu 1984) and reinforce class positions (Johnston and Bauman 2014). As Guthman (2011) argues, these class distinctions operate at the body scale, where fatness, for instance, is interpreted as resulting from poor individual choices, a symbol of weakness and moral inferiority. They also unfold at the neighborhood scale, where the presence of particular food establishments indicates desirability and reflects social hierarchies. While fast food restaurants and convenience stores often stigmatize areas, popular eateries, public gardens and healthy retailers are associated with trendiness and liveliness (Guthman 2018; Joassart-Marcelli, Rossiter and Bosco 2017; Joassart-Marcelli and Bosco 2018). As we show in this chapter, uneven urban food landscapes are intimately connected to processes of gentrification and shaped along lines of race and class by political decisions and capital flows.

In this context, "alternative" food spaces, including co-ops, community gardens and farmers' markets, have become embroiled in this process of distinction. Farmers' markets in particular have been envisioned as a way to improve food security and contribute to greener cities, although there is growing evidence that they are exclusionary spaces that cater primarily to the affluent, white and gentrifying class (Joassart-Marcelli and Bosco 2014; Slocum 2007). Furthermore, there are concerns that organic markets, community gardens and trendy eateries may undermine existing businesses, destroy neighborhood character and displace residents who cannot afford the food and/or feel excluded from these new spaces

(Anguelovski 2015; Joassart-Marcelli and Bosco 2018; Zukin, Lindenman and Hurson 2015).

In this chapter, we ask whether "alternative" and "green" food initiatives have been hijacked from their original goals and co-opted to serve the urban elite and reproduce white privilege. We first focus on the geography of farmers' markets and community gardens in the San Diego region and its relationship to gentrification. We then turn our attention to key local actors (governments, business associations and developers) that are now embracing food as a policy tool and are joining activists and community-based organizations in their support of farmers' markets and other food (re)localization efforts. We provide evidence that the alternative food movement in San Diego is part of an urban renewal agenda in which cultural food practices are used and appropriated by urban managers and developers to support neighborhood change.

Alternative food spaces, white privilege and green gentrification

Work in environmental justice points to deep inequalities in exposure to risk and access to amenities within cities. According to Pulido (2000), this is not simply the result of individual or corporate decisions to harm disenfranchised people. Instead, it reflects white privilege – an institutionalized system that confers privileges and benefits to white people because of their whiteness (Lipsitz 2006). The spatiality of these privileges entails white people securing the most desirable environments for themselves while keeping others out (Pulido 2000).

This environmental justice framework has been influential in shaping research on food justice. Scholars have shown how race and class intersect to produce unjust food environments characterized by lower access to "good" food, including fresh, healthy, affordable, diverse, culturally appropriate and sustainably grown food (Alkon and Agyeman 2011). Low-income neighborhoods of color are often described as "food deserts" or "food swamps" – metaphors meant to highlight the lack of healthy food (e.g., fresh produce) and the presence of unhealthy food (e.g., fast food) in an area (Walker et al. 2010). In response, many communities have mobilized to create local alternatives via urban agriculture, farmers' markets and greater connections between local producers and consumers. While these initiatives contribute to creating vibrant local economies, they often embrace a white habitus and a neoliberal urban agenda, which contradicts the social justice goals of locavorism.

The whiteness of farmers' markets has recently received significant attention in the literature (Alkon and McCullen 2011; Guthman 2008; Slocum 2007). Cultural geographers in particular have made important contributions by showing that farmers' markets are often white spaces where the food consumption habits of white people are normalized, leading to social exclusion. Along the same lines, observers have noted the "quality turn" that has taken place in the local food movement (Goodman and Goodman 2009) and made it out of reach for low-income people.

The neoliberal ideology underlying food localization efforts has also been the focus of recent studies (McClintock 2014; Joassart-Marcelli and Bosco 2014). In particular, the increased reliance on nonprofits and community-based organizations to solve food injustices at the local scale reflects the ongoing dismantling of the welfare state and the shift to individual responsibility, privatized solutions and apolitical notions of civil society.

To date, most of this research, including our own, has been based on case studies and in-depth analysis of social and political dynamics unfolding at specific sites. While this approach has generated much needed reflexivity in scholarship on local food (DuPuis and Goodman 2005), we argue for the need to "jump scales" (Smith 1993) and focus on urban processes that occur at the regional level to generate a new understanding of the relationship between alternative food spaces, white privilege and gentrification. From that perspective, the question is not simply whether local food initiatives fail to meet their goals of social justice, but whether they might actually contribute to injustice by encouraging gentrification.

Methods

This chapter combines quantitative data from public sources with qualitative data gathered through participant observation and media content analysis. We created lists of community gardens from the San Diego Community Garden Network (2016) and farmers' markets from the San Diego Farm Bureau (2016), Edible San Diego (2016) and the USDA (2015). We geocoded addresses and mapped them in relation to gentrification patterns estimated by using data at the census tract level from the 2000 Census of Population and Housing[1] and the 2011–15 American Community Survey.

We defined gentrification using a similar approach as Freeman (2005) and Governing (2015), but added race as a defining factor since class and race displacement are both associated with gentrification (Smith 1996). We identified tracts eligible to gentrify as those where median household income and home value were in the bottom 40th percentile in 2000, making them attractive to investors and potential gentrifiers. Gentrifying tracts were those where the 2000 to 2015 percentage change in: (1) the proportion of residents 25 and older with bachelor's degrees, (2) median home value, and (3) the proportion of non-Hispanic white residents were in the top tercile for the region. These variables reflect a rapid appreciation in real estate as well as a demographic transition towards a more highly educated and white creative class. We also relied on our knowledge of food politics in San Diego, which we acquired through five years of collaborative fieldwork and participant observation at farmers' markets and community gardens, and analyzed local media to get a better sense of how these alternative spaces present themselves and are represented by others in public discourse.

Farmers' markets and community gardens: A brief history

During the past decade, San Diego has experienced a rapid growth of alternative food initiatives. Although the county has a long history of farming and is home to approximately 6,000 farms (USDA 2012), the focus on building a local, urban food system is relatively new. The first certified farmers' market was held in 1981 in Vista – a relatively rural area close to many farms. The numbers increased slowly in the following two decades, but have grown exponentially since the turn of the millennium. Today, there are 63 farmers' markets operating in San Diego and all but four are located in urban neighborhoods. Six new markets opened in the past two years alone. Community gardens have experienced a similar growth trajectory, with many gardens less than a decade old and increasingly located in urban areas. In 2016, there were 83 gardens in the region (San Diego Community Garden Network 2016), up from 27 in 2010 (Porcella 2012), and 96 percent were located in urbanized areas.

What has been happening in San Diego is not unique. Across the United States, cities are embracing farmers' markets and urban agriculture. The number of certified farmers' markets increased from 342 in 1970 to 2,842 in 2000 (Brown 2002) and 8,674 in 2016 (USDA 2016). The more recent expansion has been associated with growing demand for fresh and local produce, as well as a variety of related food movements concerned with food justice and sustainability. Both goals – serving elite consumers and improving access to healthy foods in low-income communities of color – may help explain the fact that 80 percent of USDA registered farmers' markets are located in urban areas (Schupp 2015).

Like farmers' markets, community gardens have a long history in the United States with alternating periods of growth and decline (Lawson 2005). Following a seeming loss of interest after WWII, their numbers have grown tremendously during the past three decades. The resurgence of urban vacant lot gardens emerged primarily out of grassroots efforts to revitalize communities and improve food security (Lawson 2005; Lovell 2010). Today, the American Community Gardening Association (2016) estimates that there are 18,000 community gardens throughout the United States and Canada, up from about 700 in the late 1990s (Lawson 2005). The number of people growing food in community gardens increased from 1 million in 2008 to 3 million in 2013, with the largest increase among young adults in their 20s and 30s (National Gardening Association 2014).

San Diego's urban transformation and the alternative food landscape

Over the past fifteen years – the period during which community gardens and farmers' markets grew rapidly – San Diego became a denser and more diverse urban area, characterized by growing disparities and fragmentation. Comparisons of 2000 and 2015 US Census data for the County show that the white share of the population declined from 67% in 1999 to 46% in 2015. Based on official thresholds, poverty rates increased from 12% to 15% during that period. However, based on a threshold of 200 percent of official poverty (a more realistic approach to economic hardship in a high-cost of living place like San Diego), the increase was sharper, from 24% of the population in 1999 to 33% in 2015.

Meanwhile, median family income in the region increased from $44,009 in 1999 to $67,320 in 2015.

These broader trends hide growing disparities between cities and neighborhoods. For example, cities along the North Coast, like Del Mar, Encinitas, Solana Beach and Carlsbad, have proportions of white residents well above 70 percent, while in South Bay cities, like National City and Chula Vista, the proportion falls below 20 percent. Similarly, median household income ranges from $39,517 in National City to $103,457 in Del Mar. Neighborhood disparities, estimated by comparing Census tracts, are even wider.

The uneven socio-economic and cultural landscape of San Diego is linked to its distinct "hour-glass economy" in which middle-wage jobs are disappearing and low-wage service sector jobs in tourism and retail coexists with high-wage jobs in biotechnology and specialized fields (NUSIPR 2015). The low-wage jobs are filled primarily by immigrants and workers of color, who reside in older urban neighborhoods and inland suburban areas with lower rents. As elsewhere, the socio-economic fragmentation of the region has been exacerbated by municipal fiscal disparities and policies aimed at promoting economic growth rather than social equity. In the past three decades, the City of San Diego has actively pursued public-private partnerships to develop downtown through hotels, convention centers, and public facilities. Although these investments boost tourism, they neglect the needs of other neighborhoods that must compete with one another for resources (Davis, Mayhew and Miller 2003; Erie, Kogan and MacKenzie 2010). As a result, affluent suburban communities often engage in defensive localism to preserve their amenities and resources, while poorer urban neighborhoods pursue progressive and grassroots efforts to meet the needs of their residents (Joassart-Marcelli and Bosco 2014; Mitchell and Staeheli 2006). These contradictory trends coalesce in gentrifying neighborhoods, where it becomes unclear whether the work of nonprofits and community organizations serves the needs of long-term and typically poorer residents, or instead helps attract a new gentrifying class that further marginalizes older dwellers. Food in particular has emerged as one of the many pressing issues that animate neighborhood residents, policy makers and community-based organizations. Yet, given the multiplicity of food agendas, ranging from food security to sustainability to tourism, local alternative food initiatives are likely to have contradictory effects on the urban social and cultural landscape.

As Figure 6.1 illustrates, the location of farmers' markets and community gardens is closely related to patterns of gentrification, especially in the central urban area of San Diego where gentrification has been concentrated. Beginning in the 1990s, revitalization efforts, real estate investment and an influx of primarily white and affluent residents transformed older and declining central urban neighborhoods. Gentrification picked up after 2000 and, in the following 15 years, 39 tracts gentrified. This trend began in North Park (just north-east of Balboa Park, the city's largest green public space) and the East Village (where a new baseball stadium was built in the mid-90s) and spread to surrounding neighborhoods north, east and south of the park, including Barrio Logan and City Heights – two areas home to large immigrant populations.

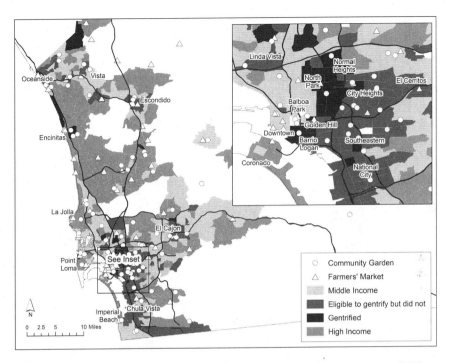

FIGURE 6.1 Alternative food spaces (2016) and gentrification by census tract (2000 to 2015), San Diego Urbanized Area

Source: Map created by authors based on data from San Diego Community Garden Network (2016), San Diego Farm Bureau (2016), Edible San Diego (2016), USDA (2015) and U.S. Census (2000, 2016)

In addition to urban neighborhoods, gentrification has also occurred at a smaller scale in cities like Oceanside, Vista, Escondido, El Cajon, National City and Imperial Beach. These historically working class communities have recently experienced an influx of higher income residents and investors attracted by lower rents and the small town atmosphere of these places. Moreover, gentrifying neighborhoods are surrounded by Census tracts ready to be gentrified due to the historical concentration of low-income households and relatively affordable housing stock. There are 153 such tracts in San Diego.

Forty-four percent of farmers' markets and 54 percent of community gardens are located within a mile of Census tracts where gentrification has been unfolding. To be sure, there are also well-established markets and community gardens in affluent and predominantly white areas like Carlsbad, Encinitas, Del Mar, La Jolla, Pacific Beach, Point Loma, Little Italy and Hillcrest. Outside of gentrifying areas, it is in these wealthier neighborhoods that some of the most active markets and gardens are located. Indeed, very few are found in middle- or low-income neighborhoods showing limited prospects of gentrification. This indicates a strong association between alternative food spaces, class and gentrification. This relationship, however, may not reflect causality. On the one hand, farmers' markets and community gardens may make some neighborhoods more attractive to white, educated, young and relatively wealthy people and thereby promote gentrification. On the other hand, residents of gentrified neighborhoods may be more likely to engage in alternative food practices and organize for the creation of spaces where they can pursue these interests. Yet, the fact that alternative food spaces are associated with neighborhood transformation highlights the role of food and foodies in creating, or at the very least reinforcing, class and race divisions and furthering displacement.

The production of the alternative food landscape: Key actors

Food localization can be understood as a spatial strategy that reflects specific agendas (Born and Purcell 2006, Joassart-Marcelli and Bosco 2014). In San Diego, there are a number of important actors that shape the expansion, spatial distribution and character of farmers' markets and community gardens. Although their goals differ, an examination of recent interventions reveal that urban renewal and real estate development have come to dominate the so-called alternative food movement.

Community organizations

Many farmers' markets and community gardens are the product of community organizing spearheaded by local nonprofits. Such organizations include the International Rescue Committee (IRC) and Project New Village that have secured vacant lots for food gardening and bring local growers together at weekly farmers' markets. These activities help address important food security issues in the low-income and racially diverse communities of City Heights, El Cajon and Southeastern San Diego.

At this time, gentrification has not occurred in Southeastern San Diego and Project New Village is consciously taking an anti-gentrification stand, putting the needs of the community first, supporting local growers and avoiding projects that will primarily attract "hipsters" from surrounding areas. In contrast, City Heights – where the IRC is most active – has undergone significant change in the past decade, and it is increasingly viewed as an extension of trendy and gentrified North Park. The work of the IRC and the alternative food spaces it has created have drawn significant attention to the neighborhood – from national media (Brown 2011) to the White House (Obama 2012) – and have contributed to its new identity as an "International Marketplace." This cosmopolitan and alternative vibe, along with comparatively lower rents, have attracted younger, whiter and more affluent residents and displaced former residents, including immigrants and refugees.

Other community organizations have decidedly more parochial goals that align more directly with the objectives of gentrification. For instance, the Golden Hill Community Garden was started in 2004 by a group of residents to "provide members an opportunity to grow their own vegetables, flowers and herbs [...] and a peaceful place to meet neighbors, experience nature, and enjoy the diversity of life" (GGHCDC 2016). Its website includes detailed garden rules, a separate page on how to lock the gate and gourmet recipes. The garden, along with the weekly farmers' market, is sponsored by the Greater Golden Hill Community Development Organization, whose board of directors is comprised almost entirely of real estate professionals and business owners who praise the "potential" of the community and aim to "build a better Golden Hill." This includes the farmers' market manager who describes himself as an "advocate for local food, local art, and local services" and runs other farmers' markets, street fairs and art walks in North Park and other nearby neighborhoods. Scholars have highlighted the connection between these sorts of festivals and gentrification (Zukin 2010). Indeed, a growing number of farmers' markets in gentrified and high-income areas are being run by private companies hired by neighborhood business associations to attract tourists and shoppers and support local businesses (Joassart-Marcelli and Bosco 2014). Similarly, gardens are emerging on corporate campuses and in private developments. These for-profit organizations often adopt decontextualized language about "community," masking their differences with grassroots nonprofits and hiding exclusionary social processes (Bosco and Joassart-Marcelli 2017).

Local governments

Until recently, relations between local governments and nonprofits involved in alternative food efforts were usually tense. Community-based organizations across the United States have long fought with local governments to secure and maintain access to land to grow food or hold farmers' markets (Lawson 2012, Saldivar-Tanaka and Krasny 2004, Schmelzkopf 2002). In the 1960s and 1970s, the most vocal advocates of urban gardens were motivated by the civil rights movement and radical responses to urban decline and, therefore, were typically perceived as working in opposition to local governments (Mares 2014). Yet, in recent years, local governments began to view these alternative food spaces as a potential tool for revitalization – a perception that aligns more closely with the views of affluent and leisure-centered gardeners.

In San Diego, community gardens and farmers' markets have become important components of urban policy, as described recently in several community plans, the climate action plan and the city-wide economic development strategy. The latter mentions that: "older commercial corridors offer a richer shopping experience that often includes authentic and diverse dining and entertainment experiences. Special events such as street fairs, restaurant walks, and farmers' markets offer residents and shoppers opportunities to experience the individual characteristics of the commercial neighborhoods" (City of San Diego 2014, 45). Hillcrest, Downtown and North Park – three early gentrifiers – are cited as examples to follow. The climate action plan, despite its disappointingly limited emphasis on food, includes pictures of community gardens and farmers' markets and suggests that they may be part of an adaptation strategy to climate change.

In the past five years, the City of San Diego has passed a number of ordinances to facilitate urban agriculture and the creation of community gardens in residential neighborhoods, following other large U.S. cities (Mees and Stone 2012). After months of community organizing, the City Council adopted an ordinance to remove zoning restrictions and waive the permitting process for community gardens in 2011. Chula Vista and Escondido had adopted similar measures to encourage community gardens in 2010 and El Cajon did so in 2013. More recently, San Diego's City Council also adopted an ordinance reducing property tax on parcels converted to community gardens, following California's 2014 Urban Agriculture Incentive Zone Act. Other cities, such as Encinitas, are considering doing the same.

These ordinances are usually envisioned as ways to revitalize neighborhoods and encourage development. For instance, the San Diego County Board of Supervisors (2015, 3–4) argued that urban agriculture incentive zones would "create vibrant green spaces out of what would otherwise be unused, vacant and blighted land [...] and help address issues of food access and promote economic resilience and community building." In short, public officials have helped reframe community gardens and farmers' markets through narratives of local entrepreneurship, sustainable neighborhoods, healthy places and strong communities that resonate with both developers seeking to generate value by rebranding "blighted" places and gentrifiers identifying with "alternative" urban lifestyles.

Public-private redevelopment partnerships

Increasingly, local governments are working with private entities in promoting economic development. Chapin (2002) warns that redevelopment projects in downtown San Diego were moving beyond the typical model of urban entrepreneurialism into what he called "municipal capitalism." Rather than simply facilitating projects through financing and permitting in the early stages, Chapin argues that the public sector is now actively driving development and focused upon investment returns (including revenue from property tax increments). Although California dismantled its redevelopment agencies in 2012, neighborhood redevelopment plans and projects in the City of San Diego have been managed by Civic San Diego, an organization owned by the city but operating as a nonprofit with private partners. Projects include housing, parks and open space, parking and new markets tax credits, and are almost entirely located downtown. The city of San Diego's partnerships with the private sector to finance redevelopment are well documented and raise questions about the equity of using public resources for private objectives (Erie, Kogan and MacKenzie 2010).

Support for small businesses along historical commercial corridors is also provided by Business Improvement Districts (BIDs) that are created by the city but similarly run by nonprofit management corporations. The vast majority of these districts are located in the gentrified or gentrifying areas highlighted in Figure 6.1, including sections of University Avenue in North Park and City Heights, Adams Avenue in University Heights and Normal Heights, El Cajon Boulevard in North Park, City Heights and El Cerrito and Imperial and Euclid Avenue in Southeastern San Diego.

On their website, in official documents and in observed conversations, both Civic San Diego and the BIDs show support for farmers' markets and community gardens as important elements of urban renewal. For instance, the Business Improvement District Council claims that "the BID associations have developed a variety of successful marketing activities that generate business for the districts. These activities range from special events such as restaurant tours, block parties, weekly farmers' markets and holiday festivals to developing public relations and marketing materials" (City of San Diego 2016). A number of projects supported by Civic San Diego also make room for farmers' markets and community gardens. For example, plans for a historic park at Horton Plaza in the center of downtown include a farmers' market. The East Village's Makers Quarter – part of the I.D.E.A. district, a major development that encompasses several blocks of public and private property – incorporates SMART Farm community garden and Silo, an outdoor gathering space for pop-up events such as the "Envision Urban Agriculture Fair," "Tacos and Beer Festival," "Plant Grow Eat," and "Vertical Garden Workshop" (Makers Quarter 2016). These symbolic components target "millennials" and "like-minded creative, tech professionals and entrepreneurs" who are attracted by the "live/work/play lifestyle" (I.D.E.A. District 2016). However, after having generated much excitement about Makers Quarters, these temporary spaces will soon be transformed and replaced with condominiums (Herstik 2016). This is not unlike the Mission Hills Farmers' Market, which lasted less than a year – long enough to help the marketers of an adjacent luxury development sell most of its units.

Real estate professionals and the media

To real estate professionals, including developers and agents, neighborhood amenities are critical in adding value to properties. Community gardens and farmers' markets have become selling points. Indeed, there is a growing literature suggesting that these alternative food sites boost property values (Voicu and Been 2008; Project for Public Spaces 2007).

In San Diego, developers and real estate professionals are using alternative food spaces to market properties. This is especially true in gentrifying neighborhoods. In September 2016, there were almost 300 recently sold and for sale properties in San Diego County that mentioned a farmers' market in their main description. Such advertising is especially common in the gentrified and gentrifying central neighborhoods of San Diego such as Hillcrest, North Park, Little Italy, City Heights and Golden Hill. For example, an ad for a condominium in University Heights invites potential buyers to "move in and leave your vehicle securely parked at home because many of the most desirable restaurants, shops and services are all conveniently located just a short distance away – including […] Whole Foods Market, Trader Joes Market, Balboa park, and the fabulous Hillcrest Farmers' Market each Sunday" (Zillow 2016).

Local business associations and media also play an important role in supporting and marketing farmers' markets and community gardens. *San Diego Magazine*, which is financed primarily through advertising by real estate companies, regularly publishes articles on San Diego's "Next Hot Neighborhoods." Of the neighbor-hoods highlighted in the 2014, 2015 and 2016 issues, over 90 percent are in already or potentially gentrified areas, including Barrio Logan and "hipster havens" City Heights and North Park, as well as "emerging neighborhoods" of "tight-knit families" and "well-educated communities" in older suburbs. Each description includes numerous mentions of food and emphasizes authentic eateries, craft breweries, restaurants and gourmet food stores. Farmers' markets and gardens are also often highlighted. For example, Oak Park in Southeastern San Diego is painted as "an ultradiverse locale where neighbors get together for gardening, community cleanups, and craft beer, [...] attracting young, community-oriented dwellers who are passionate about reinventing a place that was once run-down" (*San Diego Magazine* 2016). These and other media accounts of farmers' markets and com-munity gardens consistently emphasize their role in transforming neighborhoods into trendy places, characterized by authenticity, diversity and strong communities of highly educated and like-minded people.

Conclusion: Gentrification or food justice?

The recent popularity of farmers' markets and community gardens has been attributed to a desire to build greener cities, strengthen social connections and enhance food security. Indeed, many such spaces represent forms of resistance to a socially unjust and environmentally unsustainable food system. However, far too often, people of color and the poor are excluded from these so-called alternative food spaces (Alkon 2012; Guthman 2008; Mares 2014; Slocum 2007). While this process of exclusion can be observed in the social dynamics that characterize parti-cular gardens and farmers' markets, it is also visible in the geographic distribution of these sites and their relationships to larger processes of urban transformation. In this chapter, we have shown that farmers' markets and community gardens are primarily located in affluent and gentrifying areas and have provided evidence of a growing appropriation of alternatives food spaces by urban developers and cultural elites.

The consequences of these trends go well beyond the fact that the poor and people of color rarely shop at farmers' markets or grow vegetables in community gardens. In addition to these socially exclusionary trends, we are observing a more dramatic transformation of urban neighborhoods in which alternative food spaces attract households from higher socio-economic backgrounds, raising property values and displacing low-income residents and people of color. This process is a form of ecological or green gentrification (Checker 2011; Curran and Hamilton 2012; Dooling 2009; Gould and Lewis 2012).

The most insidious part of this gentrification process is that alternative food initiatives work against the community activists and residents who first mobilized to fight environmental injustices and provide these amenities but have significantly less political and economic clout than developers and real estate professionals. Curbing gentrification is a vexing task that requires: (1) strong community involve-ment to insure that the needs of the poorest and presumably least desirable residents are prioritized and that their voices are heard, (2) commitment from local governments to support use value over exchange value through equitable zoning policies, rent-control laws and property tax reforms in favor of long-time home-owners and (3) institutional structures such as community land trusts to maintain or strengthen community ownership, preserve affordable housing, protect access to land and build on existing resources. Ultimately, it requires slow and inclusive steps that balance new initiatives and neighborhood stability to make cities "just green enough" (Curran and Hamilton 2012; Wolch, Byrne and Newell 2014).

Note

1 We obtained the 2000 Census data from the US 2010 Project (Logan, Xu, and Stults 2014). These data use 2010 census tract boundaries, which allowed us to connect these to the 2011–15 data from the American community survey and to compute various indi-cators of neighborhood change.

References

Alkon, A.H. 2012. *Black, White and Green: Farmers Markets, Race, and the Green Economy*. Athens, GA: University of Georgia Press.

Alkon, A.H., and Agyeman, J. 2011. *Cultivating Food Justice: Race, Class and Sustainability*. Cambridge, MA: MIT Press.

Alkon, A.H., and McCullen, C.G. 2011. Whiteness and Farmers Markets: Performances, Perpetuations... Contestations? *Antipode* 43(4): 937–959.

American Community Gardening Association. 2016. *Frequently Asked Questions*. https://communitygarden.org/resources/faq/

Anguelovski, I. 2015. Alternative Food Provision Conflicts in Cities; Contesting Food Privilege, Injustice and Whiteness in Jamaica Plain, Boston. *Geoforum* 58: 184–194.

Born, B., and Purcell, M. 2006. Avoiding the Local Trap Scale and Food Systems in Planning Research. *Journal of Planning Education and Research* 26(2): 195–207.

Bosco, F.J., and Joassart-Marcelli, P. 2017. Gardens in the City: Community, Politics and Place. In WinklerPrins, A. (Ed.), *Global Urban Agriculture: Convergence of Theory and Practice between North and South*. Boston, MA: CABI International. Forthcoming.

Bourdieu, P. 1984. *Distinction: A Social Critique of the Judgement of Taste*. Cambridge, MA: Harvard University Press.

Bridge, Gary, and Dowling, Robyn. 2001. Microgeographies of Retailing and Gentrification. *Australian Geographer* 32(1): 93–107.

Brown, A. 2002. Farmers' Market Research 1940–2000: An Inventory and Review. *American Journal of Alternative Agriculture* 17(4): 167–176.

Brown, P.L. 2011. When the Uprooted Put Down Roots. *The New York Times*, October 9. http://www.nytimes.com/2011/10/10/us/refugees-in-united-states-take-up-farming.html

Chapin, T. 2002. Beyond the Entrepreneurial City: Municipal Capitalism in San Diego. *Journal of Urban Affairs* 24(5): 565–581.

Checker, M. 2011. Wiped out by the "Greenwave": Environmental Gentrification and the Paradoxical Politics of Urban Sustainability. *City & Society* 23(2): 210–229.

City of San Diego. 2014. *Economic Development Strategy 2014–2016*. https://www.sandiego.gov/sites/default/files/legacy/economic-development/pdf/economicdevelopmentstrategy.pdf

City of San Diego. 2016. *Business Improvement Districts.* https://www.sandiego.gov/econom ic-development/about/bids

Curran, W., and Hamilton, T. 2012. Just Green Enough: Contesting Environmental Gentrification in Greenpoint, Brooklyn. *Local Environment* 17(9): 1027–1042.

Davis, M., Mayhew, K., and Miller, J. 2003. *Under the Perfect Sun: The San Diego Tourists Never See.* San Diego, CA: New Press.

Dooling, S. 2009. Ecological Gentrification: A Research Agenda Exploring Justice in the City. *International Journal of Urban and Regional Research* 33(3): 621–639.

DuPuis, E.M., and Goodman, D. 2005. Should We Go "Home" to Eat?: Toward a Reflexive Politics of Localism. *Journal of Rural Studies* 21(3): 359–371.

Edible San Diego. 2016. Farmers' Markets. http://www.ediblesandiego.com/local-food/fa rmers-markets.html

Erie, S.P., Kogan, V., and MacKenzie, S.A. 2010. Redevelopment, San Diego Style: The Limits of Public–Private Partnerships. *Urban Affairs Review* 45(5): 644–678.

Freeman, L. 2005. Displacement or Succession? Residential Mobility in Gentrifying Neighborhoods. *Urban Affairs Review* 40(4): 463–491.

GGHCDC. 2016. Greater Golden Hill Community Development Corporation. Official Website. http://goldenhillcdc.org

Goodman, D., and Goodman, M. 2009. Alternative Food Networks. *International Encyclopedia of Human Geography*: 208–220.

Gould, K., and Lewis, T. 2012. The Environmental Injustice of Green Gentrification: The Case of Brooklyn's Prospect Park. In DeSena, J. and Shortell, T. (Eds.), *The World in Brooklyn: Gentrification, Immigration, and Ethnic Politics in a Global City.* Lanham, MD: Lexington Books.

Governing. 2015. San Diego Gentrification Maps and Data. Governing Data. http://www. governing.com/gov-data/san-diego-gentrification-maps-demographic-data.html

Guthman, J. 2008. "If They Only Knew": Color Blindness and Universalism in California Alternative Food Institutions. *The Professional Geographer* 60(3): 387–397.

Guthman, J. 2011. *Weighing In: Obesity, Food Justice, and the Limits of Capitalism.* Berkeley, CA: University of California Press.

Guthman, J. 2018. Can Place Cause Obesity? A Critical Perspective on the Obesogenic Environment Thesis. In Joassart-Marcelli, P. and Bosco, F.J. (Eds.), *Food and Place: A Critical Exploration.* Rowman and Littlefield.

Herstik, L. 2016. A Beer Garden Lays Down Roots for a Technology Hub. *The New York Times*, July 26. http://www.nytimes.com/2016/07/27/business/a-beer-garden-lays-down-roots-for-a-technology-hub.html?_r=4

I.D.E.A. District. 2016. Promotional Website. www.ideadistrictsd.com

Joassart-Marcelli, P., and Bosco, F.J. 2014. Alternative Food Projects, Localization and Urban Development: Farmers' Markets in Southern California. *Métropoles* 15(1): 2–23.

Joassart-Marcelli, P., and Bosco, F.J. 2018. Food and Gentrification: How Foodies are Transforming Urban Neighborhoods. In Joassart-Marcelli, P. and Bosco, F.J. (Eds.), *Food and Place: A Critical Exploration.* Rowman and Littlefield.

Johnston, J., and Baumann, S. 2014. *Foodies: Democracy and Distinction in the Gourmet Foodscape.* New York: Routledge.

Lawson, L. 2005. *City Bountiful: A History of Community Gardening in America.* Berkeley, CA: University of California Press.

Lawson, L. 2012. Cultural Geographies in Practice: The South Central Farm: Dilemmas in Practicing the Public. In Williams-Forson, P. and Counihan, C. (Eds.), *Taking Food Public: Redefining Foodways in a Changing World.* New York: Routledge.

Lipsitz, G. 2006. *The Possessive Investment in Whiteness: How White People Profit from Identity Politics.* Philadelphia, PA: Temple University Press.

Logan, J. R., Xu, Z., and Stults, B. J. 2014. Interpolating US Decennial Census Tract Data from as Early as 1970 to 2010: A Longitudinal Tract Database. *The Professional Geographer* 66(3): 412–420.

Lovell, S.T. 2010. Multifunctional Urban Agriculture for Sustainable Land Use Planning in the United States. *Sustainability* 2(8): 2499–2522.

Makers Quarter. 2016. Promotional Website. http://www.makersquarter.com

Mares, T.M. 2014. Engaging Latino Immigrants in Seattle Food Activism through Urban Agriculture. In Counihan, C. and Siniscalchi, V. (Eds.), *Food Activism: Agency, Democracy and Economy.* New York: Bloomsbury, pp. 31–46.

McClintock, N. 2014. Radical, Reformist, and Garden-Variety Neoliberal: Coming to Terms with Urban Agriculture's Contradictions. *Local Environment* 19(2): 147–171.

Mees, C., and Stone, E. 2012. Zoned Out: The Potential of Urban Agriculture Planning to Turn Against its Roots. *Cities and the Environment (CATE)* 5(1): 7. http://digitalcommons.lmu.edu/cate/vol5/iss1/7

Mitchell, D., and Staeheli, L.A. 2006. Clean and Safe? Property Redevelopment, Public Space, and Homelessness in Downtown San Diego. In Low, S. and Smith, N. (Eds.), *The Politics of Public Space.* New York: Routledge, pp. 143–175.

National Gardening Association. 2014. *Garden to Table: A Five-Year Look at Food Gardening in America.* http://garden.org/special/pdf/2014-NGA-Garden-to-Table.pdf

NUSIPR. 2015. San Diego Economic Outlook 2015. *San Diego Economic Ledger* 10(1). La Jolla, CA: National University System Institute for Policy Research.

Obama, M. 2012. *American Grown: The Story of the White House Kitchen Garden and Gardens Across America.* New York: Crown Publishers.

Porcella, A.L. 2012. *Reap What You Sow: Social Capital in Community Gardens.* M.A. Thesis. Department of Geography. San Diego State University.

Project for Public Spaces. 2007. *Estimating the Economic Impact of Public Markets.* Philadelphia: Econsult Corporation. http://www.pps.org/pdf/pps_public_markets_eis.pdf

Pulido, L. 2000. Rethinking Environmental Racism: White Privilege and Urban Development in Southern California. *Annals of the Association of American Geographers* 90(1): 12–40.

Saldivar-Tanaka, L., and Krasny, M.E. 2004. Culturing Community Development, Neighborhood Open Space, and Civic Agriculture: The Case of Latino Community Gardens in New York City. *Agriculture and Human Values* 21(4): 399–412.

San Diego Community Garden Network. 2016. *List of Community Gardens.* http://sdcgn.org

San Diego County Board of Supervisors. 2015. Implementing Urban Agriculture Incentive Zones in San Diego County. October 28. http://www.ronroberts.com/content/dam/d4/en/documents/policy/10.28.15.pdf

San Diego Farm Bureau. 2016. *San Diego County Farmers' Markets.* http://sdfarmbureau.org/BuyLocal/Farmers-Markets.php

San Diego Magazine. 2016. San Diego's Next Hot Neighborhoods. *San Diego Magazine,* February 26. http://www.sandiegomagazine.com/San-Diego-Magazine/March-2016/San-Diegos-Next-Hot-Neighborhoods/

Schmelzkopf, K. 2002. Incommensurability, Land Use, and the Right to Space: Community Gardens in New York City. *Urban Geography* 23(4): 323–343.

Schupp, J.L. 2015. Just Where Does Local Food Live? Assessing Farmers' Markets in the United States. *Agriculture and Human Values,* doi:10.1007/s10460–10015–9667-y, pp. 1–15.

Slocum, R. 2007. Whiteness, Space, and Alternative Food Practice. *Geoforum* 38(3): 520–533.

Smith, N. 1993. Homeless/Global: Scaling Places. In Bird, J., Curtis, B., Putnam, T. and Tickner, L. (Eds.), *Mapping the Futures: Local Cultures, Global Change*. London: Routledge, pp. 87–119.

Smith, N. 1996. *The New Urban Frontier: Gentrification and the Revanchist City*. London and New York: Routledge.

U.S. Census. 2000. *Census of Population and Housing*. Washington, DC: U.S. Department of Commerce. https://factfinder.census.gov

U.S. Census. 2016. *American Community Survey 5-Year Estimates (2011–15)*. Washington, DC: U.S. Department of Commerce. https://factfinder.census.gov

USDA. 2012. *Census of Agriculture. San Diego County Profile*. https://www.agcensus.usda.gov/Publications/2012/Online_Resources/County_Profiles/California/cp06073.pdf

USDA. 2015. *Local Food Directories: National Farmers Market Directory*. https://www.ams.usda.gov/local-food-directories/farmersmarkets

USDA. 2016. *Local Food Directories*. United States Department of Agriculture. Agricultural Marketing Service. https://www.ams.usda.gov/services/local-regional/food-directories

Voicu, I., and Been, V. 2008. The Effect of Community Gardens on Neighboring Property Values. *Real Estate Economics* 36(2): 241–283.

Walker, R.E., Keane, C.R., and Burke, J.G. 2010. Disparities and Access to Healthy Food in the United States. *Health & Place* 16(5): 876–884.

Wolch, J.R., Byrne, J., and Newell, J.P. 2014. Urban Green Space, Public Health, and Environmental Justice: The Challenge of Making Cities "Just Green Enough". *Landscape and Urban Planning* 125: 234–244.

Zillow. 2016. San Diego County CA Home For Sale. http://www.zillow.com/san-diego-county-ca/

Zukin, S. 2008. Consuming Authenticity. *Cultural Studies* 22(5): 724–748.

Zukin, S. 2010. *Naked City: The Death and Life of Authentic Urban Places*. Oxford: Oxford University Press.

Zukin, S., Lindeman, S., and Hurson, L. 2015. The Omnivore's Neighborhood? Online Restaurant Reviews, Race, and Gentrification. *Journal of Consumer Culture*, doi:10.1177/1469540515611203, pp. 1–21.

Zukin, S., Trujillo, V., Frase, P., Jackson, D., Recuber, T., and Walker, A. 2009. New Retail Capital and Neighborhood Change: Boutiques and Gentrification in New York City. *City & Community* 8(1): 47–64.

7

THE PRODUCTION OF GREEN: GENTRIFICATION AND SOCIAL CHANGE

Jessica Ty Miller

Green gentrification brings environmental comforts for some, such as walkways and other recreational spaces, stormwater catchment gardens, bike lanes, and other land uses that create "green" urban spaces. In Gowanus, a former industrial and transportation center in Brooklyn, New York (see Figure 7.1), physical and social changes have come long before the area will be free from contamination. Developers reacted to the promise that the area will be remediated through several cleanup processes (Miller 2015). After many years of contamination, the Gowanus Canal became a Superfund site in 2010. This designation came after years of conflict over how to clean up the canal and which government entities would be responsible for that process. This chapter will discuss how residents are responding to changes taking place in the area as a result of the renewed interest in cleaning and greening the canal.

Gowanus in context

Far from complete, research on the social impacts of gentrification and green gentrification points to a few areas that are helpful in approaching Gowanus. Some research investigates power and decision-making processes (Pearsall 2013; Hamilton and Curran 2013; Miller 2015 and 2016; Campbell and Gabriel 2016), while other researchers have focused on the tie between environmental injustice and green gentrification (Anguelovski 2016; Curran and Hamilton 2012; Checker 2011; Checker 2015; Eckerd 2011; Eckerd and Keeler 2012; Gould and Lewis 2011 and 2017; Lee and Mohai 2013; Pearsall and Pierce 2010). The "just green enough" concept (Curran and Hamilton 2012; Hamilton and Curran 2013) suggests that communities may be able to negotiate an outcome where greening occurs, but displacement does not. Miller (2015) and Wolch et al. (2014) suggest this might be a difficult balance to strike. Miller (2015) and Anguelovski (2016) suggest that greening

Gowanus Neighborhood Map

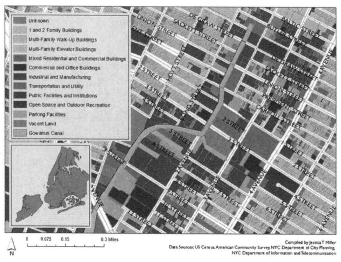

FIGURE 7.1 2014 land use map of Gowanus

may be viewed as a locally unwanted land use in favor of affordability. Miller (2016) also suggests that there are several limitations to influencing decisions at a local level concerning environmental cleanup processes. Finally, Gould and Lewis (2017) suggest that the just green enough concept may only be applicable in areas with static real estate markets. These findings suggest that the efforts towards remedying environmental harms are often obscured by limitations to taking part in planning processes and simultaneous efforts to redevelop contaminated areas.

I conducted a multi-year (2010–2014), mixed-method research project to create an account of the changing Gowanus neighborhood, including participant observation, archival research, GIS and spatial analysis, transect walks, and semi-structured interviews. These methods allowed me to catalog the historic and current activism and decision making surrounding the Gowanus Canal cleanup, and determine the current extent of gentrification and displacement taking place in the neighborhoods surrounding the canal.

A brief history of the canal

Developers located manufacturing plants, storage, distribution, and shipping facilities along the canal shortly after its construction in the mid-1800s (New York Department of City Planning 2011). Some land surrounding the canal is still industrial, but many properties now include housing, community facilities, and waterfront recreation (New York Department of City Planning 2011 and USEPA 2016). These changes are coupled with interest in remediating the canal, but few plans address the full scope of challenges that cleanup would involve.

In early 2009, the United States Environmental Protection Agency (EPA) proposed placing the Gowanus Canal on the National Priorities List (USEPA 2016). New York City created a counter proposal to clean up the canal and redevelop it quickly with its development interests ready to move in. This plan met significant community opposition. The debate between the "growth machine" (Logan and Molotch 1987), comprised of New York City government and its development interests, and the United States Environmental Protection Agency delayed the listing until 2010. The EPA investigated the extent and causes of the contamination, identified potentially responsible parties for the cleanup costs, and pushed forward with the feasibility study to select a remedy for the contamination found in the canal in 2013 (USEPA 2016). However, city, state, and community-led efforts to clean up the surrounding areas are ongoing. Vision 2020, New York City's waterfront plan, includes strategies for using waterfront areas as economic development opportunities. This plan calls for upgrades to canal infrastructure, rezoning, and cleanup of "underutilized" areas near the canal, and restoration of brownfield areas along the canal (New York Department of City Planning 2011).

Because many people in the area have long been involved in the effort to get Gowanus remediated, they have high hopes for the redevelopment of this space. Some think the area should be altered to increase waterfront access, becoming a waterfront oasis for the public to stroll through with new residential and mixed-use waterfront property surrounding it. Some would like to preserve the history of the area and create arts, entertainment, or environmental education opportunities. Some groups want the canal to remain and grow as a working waterway or industrial center, encouraging industrial, non-polluting, creative, and green businesses to move in. Some want it to be restored to its former glory as a wetland to increase the ability for wetland species to survive, and for increased opportunities for water recreation activities. Others would like to showcase the area as an innovative model for green infrastructure creation. However, there are also people who want the canal to remain filthy, therefore possibly buffering the area from high New York City rents.

Neighborhood changes

When I asked the participants about how the neighborhood is changing and how the cleanup might impact the neighborhood, most of the participants responded that the cleanup would be good for the neighborhood. Several of the participants suspected that one of the reasons the area is being cleaned up now is that new residents of the area are interested in the area being clean. One long-time landowner and developer said, "all of these buzz words – green, organic, it's what people are interested in today. People didn't care 30 years ago, but they care now" (Participant 8).

Several physical changes have taken place in the neighborhood, including new curb cuts and improved sidewalks, tree plantings, and other green infrastructure, bike lane improvements, zoning changes, new buildings, and building alterations

(Miller 2015). I asked interviewees what types of changes they have perceived to date. A few of the interviewees commented on the increased access to neighborhood amenities. One young renter and newer resident said, "I have more opportunities for doing business around the canal, more opportunities for entertainment, food and more jobs. And my young, hipster demographic is very well served by the changes that are happening around the canal" (Participant 3). He added that, "There are new woodshops and a bunch of new venues. It's become a lot more hip and interesting in the last five years" (Participant 3). Another younger male renter and business owner said, "It's nice that it's still a little bit sleepy over here. But it's nice that I can have a meeting with a client in a coffee shop now too" (Participant 10).

When I asked the interviewees how the canal itself has changed since they moved to the area, few cited any substantial changes to the physical environment of the canal. Some described seeing wildlife in the canal, or changes to the level of stench from the canal, indicating some positive change to the water quality. One older community activist and resident stated that the physical environment of the "canal has not changed, but in the realm of public understanding, there's been a tremendous increase in awareness of the environmental challenges the Gowanus Canal faces" (Participant 3). Some participants cited a reduction in crime in the area, fewer trucks, manufacturing, and noise, but reluctantly referred to these changes as positive. One long-term resident and activist said, "I miss that bit of texture. I think there is just less life and less working people" (Participant 4).

The area surrounding the canal is currently zoned as a manufacturing district and therefore has little housing supply, with some spot rezoning for new luxury housing and a Whole Foods (see Kimmelman 2016). A proposed city zoning change for the neighborhood may in the future permit residential development in the form of mixed-use buildings along the canal borders. One long-term landowner and resident said, "Rezoning probably will go through. I think it will have a big impact on the number of residential units that can be built there and I think that whatever is allowable will be maximized around the Gowanus. I'm sure there is going to be as much residential development as people can possibly build in the next 20 years" (Participant 3).

Several people who I spoke to brought up the level of transportation access in the neighborhood as either a problem that needs to be addressed or as an amenity the neighborhood offers to people moving to the area. An older landowner and developer suggested that people used to be able to live and work in the area, and the loss of that ability is partially related to the transportation infrastructure: "It is important that if people can't afford to live in a neighborhood, they can at least get there to work, or to work somewhere else" (Participant 6). An older, male landowner added, "Transportation is one of the most vital things to provide if you're going to redevelop" (Participant 7). The Department of Transportation planned bicycle lane improvements for Degraw, Nevins, Union and Sackett Streets to increase access to the area. These improvements allow bicycle connections to the

Brooklyn Greenway and two-way biking across Union Street, one of the major thoroughfares in the neighborhood (NYCDOT 2013).

Demographic shifts, gentrification, and displacement

Gowanus is becoming a neighborhood that costs more to live in and one where people with higher incomes and education levels are moving (see Table 7.1). Some interviewees reflected about neighborhood changes, citing the loss in neighborhood income diversity as an inevitability of gentrification. Some see these changes as a sign that gentrification will change the neighborhood in ways they might rather not see. An older male landowner said, "In every neighborhood, you have to have a variety of people to perform a variety of services, and if you can't have the people who cook food or do other services, and they can't afford it, than what the hell can you have?" (Participant 6).

According to the United States Census data, the population in Gowanus did not change significantly from 2000 to 2010. However, American Community Survey data suggests higher population increases. The population of the area may not have increased much yet, due to the limited available residential buildings, the largely industrial and manufacturing zoning, and many sites in transition (see Miller 2015).

The new residents of Gowanus have higher educational attainment, are whiter and wealthier than residents who have been in Gowanus for longer. The percentage of people with a bachelor's degree or higher in Gowanus has grown by over 100% since 2000. Compared to the surrounding census tracts, this is a dramatic increase. As in many of the surrounding census tracts, Gowanus became whiter since 2000 (13.4% more people identified as white). There are also fewer people in the area who were born in another country. The loss of 41.8% of the Hispanic population and 27.1% of the black population is significantly above average for the surrounding census tracts. The median income of the Gowanus area increased by 131% from 2000, which is only slightly above median income change for the rest of Brooklyn.

TABLE 7.1 Neighborhood Change Overview in Census Tract 119 (NE side of Gowanus Canal)

Tract 119 Change	ACS estimate for 2006–2010	ACS estimate for 2008–2012	% change from 2006–2012
Total population	1,635.00	1,789.00	9%
Income	$55,156.00	$72,109.00	30.70%
Median home value	$382,600.00	$658,000.00	71.10%
Median rent paid	$1,158.00	$1,458.00	25.90%
Housing units	677	774	14.30%

Source: American Community Survey.
Note: ACS data for 2014 was not compatible with the 5-year estimates, and was therefore not used.

Rent prices in the area have nearly doubled since 2000, causing some to re-evaluate their lives there. A middle-aged female resident said, "For what we're paying for our tiny apartment here, we could have an entire house. He's seriously thinking about moving" (Participant 2). The residents of Gowanus pay substantially more in rent if they moved in after 2005 than other residents of the neighborhood who moved in before them (see Figure 7.2).

The people whom I spoke to when I walked door-to-door differed from these census averages in a few ways. Most owned their homes in Gowanus, and many had lived in the area for a long time (average, 17.3 years). Significantly more respondents owned their homes than rented, which is the inverse pattern from the neighborhood characteristics that the American Community Survey and Census data show. In Gowanus, about 64% of the interview respondents owned their homes, while only 36% rented.

Several respondents told me that they knew of people who had left the neighborhood. In some cases, they felt they were "the only ones left" in the neighborhood. Peter Marcuse (1985) argued that "displacement pressure" is one of the ways a resident may experience displacement, even though they are not yet displaced. Many respondents elucidated this type of pressure in their comments.

Several residents worried about property tax increases, others moving out, the neighborhood becoming more expensive, new housing and retail development pushing them out, and real estate agents contacting them (and in some cases harassing them) to sell their property. When I asked the interviewees if they felt pressure to leave the area, or had known anyone who left already, I received mixed responses. Out of the people who I interviewed, only 14% of them immediately said they felt pressure to leave, although several more (64%) mentioned people they knew who had already left the area.

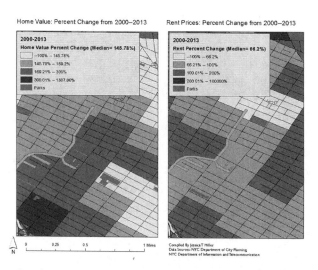

FIGURE 7.2 Median home value and rent price changes from 2000–2013 (compared to Brooklyn medians)

Based on my interviews, three groups of people were most likely to feel pressure to leave: people who rent, seniors who own their homes, and owners who feel the neighborhood is changing for the worse. An older female resident said:

> The lower income people would not be able to afford to stay here, because once condos, co-ops, Whole Foods comes in here, they can't afford to live and shop in the same neighborhood and they can't afford to pay the extra money in rent, housing, or basic necessities. Those people will move and become displaced. So I don't see how this type of development will benefit the neighborhood, because you're not investing in the people.
>
> *(Participant 1)*

Although both younger renters and older landowners have pushed for the cleanup, this participant points to the ways in which new development and the needs or desires of the new residents in the area are not the same as those long-time residents who have often invested time into pushing for the canal to be cleaned up (see Checker 2011 and 2015).

With rents increasing in the area, it is understandable that renters may feel less able to deal with this change. A woman landowner said, "Renters tend to wish they could afford to be owners in this neighborhood. But they may leave because as they have more kids, and since they haven't been able to buy a place, they may be pressured out" (Participant 2). One middle-aged woman resident explains, "In the '70s, people were leaving because of crime and danger and they were fleeing to the suburbs and it seems like most of the people who have left in my time here have left more reluctantly" (Participant 2). Stability may be difficult to obtain when rents are always increasing.

Some of the ways people are resisting this change lies in the power of the few (older) landlords who reside in the buildings they own. The few who I spoke to suggested that they are maintaining power over the space by not increasing rents in order to keep tenants and "stability" in the area. One landlord said that in all three floors of rental units, he had only increased the rent once in the last 10 years. I also spoke to one of his tenants, who confirmed this. However, when questioned further, one landlord said that he would keep rents stable for as long as possible, until he can no longer afford to maintain this practice as a result of property tax increases.

Seniors were also found to be more susceptible to displacement pressure. Participants gave several reasons for this, including shrinking parking opportunities, and unaffordability due to fixed incomes. An older landowner said, "The people leaving are those who have been priced out, mostly older people on fixed incomes" (Participant 7). Being invested in the changes to come seems to be important in keeping people in their homes: "I think we all feel that (pressure to leave), but I guess the people I know who are real die-hards, who care enough about where we live not to cave in, give up and to fight for where we live" (Participant 1).

People who dislike the changes taking place, or can envision themselves some-where else with more space, may also be more likely to feel pressure to leave: "I think when change happens, people just want to cash in and that's why they leave. I think as people see things are progressing along Gowanus, they will sell" (Parti-cipant 9). People in this group also own property; however, affordability may be more subtly impacting them through property tax increases. But due to their status as landowners, they have the flexibility to sell if they choose or feel pressure to move away from the area.

Several people suggested that not cleaning up the canal is a way to preserve the neighborhood as it is. These people tended to be residents who moved in before some of the current changes in the neighborhood were taking place. Some com-ments suggested that the area would lose authenticity through redevelopment and further gentrification (see Ahlfeldt 2011). An older male resident and developer said, "I would much rather put the resources into building factories and sewage treatment plants around the canal, not adding to its contamination. So don't fish, swim or boat in there, but keep it a working waterway and don't waste half a billion dollars to clean it up only to bring housing. I don't think it's productive effort" (Participant 6). This suggests that cleaning the area is a questionable goal to some residents.

Green economic development

Several interviewees were interested in maintaining and increasing the burgeon-ing non-polluting and creative industries along the canal. When addressing why businesses locate in Gowanus, one older woman activist asserted that, "they've gotten the boot from DUMBO, Williamsburg, Greenpoint, or wher-ever they were. Those neighborhoods probably are changing faster than Gowanus, in terms of the growth rate or the zoning and land use rules. So they've come here and found a new home and they're happy to be here, and it's exciting" (Participant 1).

Several people felt disillusioned with the redevelopment projects that have been approved in the area, because, as a younger male renter said, "Displacing everybody here by putting in a Whole Foods over there is not going to help the local economy in the long-term. It's not going to help people who live here unless they want to flip their shit [houses] and get out. Maybe that's the history of NYC in a way, but it's not a happy story" (Participant 10). Another middle-aged female resident feared that the community doesn't support the canal serving industrial purposes: "I don't have a sense that anyone on the community board is really excited about maintaining the area for manufacturing" (Participant 5). She added: "I have friends who have shops and studios down there, and they are feeling very much under siege" (Participant 5). Several others mentioned that they are worried that with increased real estate interest and rezoning potential, the area is susceptible to losing its long-term industrial character. One middle-aged male resident said:

There were a lot more larger businesses in Gowanus 20 years ago than there are today, because many of those companies have been displaced because of real estate speculation along the canal. Those were either manufacturing or warehousing. So where Whole Foods is now, there were four businesses before.

(Participant 4)

Non-polluting manufacturing in Gowanus is on the rise, and several reuse and recycling organizations have located facilities in Gowanus, using old warehouses as storage space for transportation and to store items to be reused or recycled. Build it Green, a building material reuse organization, and The Lower East Side Ecology Center E-Waste Warehouse have moved in since 2009 (Build it Green 2016; Lower East Side Ecology Center 2016).

Climate change and flooding

Superstorm Sandy brought the issue of climate change to the forefront of planning in New York. During Superstorm Sandy, many Gowanus residents were fearful of contaminated materials left by floodwaters in their basements, garages, and first floor apartments (Harris 2012). During this time, the Environmental Protection Agency conducted limited floodwater testing in two homes along the canal. They found that the water was highly contaminated with bacteria. Other pollutants were found to be "below levels of concern" (USEPA 2012). However, the threat of flooding did not disappear with the receding floodwater.

In January of 2013, only a few months after Superstorm Sandy, the State of New York announced a "retreat from the shore" plan (New York State Office of the Governor 2013) for buying and demolishing coastline property damaged during Sandy to prevent redevelopment from occurring along areas likely to flood again in the future. As of now, this program will only address homes along the Atlantic coastline, the areas hit worst during Sandy. However, many areas near the harbor and along the waterfront, including Gowanus, sustained significant flood damage and will also experience increased flooding in the future.

The Federal Emergency Management Agency's (FEMA) updated flood zone maps include twice as many building structures as the last update, which was completed in 1986 (Buckley 2013). However, these maps do not reflect anticipated sea-level rise. They also reflect a much smaller area than the total area of land impacted by Sandy, indicating they may be conservative estimates of future flooding risks (Columbia Climate Law Center 2013).

City plans have in the past been slow to adjust to increased flooding, in favor of traditional economic development over climate change responsive development. However, updated city zoning regulations may be able to shape the future of Gowanus in a way that might not have been considered pre-Sandy. In response to the storm, New York City released a 2013 plan, *A Stronger, More Resilient New York*, which outlines planning and coordination strategies for increasing resilience to future storms (City of New York 2013).

One older male landowner told me that the planning visions for the neighborhood post-Sandy reflect that planners are starting to have "A realization that you have to be more in balance with nature" (Participant 6). Yet, if Gowanus stands as a reflection of citywide economic development priorities, the large-scale (mostly market rate housing with retail on the ground floor) complexes will be permitted to build in flood zones, adding additional runoff into an already difficult to manage waterway. One participant said that, "All of the sudden, people have to have access to the water ... until they're under water" (Participant 6).

One older woman I spoke to when walking door-to-door told me that her home had been flooded during Sandy, and she was finishing up a remodel in April of 2013 after the damage. She said that she "can't afford to remodel again if it floods again" (Participant 12). She also said that after the storm, she could no longer afford to buy flood insurance due to the increased price of premiums, indicating that she would have to leave the area if another storm destroys her home. This story points to the limited ability for lower-income people to develop resilience to climate change impacts, and therefore, to resist displacement as a result of flooding. Developers of new commercial and residential space will be able to integrate plans for new buildings to withstand damage from future storms by building higher or integrating parking onto the first floor of a building or in other most likely to flood areas, but residents of smaller buildings may not be able to do so.

Discussion

The Superfund designation and Superstorm Sandy may have slowed some of the redevelopment plans, but the area continues to change rapidly. The social and cultural shifts taking place in Gowanus indicate that there is a wave of difference between what has been there (manufacturing, vacant lots, few commercial areas, little housing supply, crime), what is currently taking place (spot rezoning for luxury housing with green space surrounding buildings, offices, street infra-structure improvements, restaurants, and venues), and the future cleanup of the canal, which is likely to bring more of these changes to the area. Recently, "anticipated development" led to a vacant lot selling for $338 per square foot of buildable area (Albrecht 2016). While gentrification was underway long before the area is likely to be clean, it coincided with future plans to remediate the area. While there still may be room to shape the outcomes of these shifts, the cleaning and greening of the area is shaped mostly by large development projects and government agencies. One respondent summed up the relationship between cleanup and development in this way:

> I see gentrification driving the desire to clean it up. Not to say there wasn't an effort before. But property values start to increase and it creates pressure closer and closer to the canal and people are like, this property would be worth a lot if only the canal didn't smell so bad. When these houses weren't worth

anything, no one would have thought to clean up the canal because what did it matter, but now, there's this pressure.

(Participant 2)

The potential for residents and activists to impact development plans is limited by the ability for large landholders to enter into negotiations with developers that do not consider community needs.

As the area gentrifies, residents in the area are feeling the changes in positive and negative ways. Even though the area has become more expensive to live in, I found only a few people who said that they feel pressure to leave. Many of the people I spoke with told me that they approve of some of the changes, because the area feels safer than it used to, citing more foot traffic and street activity or fewer prostitutes and drug dealers as proof of this change.

Many more residents discussed the pressure they feel to leave in other ways, such as their unhappiness about the rapidly decreasing affordability of the area or other changes in the neighborhood, such as access to transit or parking. But the older residents and residents who have lived there for several years want to stay put for as long as they can, and some resist change by maintaining stable rents in their rental units. They would like to maintain the lives they have had in Gowanus for years. Stability, or the notion of it, comes in several forms, depending on the needs and desires of particular groups.

This paper speaks to the need to conduct macro-scale research on the social impacts people feel when gentrification occurs (Curran 2007; Newman and Wyly 2006; Slater 2006). It also suggests that the just green enough (Curran and Hamilton 2012) potential is limited by the impacts of the city-supported development and the demographic shifts taking place along the canal. The added complication of greening and cleaning the area is that it obscures that this area is being re-created in the interests of wealthier, whiter, and more educated people, leading some long-time residents to reject the desire to make the area free of contamination, or what I refer to as seeking "polluted protection" (Miller 2015). In order to change the potential outcomes in places like Gowanus, solutions such as land trusts or cooperative housing arrangements could be helpful. However, when land is as expensive as it is in New York City, these arrangements may have limited room to grow. Housing policy should protect low-income residents from displacement, and local policymakers need to consider updates to rent stabilization and the extremely limited rent control that exists in New York City. The promise of a cleaner environment has broken some barriers to redevelopment in the area, while placing pressure on the very residents who have pushed for years to get the canal cleaned up. This shuffling of residents from one dirty place to another creates concerns that both environmental justice and green gentrification researchers will grapple with for years to come.

References

Ahlfeldt, G. M. 2011. Blessing or curse? Appreciation Amenities and Resistance to Urban Renewal. *Regional Science and Urban Economics* 41(1): 32–45.

Albrecht, L. 2016. "Anticipated Development" Drives Record Sale of Gowanus Empty Lot. *DNA Info*. https://www.dnainfo.com/new-york/20160328/gowanus/anticipated-deve lopment-drives-record-sale-of-gowanus-empty-lot

Anguelovski, I. 2016. From Toxic Sites to Parks as (Green) LULUs? New Challenges of Inequity, Privilege, Gentrification, and Exclusion for Urban Environmental Justice. *Journal of Planning Literature* 31(1): 23–36.

Buckley, C. 2013. Twice as Many Structures in FEMA's Redrawn Floodzone. *The New York Times*. Jan. 28. http://www.nytimes.com/2013/01/29/nyregion/homes-in-flood-zone-doubles-in-new-fema-map.html

Build It Green. 2016. About. http://www.bigreuse.org/about/

Campbell, L. K. and Gabriel, N. 2016. Power in Urban Social-Ecological Systems: Processes and Practices of Governance and Marginalization. *Urban Forestry & Urban Greening* 19(1): 253–254.

City of New York. 2013. *PlaNYC: A Stronger, More Resilient New York*. http://www.nyc. gov/html/sirr/html/report/report.shtml

Checker, M. 2015. Green Is the New Brown: Old School Toxics and Environmental Gentrification on a New York City Waterfront. In Isenhour, C., McDonogh, G.W., and Checker, M., eds., *Sustainability in the Global City: Myth and Practice*. New York, NY: Cambridge University Press.

Checker, M. 2011. Wiped Out by the Greenwave: Environmental Gentrification and the Paradoxical Politics of Urban Sustainability. *City & Society* 23(2): 210–229.

Columbia Climate Law Center. 2013. New FEMA Maps for New York Do Not Consider Sea Level Rise. http://blogs.law.columbia.edu/climatechange/2013/02/14/new-fema-flood-maps-fornew-york-do-not-consider-sea-level-rise/

Curran, W. 2007. "From the Frying Pan to the Oven": Gentrification and the Experience of Industrial Displacement in Williamsburg, Brooklyn. *Urban Studies* 44(8): 1427–1440.

Curran, W. and Hamilton, T. 2012. Just Green Enough: Contesting Environmental Gentrification in Greenpoint, Brooklyn. *Local Environment* 17(9): 1027–1042.

Eckerd, A. 2011. Cleaning Up Without Clearing Out? A Spatial Assessment of Environmental Gentrification. *Urban Affairs Review* 47(1): 31–59.

Eckerd, A. and Keeler, A. 2012. Going Green Together? Brownfield Remediation and Environmental Justice. *Policy Sciences* 45(4): 293–314.

Gould, K. and Lewis, T. 2011. The Environmental Injustice of Green Gentrification: The Case of Brooklyn's Prospect Park. In DeSena, J. and Shortell, T., eds., *Gentrification, Immigration, and Ethnic Politics in a Global City*. Lanham, MD: Lexington Books.

Gould, K. A. and Lewis, T. L. 2017. *Green Gentrification: Urban Sustainability and the Struggle for Environmental Justice*. New York and London: Routledge.

Hackworth, J. and Smith, N. 2001. The Changing State of Gentrification. *Tijdschfiftvoor Economische en Sociale Geografie* 92: 464–477.

Hamilton, T. and Curran, W. 2013. From "Five Angry Women" to "Kick-ass Community": Gentrification and Environmental Activism in Brooklyn and Beyond. *Urban Studies* 50(8): 1557–1574.

Harris, E. 2012. In Brooklyn, Worrying About Not Only Flooding, but What's in the Water. *The New York Times*, November 5.

Kimmelman, M. 2016. In Gowanus, a People's Housing Plan to Challenge the Mayor's. *The New York Times*, August 1. http://www.nytimes.com/2016/08/02/arts/design/in-gowanus-a-peoples-housing-plan-to-challenge-the-mayors.html?_r=0

Lee, S. and Mohai, P. 2013. The Socioeconomic Dimensions of Brownfield Cleanup in the Detroit Region. *Population and Environment* 34(3): 420–429.

Logan, J. and Molotch, H. 1987. *Urban Fortunes: The Political Economy of Place*. Berkeley: University of California Press.

Lower East Side Ecology Center. http://www.lesecologycenter.org/programs/ewaste/

Marcuse, P. 1985. Gentrification, Abandonment and Displacement: Connections, Causes and Policy Responses. *Journal of Urban and Contemporary Law* 28: 195–240.

Miller, J. T. 2015. *Super Fun Superfund: Polluted Protection Along the Gowanus Canal*. City University of New York. Unpublished PhD Dissertation.

Miller, J. T. 2016. Is Urban Greening for Everyone? Social Inclusion and Exclusion along the Gowanus Canal. *Urban Forestry & Urban Greening* 19. doi: 10.1016/j.ufug.2016.03.004

Newman, K. and Wyly, E. (2006). The Right to Stay Put, Revisited: Gentrification and Resistance to Displacement in New York City. *Urban Studies* 43(1): 23–57.

New York State Office of the Governor. 2013. Governor Cuomo Seeks Federal Approval of NY State Plans for Housing and Business Storm Recovery Programs. https://www.governor.ny.gov/news/governor-cuomo-seeks-federal-approval-ny-state-plans-housing-and-business-storm-recovery

Pearsall, H. 2013. Superfund Me: A Study of Resistance to Gentrification in New York City. *Urban Studies* 50(11): 2293–2310.

Pearsall, H. and Pierce, J. 2010. Urban Sustainability and Environmental Justice: Evaluating the Linkages in Public Planning/Policy Discourse. *Local Environment* 15(6): 569–580.

Slater, T. 2006. The eviction of critical perspectives from gentrification research. *International Journal of Urban and Regional Research* 30(4): 737–757.

New York Department of City Planning. 2011. *Vision 2020: New York City Comprehensive Waterfront Plan*. http://www.nyc.gov/html/dcp/html/cwp/cwp_2.shtml

New York City Department of Transportation (NYCDOT). 2013. *Current Projects*. http://www.nyc.gov/html/dot/html/about/current-projects.shtml

United States Environmental Protection Agency Archive. 2012. *Hurricane Sandy Response Efforts*. https://archive.epa.gov/region02/sandy/web/html/response_12-4-12.html

Wolch, J. R., Byrne, J., and Newell, J. P. 2014. Urban Green Space, Public Health, and Environmental Justice: The Challenge of Making Cities "Just Green Enough." *Landscape and Urban Planning* 125: 234–244.

PART III

State-led environmental gentrification

8

ENVIRONMENTAL GENTRIFICATION IN METROPOLITAN SEOUL: THE CASE OF GREENBELT DEREGULATION AND DEVELOPMENT AT MISA RIVERSIDE CITY

Jay E. Bowen

Introduction

In 2008, South Korean President Lee Myung-bak initiated his Bogeumjari (Nest) Housing Area (*Pogŭmjarijut'aekchigu*) plan to increase public and affordable housing in the Seoul Capital Area (SCA). On September 28th, 2009, the Ministry of Land, Transport and Maritime Affairs (now the Ministry of Land, Infrastructure and Transport) announced the designation of a Bogeumjari Housing Area (BHA) at a 5.47 km^2 site in Hanam City, adjacent to Seoul's Gangdong District, and in the city's vast peripheral greenbelt, or Development Restriction Zone (*Kaebaljehan'guyŏk*) (MLTMA 2009, Kim 2014), simultaneously announcing the deregulation of greenbelt land use restrictions. In the face of widespread discontent among local landowners, residents, and workers, the government-run Korea Land and Housing Corporation (LH) began seizing the mostly agricultural properties through eminent domain, preparing the Hanam Misa Bogeumjari Housing Area for redevelopment. Nearly four years later, shortly after her inauguration, President Park Geun-hye declared Lee's Bogeumjari Housing implementation plans invalid, partly due to fears of price suppression of real estate in Seoul (Ju 2013). On May 5th, 2013, the Board of Audit and Inspection of Korea released an audit of LH, warning of the economic infeasibility of its Bogeumjari Housing Program (BAIK 2013). In an effort to counter LH's supposed oversupply of low-income housing, Hanam Misa Bogeumjari Housing Area was reborn as Misa Riverside City (*Misagangbyŏndoshi*). The new plans tout a "sustainable" mix of public and luxury housing, inlaid and encircled with a harmonious diversity of urban and ecological amenities.

This study examines Misa Riverside City within the context of the emerging literature on environmental gentrification and multi-scalar approaches to understanding neoliberalism in East Asian developmental states. The rollout of the project through stages of planning, revision, and activation amidst greenbelt deregulation, dispossession by eminent domain, and citizen protest presents a case of gentrification through direct state intervention. Through the upgrade and promotion of devalued environmental characteristics as ecological amenities, and an explicit encouragement of sustainability through creative industries, the state engaged more precisely in a localized example of environmental gentrification that unmade the variety of "just green enough" adaptations users of the green belt had constructed.

As a number of recent studies demonstrate, the production of urban sustainability is a contested process wherein environmental improvements often increase real estate prices and lead to the dislocation of lower-income residents (Dooling 2009; Quastel 2009; Curran and Hamilton 2012; Pearsall 2012; Wolch et al. 2014). The case of Misa Riverside City presents a tangible contestation of sustainable development. Conflicting notions of deserving and undeserving poor shaped the planning process. Ideas about green urbanism and environmental protection reworked development restriction spaces into speculative nodes. Internal disagreement among government agencies over how to manage competing objectives of poverty management and real estate market correction met resident and local business opposition. Finally, criminal corruption charges against a local politician and organizer undermined the potential of civil opposition to the development. The outcome of the project rested on several rounds of readjustment to changing technocratic directives and citizen protest, moving from a public housing initiative on deregulated greenbelt, which disadvantaged area residents, farmers, business people, and landowners, to a predominantly luxury development advertising green amenities.

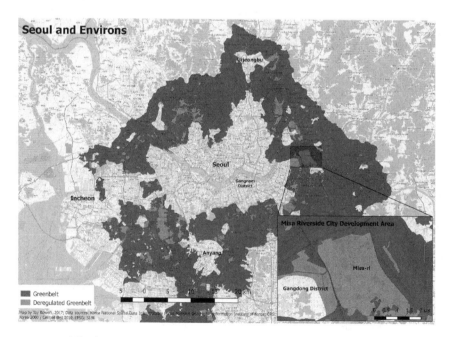

FIGURE 8.1 Misa location

Gentrification locally situated

Gentrification is not a commonly used term among the Korean public, only recently gaining limited familiarity. In-situ neighborhood upgrading and real estate price increases common in US cities are not yet widespread in Korea (Ha 2015; Shin and Kim 2016) though it is now observable in inner-city neighborhoods like Samcheong-dong, Ikseon-dong, and Seongsu-dong. Rather, neighborhood upgrade, real estate speculation, and price inflation are distinctly associated with large-scale demolition and infill developments, which have successively rearranged and rebuilt the city since the Korean War. As opposed to gentrification, the terms redevelopment (*chaegaebal*) and reconstruction (*chaegŏnch'uk*) are more widely known as a ceaseless aspect of urbanization. Despite countless neighborhood-scale protest movements over dispossession, displacement, and unfair compensation, public discourse generally welcomes and praises these forms of urban renewal as a point of national pride in rapid modernization. Beyond local-scale contestations, criticism of Seoul's massive urban renewal projects has long been treated with some bewilderment or hostility. Additionally, national-scale discourse has reframed anti-redevelopment protests as antagonistic to national stability and progress, and there is an evident scarcity of literature critiquing gentrification in Korea (Shin and Kim 2016). In order to capture issues of social injustice through real estate speculation and improvement in Seoul, a broader notion of gentrification is needed, encompassing large-scale bureaucratic intervention and planning, joint corporate and landowner investment in demolition, redevelopment, and sale, and its impacts on the dispossession of poorer residents through both coercion and rising prices.

Examples from Korea emphasize the central, though not exclusive, role of the state in activating gentrification, demonstrating that "gentrification researchers need to pay much closer attention to government policies on gentrification as neoliberal models of governance" (Lees 2012). The case of Misa Riverside City exemplifies a growing global phenomenon of environmental gentrification. Here, the displacement of the poor occurs through a revanchist reworking and provision of green amenities and multiuse redevelopment (Smith 1996; Heynen and Perkins 2005). This supports the social reproduction of privileged classes of mixed-income citizens at the expense of certain long-term residents and workers, whom new public-private urban planning regimes marginalize as redundant in a sustainable city.

In addition to the critique of environmental gentrification, an assessment of Misa Riverside City should acknowledge the critical benefits of a scalar re-theorization of the developmental state. Developmental state theorists prioritized the agency of the admittedly powerful post-war authoritarian state in promoting economic growth, overlooking important aspects of internal uneven development, local-scale political agency, and supranational influences. The developmental state thesis (DST) was critically important to challenging neoclassical economic presumptions that minimal state intervention drives economic development. However, it has influenced an overly simplistic dichotomy between the pre-democratic economic interventionism of the developmental state and the post-democratic activation of civil society and neoliberalism.

More recent academic observations have highlighted the continuities of political and economic activities between the phases of authoritarianism and democratization in Korea. These studies demonstrate how identifiably neoliberal practices flourish within and through the developmental state (Park 2005; Choi 2012; Park and Lepawsky 2012). Moreover, it is clear that local and regional citizens and political actors competed intensely for government assistance, infrastructural improvements, free trade zones, and foreign investment throughout the authoritarian developmental state era (Moore 1984; Park and Choi 2014; Hwang 2016). Likewise, in processes of gentrification through the real estate sector, there is obvious continuity between the "consignment redevelopment" and Joint Redevelopment Program (JRP) of the past and the more recent New Town Program (NTP) introduced during Lee Myung-bak's term as Seoul mayor (Shin and Kim 2016).

In 1966, more than one-third of all housing in Seoul consisted of illegal structures (Seoul Metropolitan Government 1973, cited by Shin and Kim 2016). Beginning in 1972, the government began strict enforcement against the construction of new illegal housing and, in 1973, enacted legislation to prohibit the upgrading of illegal dwellings. For this reason, in-situ gentrification was never a major component of Seoul's history of real estate speculation. Simultaneously, the city government introduced a pilot project of "consignment redevelopment," whereby owner-occupiers in substandard neighborhoods were required to form committees to delegate the clearance of their homes to a construction company, which would then build apartment blocks. This program incurred heavy burdens on owner-occupiers through costs of reconstruction and interim relocation and was terminated. However, the city's JRP of 1983 proved a more enduring blueprint for urban renewal and gentrification in Seoul.

Shin and Kim (2016) note that the state used the JRP to channel revenue from over-accumulation in the industrial sector into the real estate market, and foster the growth of the rising middle class in the process. The JRP rested not only upon the power of the authoritarian developmental state, but also on the collaboration between real estate conglomerates and property owners. In many cases, the construction firms were, and remain, divisions of the same corporations involved in heavy industries: Samsung, Daewoo, Hyundai, LG. In Korea, it is feasible to live in an apartment block constructed by the same corporation that produced your household appliances, television, phone, computer, and personal automobile. In JRP districts, the owner-occupiers organized redevelopment associations. The redevelopment associations and construction firms financed these projects by selling additional units ahead of construction to investors at the market rate. Government incentives helped resident-owners purchase new units at the cost of construction. Poorer property owners were compelled to sell their right to a new unit at a price determined between the price of their current unit and the subsidized price of the new unit. Because this scheme resulted in the dislocation of poorer resident-owners and the influx of absentee landlord speculators and renters, later JRP redevelopment associations were largely comprised of people who did not live in the neighborhoods being redeveloped.

In 2002, Mayor Lee Myung-bak initiated the NTP to target the redevelopment of Seoul's remaining redbrick detached housing (*chut'aek*) into modern high-rises. Lee's NTP followed the same financial structure as the JRP, with large-scale demolition and redevelopment, impacting 850,000 city residents (Shin and Kim 2016). Initially, property owners and residents welcomed NTP projects because of a faith in the inevitability of trickle-down revenue. However, an increasing number of owner-occupiers were unable to afford the new units, leading to more requests for compensation, in turn leading to inflated apartment prices and rents. Widespread coercion of remaining residents to leave without compensation also led to growing dissatisfaction. Redevelopment slowed, and pervasive discontent led Seoul's current mayor, Park Won-soon, to terminate the NTP in 2012 (Berg 2012). This is important to the development of Misa Riverside City, because the scale of the NTP would eventually create enormous overall instability in Seoul's real estate market and lead to extensive resident dislocation, justifying Lee's later BHA as president.

Spatiotemporal context

At Misa Riverside City, government housing initiatives, private development interests, and real estate market speculation converged with state-directed land use deregulation and eminent domain to propel the environmental gentrification of peri-urban farmland. Underpinning the development was the national government's decision to green light the deregulation of 5.47 km^2 of greenbelt, which maintained agricultural land uses in the region since the third phase of Seoul's greenbelt designation in 1972. The concomitant stress placed upon local residents, workers, and landowners, tossed from state regulated development prohibition to public-private redevelopment by eminent domain, highlights the confluence of the developmental state and neoliberal gentrification in Seoul.

Mapped across the SCA, the greenbelt suggests a positive swath of green amenity, cloaking the internal diversity of land uses. The greenbelt hosts not only mountain parks, bike paths, and temples, but also farms, greenhouses, fish markets, small workshops, government facilities, military checkpoints, bunkers and bases, Gimpo International Airport, and myriad illegal land uses. Furthermore, the greenbelt tends to conceal the feelings of in-situ dispossession felt by many of its landowners, who have been deprived of an ability to cash in on Seoul's rapid development. Likewise, the free market rhetoric surrounding greenbelt deregulation and the redevelopment of "obsolete" farmland disguises the ongoing inability of local denizens and laborers to take full advantage of market liberalization. The production of the greenbelt, as well as its piecemeal deregulation, hides many consequences.

President Park Chung-hee established Seoul's 1567 km^2 greenbelt, or Development Restriction Zone, in four successive expansions between 1971 and 1976 (Bae 1998). Park "greenwashed" social injustice by presenting the greenbelt as a public

FIGURE 8.2 Greenbelt farmland and residential high-rises in Gangdong district

environmental benefit. However, Seoul's greenbelt was a uniquely militarized green space – a desperate authoritarian effort to fortify the city against North Korean attack and political intrigue and prevent the proliferation of unlicensed informal settlements in the capital's periphery. While Smith (2002) claims that Asian metropolises have an edge in global gentrification, because of a sort of *tabula rasa* lacking the political economic girders of a Keynesian past, the unfolding of the Misa Riverside City development presents a reality much more akin to Schein's (1997) concept of palimpsest. The site is an intersection of multiple state and local discourses exhibiting a constant process of erasure, continuity, and rewriting of the landscape by the overlapping objectives of different actors across scales. Rather than simply a strong state producing spaces of capital accumulation in real estate upon a disentangled blank slate, the Misa Riverside City project has encountered a wide range of conflicting discourses over the production of space in one part of Seoul's greenbelt.

In its earliest materialization as a regulatory spatial regime, Seoul's greenbelt was a peri-urban parallel to spaces of "fortress conservation" and "conservation territories" (Neumann 2004; Zimmerer 2000; Mutersbaugh 2006). The designation of the greenbelt established a strict land use scheme, preventing Seoul's evicted urban poor from accessing the land for new informal settlements and freezing existing land uses for the remaining inhabitants. Greenbelt residents were frozen in time on agrarian islands between the inner city and dense, industrial, state-planned satellite cities.

The greenbelt's development regulations were strict and included prohibitions on new buildings, changes in land use, and changes in the use of already built structures. Increasingly, greenbelt restrictions faced popular opposition from residents and landowners, as a massive rent gap grew between the greenbelt and proximate urban areas on either side. Consequentially, the national government began to loosen land use and building restrictions during the 1990s, with sweeping greenbelt reforms announced in July 1999 (Bae, Jun, and Richardson 2011). In 2008, the national government under President Lee passed a law allowing the deregulation of greenbelt land with "low preservation value" for public housing construction (MLTMA 2010). In turn, much of the land chosen for Lee's public BHA, of which Misa Riverside City was planned as a pilot project, consisted of commercial greenbelt farmland.

This easing of restrictions and release of greenbelt land arose in tandem with democratization and ongoing efforts to liberalize the economy. However, it would be an overly simplistic reading of Korean neoliberalism to claim that the relaxation of restrictions and deregulation of greenbelt land represents a democratization of land use and ownership, or a withering of state control. The degree to which a policy and its implementation appear to be a continuation of developmental state control, or a tendency towards neoliberalism, often depends on the individual policy and the scale at which it is observed.

Misa Riverside City: Environmental gentrification through developmental neoliberalism

In Seoul's greenbelt at Misa-ri, farmers once lauded as necessary for urban food security and for feeding Korea's industrialization were also always at risk of being declared "indolent," or a "slumbering" backwards peasantry (Park 1979; Moore 1984). Within the shifting plans and objectives for public housing within the Misa Riverside City project, the intended beneficiaries of the state-supported project also changed alongside mercurial political narratives. President Park replaced Lee's BHA with her own Haengbok (Happiness) Housing Areas (HHA), focusing on producing urban sustainability through the creative class. In this movement, it is imperative to investigate how, as Soja (1989) says, "space can be made to hide consequences."

At Misa, environmental gentrification occurred not simply as a process by which the provision of green space induced rising property values and an influx of wealthier residents, but also in the sense that it repurposed the "obsolete" environmental amenity of greenbelt farmland into a trendy mixed-use development replete with a river walk. Additionally, the developmental plans themselves went through a revision, suggesting a movement from a sort of localized "just green enough" strategy tilted towards improving housing affordability, to an outcome more centrally focused on luxury. Simultaneously, the reimbursement demands of dispossessed local citizens preceding construction placed further financial pressure upon the state and corporate developers, ultimately helping to justify a rebalancing of planned housing stock towards higher-income consumers and investors.

The origins of the mega development at Misa rest upon national legislation allowing for the deregulation of greenbelt land, which the Minister of Land,

Infrastructure and Transport designates as "damaged" or having "low conservation value" (Choi et al. 2010). Therefore, decisions about where to develop revolve around a social discourse about what sorts of green spaces, land uses, and livelihoods are not green enough to count as generative of urban sustainability. Also, developmental neglect of areas under greenbelt regulation for nearly four decades became a self-fulfilling justification for a kind of high-rise redevelopment that would raise eyebrows on green space more integrated with Seoul's urban amenities. In the greenbelt, the criteria for low conservation value are based not just on an environmental impact assessment, but also on the land's urban infrastructure connection potential. Thus, the ministry does not necessarily choose the most environmentally degraded greenbelt land for redevelopment, but more likely selects land combining great speculative potential with socially devalued land uses.

Before redevelopment began at Misa, the composition of the land was largely devoted to farming, warehouses, a seafood distribution center, and an agricultural school. These land uses comprise the notion of environmental damage and lack of conservation value upon which the Lee Administration justified the deregulation and construction of its BHA projects in Seoul's greenbelt. Lee's BHA program was meant, in part, to address the lack of affordable housing and housing market instability incurred by his NTP as Seoul Mayor. Officially, the project would provide subsidized housing to low-income families to minimize the effects of income inequality and facilitate home ownership for the lower middle class.

On September 28th, 2009, the Ministry of Land, Transport and Maritime Affairs deregulated the 5.47 km^2 greenbelt site at Misa, and LH began acquiring land and

FIGURE 8.3 Commercial farming in the greenbelt

reimbursing landowners for the planned BHA. The financial feasibility of the project rested upon LH's faith that it could obtain greenbelt land at relatively low prices, compared to comparable unrestricted land. This would prove to be a false expectation as residents resisted their dislocation due to a widely shared sentiment that LH was defrauding them of anticipated profits and rising property values. Area property owners organized the Hanam Misa Area Citizens' Countermeasures Committee under Park Deok-jin, arguing that the land reimbursements were below the market price (Lee and Hong 2011). Citizens began an information campaign, posting signs across the district to warn about insufficient compensation or promote the cancellation of the public housing project. Residents also began filing official complaints to the president and the Ministry of Land, Transport and Maritime Affairs. Still, area landowners were not necessarily *against* the BHA development as much as they were *for* what they perceived as fair recompense for their land. This local-scale campaign effectively delayed construction and pressured state-owned LH, already facing accruing debt and financial insecurity.

With project delays dogging the BHA rollout at Misa and the inauguration of President Park Geun-hye in early 2013, the new president sought to establish her own legacy by replacing former President Lee's public housing initiative with her own Haengbok Housing Area (HHA) program. Calling for a plan to correct the real estate market, Park declared on April 1st, 2013 that the Bogeumjari Housing implementation plans were no longer valid (Ju 2013). One month later, with pressure from the new presidency, the Board of Audit and Inspection of Korea released their audit of LH, declaring the BHA projects economically unsustainable (BAIK 2013). The report criticized the BHA project for being too big and suffering from a lack of buyers for low-middle-income units and further identified finance problems due to the diversion of funds to the Misa project and construction delays causing a shortage of new revenue. Moreover, LH planned to dramatically increase Bogeumjari Housing supply without considering their financial solvency, resulting in an inability to fully compensate landowners. Finally, the audit asserted that the income-based criteria were flawed and provided housing to undeserving residents who were actually "wealthy."

Four days later, in a move to revamp the Hanam Misa BHA into a revenue-generating government project, LH announced a shift in concept and renamed the project Misa Riverside City, emphasizing the desirability of its location near the Han River (Lee 2013a). The resultant changes in housing composition and urban planning reflected the new administration's push for further market liberalization to meet national planning and development objectives. After the name change, LH began promoting the project through a prism of speculative and aspirational assets, asserting that "city function," rather than affordable housing, would be the new focus (Lee 2013a). A representative of LH affirmed that Misa Riverside City would promote its locational advantage along the river, which it would amplify with an increase in zoning for self-sufficient facilities. In Korea, the zoning designation of self-sufficient facility (*chajoksisŏlyongji*) includes venture enterprise centers, software development facilities, hotels, public halls, conference centers, exhibition halls, education and research institutes, and urban agriculture facilities, and is a targeted measure to stimulate the creative industries. With LH's statements on the change in plans, there was an obvious pivot towards a direct promotion of gentrification through appeals to the creative class and economic growth-oriented sustainability.

On May 31st, 2013, President Park declared that 9.5 trillion KRW (about 8.7 billion USD in 2013) would be cut from the Bogeumjari Housing Project over five years in order to fund her Haengbok Housing Project, targeting young citizens and the creative class in place of the long-term poor and vulnerable groups better served by the previous public housing initiative (Ju 2013). Eighty percent of housing in Park's new HHAs was to be furnished to newlyweds, university students, and "career starters," while only 10% of the remaining units would go to "under-privileged and residentially vulnerable classes" (Kim and Lee 2014). Moreover, in a further dismissal of the region's urban poor, state-supported Haengbok Housing would comprise a smaller portion of the overall housing at Misa Riverside City. LH would sell much of the rest of the land to a small group of Korean conglomerates (*chaebŏl*) with construction and real estate divisions.

Declaring the HHA a "public housing policy for sustainable development," Kim and Lee (2014) state that, through the provision of HHAs, which integrate in-demand cultural spaces, parks, and green lands, "urban regeneration can be accelerated" by attracting an "economically active population." In the switch from a large public housing area for low-income residents to a mix of luxury private housing and public housing for the creative class, along with a provision of specific kinds of environmental amenities, a clear process of environmental gentrification was visible. This process plainly redefined the state's notion of the deserving poor as young, creative, and motivated people, who would promote business and draw in wealthier residents and investors. Moreover, the plans deepened the reframing of urban ecological amenity from spaces of professional agriculture to leisure spaces for the creative class.

In 2013, with the sale of land and housing, LH was able to raise 22.1 trillion KRW (roughly 20 billion USD), resulting in a 30% increase in revenue over 2012 (Woo 2014). In order to reduce their debt further, as well as to resolve their resident compensation issues at Misa, LH announced that they would initiate public-private partnerships to contract with private corporations to buy land and build public housing. Although LH was able to distribute acceptable compensation to most inhabitants by July of 2013, organized occupations continued to delay construction, making the planned initial move-ins of June 2014 impossible to achieve (Choi 2013; Lee 2013b). Simultaneously, as investigations later revealed, the politician leading the Hanam Misa Area Citizens' Countermeasures Committee (Park Deok-jin) was accepting bribes from construction and materials companies for contracts at Misa while he was protesting the development (Kim 2016). For these bribes and political corruption, officials would later sentence Park to five years in prison.

Considering the conflicts of interest between Park Deok-jin's personal and political objectives, the citizens' movement against Misa's redevelopment was impaired from the start. However, other organizations and entities continued their

FIGURE 8.4 Construction at Misa Riverside City from the Han River bike paths

own protests to refuse reimbursement and relocation. These included business owners in the Hanam Marine Products Distribution Center, the Gana-an Farmers' School, the Daehyung Ready-Mix Concrete Factory, and twenty small businesses. Initially trying to avoid forceful evictions, LH proceeded with complex negotiations involving all of these individual entities, which intensified anger among investors and residents desiring to move in (Choi 2013). With pressure mounting from this side, LH began charging rent to remaining occupiers, who held out in an attempt to extract maximum benefit before their imminent removal (Lee 2013b). In this way, some of the dispossessed occupants of once devalued greenbelt land successfully captured some of the added revenue from the gentrification process that sought to exclude them.

In the case of the Hanam Marine Products Distribution Center, business owners initiated a movement both to profit from their dispossession and to push for reintegration of their businesses in the Misa Riverside City development. By organizing the Hanam Marine Product Retailers' Cooperative, retailers weathered five years of challenges to their continued presence, delaying scheduled construction and move-ins. In the end, LH enforced violent removals amidst charges of broken promises regarding reimbursement and relocation. In the case of the Gana-an Farmers' School, LH reimbursed the school with 24 billion KRW (about 21.7 million USD) in 2011, but the school principal argued that this was too little for relocation and refused to leave. The principal claimed that initially they accepted this amount because LH had promised to help with relocation, which LH later denied (Jang 2013). Meanwhile, the Hanam Marine Product Retailers' Cooperative was caught in a legislative tango between LH and Hanam City for five years. "During negotiations with LH over the last five years for a smooth development process, LH offered us a temporary relocation site. Regardless of the large cost for temporary structures necessary for seafood retail, we were compelled to accept" (Bae 2015). However, Hanam City refused to grant permits to the retailers after they paid relocation and rebuilding fees. For planners, investors, and new residents, a malodorous fish market was not conducive to the profit and gentrification-oriented goals of the new development. Furthermore, as the businesses handled 35% of the domestic wholesale market in live seafood, allegations surfaced over water and soil contamination, damage to street trees, and reduced living conditions due to heavy traffic (Lee 2015). While the retailers successfully sued LH in 2014, LH responded by refusing their relocation to a previously designated site within the project area. In February of 2015, LH hired 600 enforcers and employed heavy machinery to demolish sixteen stores and forcibly remove the remaining occupants (Lee 2015).

Amidst the unresolved conflict between the live seafood wholesalers, LH, and Hanam City, nationwide newspapers began the promotion of Misa Riverside City's investment potential in advance of planned move-ins for late 2014 and early 2015. Touting its locational advantage and planned supply of luxury housing, *The Korea Economic Daily* pronounced, "The location combines the three most important factors driving demand for housing in the Seoul region: Gangnam (a popular upscale consumption and entertainment district) accessibility, Han River proximity, and parks" (Kim 2014). Newspapers also listed the names of envied apartment developers and brands (Posco The Sharp, Daewoo Prugio, GS Xii, etc.) that had bought housing blocks from LH, along with how many units of luxury housing were on the market. With this, national housing and development policy finalized an on-the-fly environmental gentrification process, which began with "upgrading" blue-collar and agricultural greenbelt land uses to housing for low-income residents priced out of Seoul, eventually leading to state collaboration with private interests for a luxury development. This turn rested upon an upgrading of the state's notion of a model public housing candidate from simply low-income to a temporarily low-income member of the creative class. By mixing public housing for the creative class with luxury housing, the state could use public revenue to support the individualized cultural activities that are believed to foster urban rejuvenation and liveliness for the benefit of higher-income urbanites.

Conclusion

The rollout of the Misa Riverside City development is a site-specific example of environmental gentrification within a multi-scalar process of developmental neoliberalism. It is a case where a sort of "just green enough" space succumbed to the rhetoric of obsolescence, labeling it "not green enough." The state deregulated

Misa's greenbelt for residential development, dislocating many area residents, farmers, and businesses for new, more generalizable, urban aspirations. The local-scale interests of these inhabitants coalesced in protest organizations, which were generally successful in terms of winning acceptable monetary compensation. Simultaneously, the pressure these organizations exerted made LH appear financially vulnerable, justifying a reorganization of the project goals to target luxury housing for urban elites and public housing for the creative class. The two reiterations of the project phased out both the interests of the area's initial inhabitants and the previously dislocated urban poor.

Additionally, Misa Riverside City is a unique case where a president restructured a national public housing initiative to facilitate gentrification through new notions of sustainable development resting on the creative class thesis. President Park's Haengbok Housing Project redefined sustainability as an economically oriented concept. The Ministry of Land, Infrastructure and Transport identified "damaged" land, regulating out supposedly unproductive greenbelt land uses, once thought to sustain urban industrialization (Ministry of Land, Infrastructure and Transport 2013). Then, LH integrated the Haengbok Housing Project and luxury developments within the Misa Riverside City project. Finally, the development process overhauled local green space to satisfy the recreational and cultural demands of new, idealized, residents.

In any instance of professed sustainable development, it is important to identify who and what must be sustained or become sustainable. Although environmentalist perspectives are commonly a component of efforts to establish economic sustainability, the prevailing focus on free market economic benefits usually results in the production of green spaces that do not consider the sustained social reproduction of the most vulnerable, much less a rational metabolism that recognizes the integration of society and cities in nature. The production and promotion of green spaces, consumption fund amenities, and cultural spaces specifically directed at urban "rejuvenation" and "regeneration" reinforces and intensifies uneven urban development. Moreover, the case of Misa Riverside City, with its integrated public housing, demonstrates that even the state can employ the provision of subsidized low-income housing to stimulate gentrification and all of its inherent social and environmental injustice.

Considering the vociferous protests of local residents and workers, the events at Misa iterate how even those appearing to oppose development become enrolled in their own dispossession. These apparent "anti-development" protests take little issue with the state politics and economic rationalities that allow outside speculation, as long as they get their perception of a fair cut. Insofar as they too buy into the notion of their land as an investment, such mega-scale gentrification projects continue across the SCA, expecting similar opposition movements as a type of high-stakes bartering. Without confronting and seeking to reform the economic structures that reproduce unevenness, these local movements extract momentary financial gains from the gentrification processes that ultimately marginalize their livelihoods.

References

Bae, B.I., 2015, June 25. The Gyeonggi Hanam marine product retailers' cooperative protest at LH Headquarters. Gyeongnam Domin Shinmun: Demand permit for Misa Riverside City self-sufficient facilities site. http://www.gndomin.com/news/articlePrint.html?idxno=87393 [In Korean]

Bae, C.H., 1998. Korea's greenbelts: Impacts and options for change. *Pacific Rim Law & Policy Journal* 7(3): 479–502.

Bae, C.H., Jun, M.J., and Richardson, H.W., 2011. Greenbelt policy. In C.H. Bae and H.W. Richardson (Eds.), *Regional and urban policy and planning on the Korean Peninsula* (pp. 75–90). Cheltenham, UK and Northampton, MA, USA: Edward Elgar.

Berg, N., 2012, February 6. Seoul ends failed "New Towns" project. *The Atlantic*. http://www.citylab.com/housing/2012/02/seoul-ends-failed-new-towns-project/1149/

BAIK (Board of Audit and Inspection of Korea), 2013, May 8. Review of basic housing stability measures. Inspection results. https://www.bai.go.kr/bai/cop/bbs/detailBoardArticle.do?mdex=bai20&bbsId=BBSMSTR_100000000009&nttId=1489 [In Korean]

Choi, I.H., Jin, M.Y., and Kim, J.Y., 2010, September. *Current issues and future development plans for the supply of Bogeumjari Housing*. Seoul: Korea Planning Association. http://www.auric.or.kr/user/rdoc/DocCmag.aspx?returnVal=CMAG&dn=172891#.WDaDkCN94Us [In Korean]

Choi, B.D., 2012. Developmental neoliberalism and the hybridity of the urban policy of South Korea. In B.G. Park, R.C. Hill, and A. Saito (Eds.), *Locating neoliberalism in East Asia: neoliberalizing spaces in developmental states* (pp. 86–113). West Sussex, UK: Blackwell.

Choi, S.Y., 2013, July 4. Misa Riverside City "residents see the fire of their own demise." *Jonghap News*. http://www.jonghapnews.com/news/articleView.html?idxno=119608 [In Korean]

Curran, W. and Hamilton, T., 2012. Just green enough: contesting environmental gentrification in Greenpoint, Brooklyn. *Local Environment* 17(9): 1027–1042.

Dooling, S., 2009. Ecological gentrification: a research agenda exploring justice in the city. *International Journal of Urban and Regional Research* 33(3): 621–639.

Ha, S.K., 2015. The endogenous dynamics of urban renewal and gentrification in Seoul. In L. Lees, H.B. Shin, and E. Lopez-Morales (Eds.), *Global gentrifications: uneven development and displacement* (pp. 165–180), Bristol, UK: Policy Press.

Heynen, N. and Perkins, H., 2005. Scalar dialectics in green: urban private property and the contradictions of the neoliberalization of nature. *Capitalism, Nature, Socialism* 16(1): 99–113.

Hwang, J.T., 2016. Escaping the territorially trapped East Asian developmental state thesis. *The Professional Geographer* 68(4): 554–560.

Ju, J.W., 2013, June 3. No land for Bogeumjari to stand. *Korea Joongang Daily*. http://news.jtbc.joins.com/article/article.aspx?news_id=NB10287063 [In Korean]

Jang, E.K., 2013, October 28. Will the first stage of move-ins be delayed for the Hanam Misa Area? Obstacles in the way of the relocation of the Gana-an Farmers' School. *Incheon Ilbo*. http://www.incheonilbo.com/news/articleView.html?idxno=502887 [In Korean]

Kim, H.N., 2014, April 8. Sandy fields that turned to gold now appear unrecognizable. *The Korea Economic Daily*. http://land.hankyung.com/news/app/newsview.php?aid=201404073862e [In Korean]

Kim, O.Y. and Lee, J.P., 2014. Revitalization of urban regeneration through the Happiness Housing Project as public housing policy. *LHI (Land and Housing Institute) Journal of Land, Housing, and Urban Affairs* 5(3): 151–167.

Kim, Y.K., 2016, November 18. Former Hanam City Boss, Park Deok-jin, who gave development information for bribes, imprisoned. *Kukmin Ilbo*. http://news.kmib.co.kr/article/view.asp?arcid=0011076134&code=61121111&cp=nv [In Korean]

Lee, D.H., 2013a, May 12. Hanam Bogeumjari changed to "Misa Riverside City." *Kyonggi News*. http://www.kgnews.co.kr/news/articlePrint.html?idxno=343109 [In Korean]

Lee, D.H., 2013b, July 9. "Leave because we paid you" vs. "We have nowhere to go with that money." *Kyonggi News*. http://www.kgnews.co.kr/news/articleView.html?idxno=349558 [In Korean]

Lee, E.A. and Hong, C.W., 2011, July 21. Misa Area compensation 300 billion won lower than expected. Land Exchange Permit Area restrictions enforced. Land owners in double bind. *Maeil Business News Korea*. http://news.mk.co.kr/newsRead.php?year=2011&no=475276 [In Korean]

Lee, W.S., 2015. Hanam Marine Product Retail Distribution Center experiencing "relocation conflict" forcefully removed after four years. *Yonhap News*. http://www.yonhapnews.co.kr/bulletin/2015/02/05/0200000000AKR20150205126900061.HTML [In Korean]

Lees, L., 2012. The geography of gentrification: thinking through comparative urbanism. *Progress in Human Geography* 36(2): 155–171.

Ministry of Land, Infrastructure and Transport, 2013, April 23. Making Happy Housing into the creative space of the sustainable city. *Land, Infrastructure and Transport News*. http://www.molit.go.kr/USR/NEWS/m_71/dtl.jsp?lcmspage=1&id=95071954 [In Korean]

MLTMA (Ministry of Land, Transport and Maritime Affairs), 2009, September 28. Hanam Misa Bogeumjari housing area. Land use regulations information system. http://luris.go.kr/web/actreg/mapboard/ArMapBoardView.jsp?seq=3338 [In Korean]

MLTMA (Ministry of Land, Transport and Maritime Affairs), 2010. Early budget execution for 2010. http://english.molit.go.kr/USR/WPGE0201/m_33143/DTL.jsp#mltm

Moore, M., 1984. Mobilization and disillusion in rural Korea: the Saemaul Movement in retrospect. *Pacific Affairs* 57(4): 577–598.

Mutersbaugh, T., 2006. Certifying biodiversity: conservation networks, landscape connectivity, and certified agriculture in Southern Mexico. In K.S. Zimmerer (Ed.), *Globalization and new geographies of conservation* (pp. 49–70). Chicago: University of Chicago Press.

Neumann, R.P., 2004. Toward a critical theorization of conservation enclosures. In R. Peet and M. Watts (Eds.), *Liberation ecologies: environment, development, social movements, second edition* (pp. 179–199). New York and London: Routledge.

Park, C.H., 1979. *Korea reborn: A model for development.* Englewood Cliffs, NJ: Prentice-Hall.

Park, B.G., 2005. Spatially selective liberalization and graduated sovereignty: politics of neoliberalism and "special economic zones" in South Korea. *Political Geography* 24(7): 850–873.

Park, B.G. and Choi, Y.J., 2014. Relations between the state and the local in the construction of Masan Export Processing Zone. *Journal of the Korean Geographical Society*, 49(2): 113–138. [In Korean]

Park, B.G. and Lepawsky, J., 2012. Spatially selective liberalization in South Korea and Malaysia: neoliberalization in Asian developmental states. In B.G. Park, R.C. Hill, and A. Saito (Eds.), *Locating neoliberalism in East Asia: neoliberalizing spaces in developmental states* (pp. 114–147). West Sussex, UK: Blackwell.

Pearsall, H., 2012. Moving out or moving in? Resilience to environmental gentrification in New York City. *Local Environment* 17(9): 1013–1026.

Quastel, N., 2009. Political ecologies of gentrification. *Urban Geography* 30(7): 694–725.

Safransky, S., 2014. Greening the urban frontier: race, property, and resettlement in Detroit. *Geoforum* 56: 237–248.

Schein, R.H., 1997. The place of landscape: a conceptual framework for interpreting an American scene. *Annals of the Association of American Geographers* 87(4): 660–680.

Shin, H.B. and Kim, S.H., 2016. The developmental state, speculative urbanization and the politics of displacement in gentrifying Seoul. *Urban Studies* 53(3): 540–559.

Seoul Metropolitan Government, 1973. *Municipal administrative outline*. Seoul: Seoul Metropolitan Government.

Smith, N., 1996. *The new urban frontier: gentrification and the revanchist city*. London: Routledge.

Smith, N., 2002. New globalism, new urbanism: gentrification as global urban strategy. *Antipode* 34(3): 427–450.

Soja, E.W., 1989. *Postmodern geographies: the reassertion of space in critical social theory*. London and New York: Verso.

Wolch, J.R., Byrne, J., and Newell, J.P., 2014. Urban green space, public health, and environmental justice: the challenge of making cities "just green enough". *Landscape and Urban Planning* 125: 234–244.

Woo, J.Y., 2014, February 23. In order to reduce debt, LH enters a public-private partnership to develop Hanam Misa Bogeumjari. *Maeil Business News Korea*. http://estate.mk.co.kr/news2011/view.php?TM=V1&PTM=N6&MM=A2&sc=90600032&cm=%C7%CF%B3%B2%BD%C3&year=2014&no=290801&relatedcode=&sID=NEWS&sm= [In Korean]

Zimmerer, K.S., 2000. The reworking of conservation geographies: nonequilibrium landscapes and nature-society hybrids. *Annals of the Association of American Geographers* 90(2): 356–369.

9

DISPLACEMENT AS DISASTER RELIEF: ENVIRONMENTAL GENTRIFICATION AND STATE INFORMALITY IN DEVELOPING CHENNAI

Priti Narayan

It had been raining continuously for many hours, but at about 8 p.m. on December 1, 2015, homes started to flood in Surya Nagar, in the Kotturpuram area of Chennai, the capital of Tamil Nadu state in India. The abutting Adyar River, which had steadfastly held fort all day, just could not contain the flood anymore. Water rose up to about eight feet, while residents panicked and rushed to take shelter in a nearby school. They stayed there for the next few days, tended to by relief workers, before they moved back to their homes in Surya Nagar when the water had receded.

Multiple homes were flooded in Chennai that day, rich and poor alike. The floods were rather indiscriminate in their destruction of homes, belongings, and lives. Yet, there was a difference. Less than a week after the floods, then-Chief Minister of Tamil Nadu J. Jayalalithaa announced that those who had lost their huts to the deluge will be given permanent homes; 10,000 tenements built by the Tamil Nadu Slum Clearance Board in the outskirts of the city were to be allotted to these hut dwellers (PTI 2015a). The goal was not just to resettle people "who had lost their hutments" but also "to facilitate the free flow of rain water in such waterways" (PTI 2015b). The underlying assumptions were multifold: a) that the way to provide relief to slum dwellers was by providing them alternate homes built by the government in the peripheries, and b) that slums were inhibiting the free flow of water, and their removal from riverbanks would facilitate flow in the waterways.

This chapter seeks to place government action post the 2015 floods in the context of ongoing developmental efforts in Chennai. Through the theoretical frameworks of environmental gentrification and state informality, it illustrates how compensation after the floods is only an extension of the development project which punishes the urban poor through a process of criminalization, eviction, and resettlement in precarious locations, while rewarding corporate and middle class interests.

The floods: What happened

The annual northeast monsoons brought the most rainfall in a hundred years to the state of Tamil Nadu (PTI 2015c). The weather phenomenon El Niño was deemed to be largely responsible for the high amounts of rainfall; the city received three times the average rainfall expected in November and December, receiving a record-breaking 72 mm of rainfall in just 12 hours, on December 1, 2015 (Skymet 2015; Krishnan 2015). The floods in Tamil Nadu killed more 470 people according to official estimates (PTI 2016), and displaced anywhere between 1.8 to 2 million people (DTE staff 2016; Voinea 2016)

While it was acknowledged that the amount of rainfall was unprecedented, criticism of the government was swift. Multiple news reports claimed that it was, in fact, government mismanagement that inundated the city. Despite multiple warnings from the India Meteorological Department, the state department failed to act in time to mitigate the effects of the floods. There were bureaucratic difficulties and delays in opening sluice gates of the overflowing Chembarambakkam reservoir during the rains, and after they were eventually opened, the Adyar River, which originates from this reservoir, could not hold the water, and flooded its embankments in hours (Chakravartty et al. 2015; Anwar 2015). The comptroller and auditor general (CAG) had, earlier in 2013 and 2014, urged the Chennai City Corporation to undertake measures to avoid flooding given the flood-proneness of Tamil Nadu's coastal districts due to cyclonic storms, but the city had failed to do so, citing high costs (Philip 2015). The chief urban planning agency, the Chennai Metropolitan Development Agency, had been working with outdated hazard profiles, and the state did not have disaster management rules to work with, or a functioning disaster management authority (Chakravartty et al. 2015). The CAG declared that the city was thoroughly unprepared for disaster, not having put in adequate early flood warning systems, or systems to ensure the gradual release of water from overflowing water bodies (Sample Survey of Losses 2016).

According to a parliamentary standing committee that examined the Chennai floods, the main reason for the flooding was not just the ill-preparedness of the government at the time of disaster, but the unbridled, unplanned nature of urbanization itself that has rendered the city incapable of handling flood events (DTE Staff 2016). The rate of urbanization in Chennai has increased by 20 times in the last four decades, leading to increased pressure on the city's water bodies. All of the city's three rivers, Cooum, Adyar, and Kosathalaiyar, and its various other smaller water-bodies and marshlands, have been subject to encroachments and overpollution from untreated sewage (Chakravartty et al. 2015; Anwar 2015). Despite multiple reports recommending that the rivers and waterways be cleared and rejuvenated, the government has failed to do so for many years (Anwar 2015), reducing the carrying capacity of the city's water bodies when it mattered. Thus, in all respects, the floods were a manmade disaster, caused by unbridled development and governance failures.

The government, while reluctant to accept culpability or accountability for the floods (ibid.), was quick to announce that slum households who have lost their homes in the floods will be relocated to tenements constructed by the Tamil Nadu Slum Clearance Board in Perumbakkam outside Chennai Corporation boundaries. Almost a year since the deluge, monetary compensation promised to flood-affected has not reached all slum residents yet,[1] but over 4,100 families living along the Adyar River have been relocated.[2]

Although the floods affected the rich and the poor alike, the poor have had to bear the disproportionate burden of the floods. The sluice gates of the Chembarambakkam Lake were opened without giving notice to many areas. In most neighbourhoods surveyed by activists to compile the Sample Survey of Losses Sustained During Chennai Floods (2016), slum residents reported witnessing their belongings being destroyed in a matter of mere minutes as water levels suddenly rose within their homes. People spent at least 25 days at relief camps and other public places such as railway stations, accessing relief materials provided by both the state as well as non-state relief workers. Slum residents reported having spent up to Rs. 5000 (about $77) the first few days, in order to access essential rations such as milk, water, and medical supplies. In addition, they reported having to spend a lot more money repairing or replacing walls and floors in their homes, as well as household appliances and their tools of trade, such as masonry and carpentry tools, vending tricycles, tailoring machines, etc. Daily wage workers, with daily wages ranging from Rs. 250–500 ($3.8–$7.7), lost multiple workdays to the flood. Migrant workers and single women reported worse impacts, being unable to receive flood relief, and plunging deeper into indebtedness. The government only dispensed flood relief of Rs. 5000 ($77) per household, which all households reported was not adequate to cover the damages caused by the floods. Since the floods were, in fact, a result of government mismanagement, the aim of the *Sample Survey Report* was to demand reasonable and adequate compensation for the poor.

What the government considers "compensation" – the relocation of 10,000 households along the Adyar River to tenement colonies in Perumbakkam and Ezhil Nagar in the city's peripheries – is interesting. Perumbakkam and Ezhil Nagar themselves fared badly during the floods. During a visit to Ezhil Nagar right after the floods, residents reported[3] being marooned for at least three days because not only was there flooding in the ground floor, there were also snakes and insects in the water. Relief supplies had to be airdropped from helicopters for the first few days; residents ruefully described the immense wastage of precious food as food packets fell into the water or split open on the ground. They felt grossly neglected during the floods and did not think they received enough relief through the disaster. At least six people in the occupied resettlement colony of Semmencherry,[4] located right next to Perumbakkam, died of snake bites during the floods (Unorganized Workers Federation 2016). The reason these peripheral resettlement colonies were flooded this badly is because they are located on water bodies themselves.[5] In effect, people who had lost their homes and belongings were moved to equally, possibly more, precarious locations.

However, the threat of eviction and resettlement to the peripheries is one that is not new to Chennai's slum dwellers, or unique to the flood situation. The threat of eviction is a constant one, especially to those slums located near the city's rivers.

Slums, and slums along waterbodies

The state has never taken kindly to slums, those along water bodies in particular. The very first legislation on slum areas in Tamil Nadu state, the Tamil Nadu Slum Areas (Improvement and Clearance) Act 1971, officially recognizes 1,202 slums in Chennai (then Madras). Yet, alongside, it also identifies a list of slums as lying along the major rivers; these are not officially recognized and are stated as slums to be evicted at some future date because they lie along water bodies. Since this time, multiple surveys undertaken by the Tamil Nadu Slum Clearance Board (TNSCB), as well as the website of the Board, identify slums along river margins (as well as those on road and rail margins, and in "places required for public purposes") as "objectionable" slums. The understanding is that government recognition of them as "objectionable" renders them and their residents "encroachers," vulnerable to clearance.

The term "encroacher" in urban parlance is one that is reserved for the unpropertied urban poor. Over the past few decades, Indian courts have turned largely unsympathetic to the right to livelihood of the poor, criminalizing them for their "illegal" occupation of public space (Upadhyay 2003). From the 1990s, the environment and its protection started to feature in planning documents in Chennai proclaiming the need for a "Singara Chennai" (beautiful Chennai) that can be achieved by cleaning the Cooum River. All these projects have identified the need to remove slum dwellers along the Cooum as necessary for the restoration of the river, and even succeeded in evicting thousands of families, even if none of the projects were actually implemented (Coelho and Raman 2010). The latest one to be floated is the Cooum River Restoration project, entrusted to the government-constituted Chennai Rivers Restoration Trust. At a National Green Tribunal hearing[6] on the Cooum River Restoration Project in Chennai, these "encroachers" had been identified as the major polluters of the Cooum River in Chennai, and their removal deemed necessary for the restoration of the canal (Ravi 2015). The project document reveals that Rs. 1087.63 crores (~$167 million), that is, 56% of the project cost,[7] are to be spent on resettling the 14,257 slum families who are to be affected by this project (LKS 2014).

Policymaking in Chennai thus fits what Dooling (2009, p. 631) calls *ecological gentrification*,[8] a convergence of "processes of converting uses of public (city-owned land), the ecological rationality driving this conversion and the consequences for a group of individuals who, although not private-property owners, are vulnerable to the economic and political consequences of gentrification." Policymakers are laying claim to land hitherto unclaimed by them, justifying their claims through a narrative that deems slums a blight on modern landscapes and polluters of waterbodies, even enfolding the displacement of the poor within their policy budgets.

The idea that slum dwellers must be removed from the city is one that is also increasingly gaining traction from the middle classes, property owners and the media, even justified in the name of "environmental improvement" (Ghertner 2012). Rich and middle class citizens alike have increasingly begun to take legal action against poor residents living along water bodies, by means of a constitutional tool called the Public Interest Litigation (see Narayan 2015, for example). Slum removal has become a matter of "public interest," at least in the eyes of the landowning public and the courts.

However, slum removal in India is not just the result of an emerging rationality more sensitive to ecological conservation than to social justice (as illustrated by Pearsall and Pierce 2010). Ecological conservation is part of a larger mechanism aimed at developing the city through state processes that can be described as informal.

Development and state informality-induced displacement

At least 150,000 people from 63 slums in Chennai have been removed from their homes in the last ten years (Transparent Cities Network 2015). With infrastructure being hailed as the material embodiment of modernity and the means for carrying the city and nation forward (Baviskar 2010; Graham and Marvin 2001), landscapes have been dramatically transformed in the post-liberalization Indian city, subsequently deepening forms of spatial segregation. Land owned by the state has increasingly been released into the market as opportunities for major revenue gains from public asset sales have materialized. The resulting development projects have been dispossessing the poor of the land they had been living on for years, in a classic case of what David Harvey (2004) calls "accumulation by dispossession."

This accumulation of land and capital and the subsequent eviction of the urban poor is enabled by informal yet purposive acts of the state, what Ananya Roy (2009) describes as "calculated informality." The state regularly gives away urban land, suspends laws and creates exceptions for corporate investors and middle class homeowners to aid development, real estate growth and the aesthetic appeal of a world-class city, often justified by public calls for beautification and environmental improvement (Ghertner 2015; Chatterjee 2004; Baviskar 2003). Thus, environmental gentrification in the Indian city can be thought of as only one among multiple mechanisms aimed at "developing" the city, while being deeply imbricated with these other developmental mechanisms and enabled by state informality.

Data collected by the Transparent Cities Network (2015) on the 63 evictions in Chennai city over the last ten years reveal that at least seven of the evicted slums were officially recognized; meaning that the residents held the right to live and access basic services where they lived, and for which they paid taxes. However, their eviction means that official slum recognition does not offer protection against evictions anymore. In other words, it does not matter, whether you are a taxpaying resident or not; if you live in a "slum," you can be evicted, often without due process. Only in six cases was advance notice given to slum residents before evictions. In most cases, evictions happen in an arbitrary manner, with no stipulated notice period and no standard compensation package for evictees. Different development projects planned on or near slum lands produce different eviction outcomes for slumdwellers. In many cases, slumdwellers have been evicted for projects that ultimately were never built. Often, there is a lack of clarity on the department in charge of eviction of a particular slum, meaning that residents do not know where to go to seek information or relief. In addition, residents often face intimidation and violence during evictions. The opacity in eviction practices and the lack of due process ensure that the urban poor do not have adequate opportunities to defend their homes legally or respond effectively to the threat.

Most evictees then, are offered compensatory housing in peripheral resettlement colonies, built using large fund tranches that have been made available by the central government since the late 1990s for flood alleviation, housing development and urban renewal (Raman 2011). In fact, the first set of 3,000 homes built in Chennai's first, and now Asia's largest, resettlement colony, Kannagi Nagar, was built using funds made available through the "Flood Alleviation Programme." A host of slumdwellers living on river banks were evicted and rehoused here (ibid.). Since the construction of tenements in Kannagi Nagar, the TNSCB has been using significant amounts of money made available through central government urban renewal and housing schemes to simply construct housing stock in various peripheral locations. About 20,000 homes are in various stages of completion in the newest site, Perumbakkam.[9] Displaced communities who are moved here face poor access to basic amenities, limited social infrastructure, and few employment and educational opportunities (Lakshman 2009; Ramakrishnan 2009). These government-created ghettoes are also characterized by high crime and suicide rates (Tejonmayam 2014; Special Correspondent 2011).

Development + disaster

These resettlement tenements stand as a solution not just when barriers to accumulation are encountered, but also when disaster occurs. Disaster relief was the face of dispossession after the tsunami in 2004. Land on the beach near Loop Road was freed up through the resettlement of slumdwellers from Pattinampakkam into tenements in Ezhil Nagar in the outskirts, whose construction was funded by the Emergency Tsunami Rehabilitation Project (ETRP) funds.[10] The government also attempted to remove fishing villages from the coast in a bid to protect fishermen from future risks, while simultaneously promoting large-scale, upscale development along the coast in the form of luxury housing and resorts (Coelho 2016). This is part of a larger trend of removing slum settlements from prime real estate in the city, whenever slum fires (widely alleged to be arson by the government) and routine flood events occur (ibid.) Now too, after the floods, the city is poised to witness large-scale evictions of slums along water bodies.[11] Disaster has only been an excuse to resettle the poor and expedite the clearance of valuable land for the development of the central city.

Losses during the floods amount to the order of up to Rs. 50,000 crores (~$7.6 billion), according to some estimates (Kotteswaran 2015). This loss includes the loss of multiple cars and consumer goods in middle class and rich households, in addition to losses suffered by industries, agricultural farms, hotels, and shops. Loss to property and business alone, including those insured, ran to over Rs. 14,602 crores (~$2.2 billion) (ENS Economic Bureau 2016). The nature of compensation offered was mostly monetary (Special Correspondent 2015; PTI 2015a). Only slum dwellers were asked to move to alternate housing in the peripheries less than a week after the floods; this indicates both their abject housing conditions as well as the discriminatory nature of relief.

Civil society and media discourse on the floods threw into sharp relief the encroachments made by the rich and middle class into ecologically sensitive areas of the city that ultimately drowned it. Activists have written about how the Pallikaranai marsh, for instance, has shrunk to less than a tenth of its size in the last few decades, making way for the famed IT corridor in South Chennai. Multiple tanks and lakes have shrunk or gone wholly missing in various parts of the city thanks to unbridled construction of gated residential colonies, industry Special Economic Zones, and private colleges (Jayaraman 2015a). In fact, right next to the Surya Nagar slum along the Adyar River, even a few meters closer to the river, many upscale apartments continue to stand intact, unthreatened by government removal. Automotive multinationals such as Hyundai, Daimler Benz, Renault Nissan and Ford have all located their factories on hydrologically sensitive catchment areas in Chembarambakkam and Oragadam (Jayaraman 2015b; incidentally, these companies had to suspend operations temporarily due to intense flooding and suffered huge losses). In addition to approving these constructions and/or turning a blind eye to corporate, private interests, the government itself is perhaps the largest encroacher on water bodies. In its aspiration to be a world-class city, infrastructure such as bus terminals, expressways, the Mass Rapid Transit System, and the Kamarajar Port have all been approved to be built on lakebeds, flood plains and other water bodies (ibid.; Coelho 2016). The government has routinely created housing stock on lakebeds: Perumbakkam and the various "eri" schemes implemented by the Tamil Nadu Housing Board are examples. Yet, no punitive action has been taken against any of these encroachers. The Parliamentary Standing Committee on the floods had demanded "strict action against illegal encroachments" and asked the government "to check real estate mafia involved in illegal construction and usurping of water bodies" (DTE Staff 2016). In response, the government had promised to remove only 11 unauthorized constructions (ibid.). No action seems to have been taken so far.

This means that while slum dwellers living along water bodies have been historically and routinely criminalized and removed, industries, big businesses and government buildings (including resettlement tenements) have been allowed to flourish in similar ecologically sensitive locations, because they aid the vision of a developing city. Environmental concerns have only emerged with respect to slum dwellers along water bodies, while other gross encroachments onto ecological sensitive areas by developers have been tolerated, leading to the colossal flood event in 2015. The government's reaction to the floods extends and highlights this discriminatory treatment: blame has been placed on the shoulders of the poor, and their "compensation" has taken the form of peripheral resettlement. Resettlement of the poor to the peripheries clears land within the city for further development and the absence of punitive action for proven affluent rich encroachers can only be taken as encouragement to the development project. The government's approach, then, is selective: an ecological rationality is an essential part of its pro-development rhetoric, even a front for development projects themselves, but does not feature in disaster planning or management practices, given the government's inaction to prevent disaster and the fact that the tenements offered as compensation were themselves built on lake beds and devastated by the floods. Such an ecological rationality only punishes the poor by uprooting them and placing them in precarious locations, while actively rewarding developer and middle class resident interests. This selective, discriminatory nature of state action itself can be understood within the larger theoretical framework of state informality in India, and the historical precedents of development and disaster management practices in Chennai.

Slum residents and activists have long been protesting against resettlement as a housing option for the poor because of the poor access to livelihoods, education and basic services. Resettlement in Chennai has been a failure by all measures; fewer than 50% of the original beneficiaries of tenements in Kannagi Nagar continue to live there (Lopez 2012). Despite the government's recent attempts to mitigate the adverse effects of resettlement by providing moving allowances, expediting local school admissions for children and so forth, the overarching problems associated with eviction and resettlement remain. Intimidation remains an oft-used method to make people move (in Surya Nagar; also see Unorganized Workers Federation 2016). Basic services and infrastructure remain inadequate. Based on an assessment of infrastructure and access to services at Ezhil Nagar conducted by Transparent Cities Network (2015), water is only supplied once in two hours. Sewerage connectivity is not complete, leading to overflowing sewerage on the streets. Childcare facilities, schools, transport facilities and ration shops are disproportionately few compared to the population. There are no government healthcare services in the settlement. Despite the job trainings provided to those resettled, these have not resulted in better access to job opportunities in the peripheries (interview notes January 2016; Express News Service 2016). Yet, the Tamil Nadu government seems convinced that resettlement is the primary road to take.

The Surya Nagar story: An illustration

About 67 houses in Surya Nagar, located along a meander of the Adyar river, were washed out by the floods. Having lost all their belongings, these families wrote petitions to the Mayor and the Chief Minister asking for a solution. In January 2016, a camp was set up in Surya Nagar where not only those 67 families were allotted homes in Perumbakkam, but other residents were told that they could receive homes as well. "A combination of methods were used," Senthil, a Surya Nagar resident recalls. "They subtly threatened to cut off our power supply and demolish our homes. Alongside, they plied people with the promise of a moving allowance of Rs. 5000 and a subsistence allowance of Rs. 2500 every month for a year, in addition to claiming that the houses they will receive in Perumbakkam were worth Rs. 27 lakhs (~$41,530)," he says. Government officials from various government departments including the city corporation and the Revenue Department, as well as the police, arrived to convince people to leave (in trucks that had suddenly arrived), all the while reassuring the skeptics among the residents that the people "were not being forced, but were moving voluntarily."[12] Some families got multiple resettlement homes as a reward, and many managed to get homes even without the necessary identification documents, while the more skeptical among them collaborated with members of the Communist Party of India (Marxist), or CPI(M), to mobilize.

Four days into the government's intervention into Surya Nagar, the media was invited to watch as some residents first asked the police to leave. Upon the police's refusal and their ensuing threats to arrest, one group of residents, mostly women, defied the police to advance towards the arterial Gandhi Mandapam High Road, while another group found its way out by walking down the river and exiting the slum through an alternate route. They disrupted traffic by staging a spontaneous *road roko*, gave interviews to the media, and signed petitions circulated by the CPI(M) for a good 15 minutes before the police requested them to leave.

Since then, the residents of Surya Nagar have neither seen the police in the neighbourhood, nor witnessed any further demolition of homes. Attempts by the local police inspector and the District Collector to negotiate evictions have failed, as people have stood their ground, refusing to move. About 700 families have relocated to Perumbakkam, but of the remaining 200, 175 have come together to secure their homes legally. On the basis of the fact that Surya Nagar is a declared slum and residents have been paying all the requisite taxes, they have received an interim stay order against evictions. Residents continue to go to court in the hope of obtaining some form of more permanent legal access to the land they have been living on for the last 60 years.

The next monsoons arrived, yet few things had changed and few lessons had been learned. Residents of upscale apartment complexes right by Surya Nagar have returned to their normal lives, while Surya Nagar looks like a ghost town, with so many of its homes abandoned or reduced to wreckage, thanks both to the floods and the eviction that ensued. A mere few months after the floods, construction work on a new set of apartments right along the river next to Surya Nagar, closer to the water than Surya Nagar, had commenced. Seeming untouched by the floods, right across the river, along its other bank, lies a golf course, its manicured grounds protected by a shiny high wall. It is business as usual in Chennai.

Notes

1 Field notes, August–October 2016.
2 Interview with TNSCB official, August 8, 2016.
3 Field interviews, January 9, 2016.

4 Semmencherry is a peripheral resettlement colony consisting of 6,734 apartments, most of which are occupied. The first set of tenements on this site were given to families affected by the 2004 tsunami.

5 This is consistent with the Tamil Nadu Housing Board (TNHB) and the TNSCB's practice of creating housing layouts on lake beds (the "eri" schemes) and canals (Coelho 2016; Radhakrishnan 2015).

6 The National Green Tribunal was set up in 2010 to handle cases relating to environmental protection and conservation of forests and other natural resources.

7 The total project cost is estimated to be Rs. 1934.88 crores (~$297million). Apart from resettlement, funds are to be allocated to the "sanitation sector," solid waste management, inundation plan, riverfront development, and biodiversity.

8 Ghertner (2014), however, suggests that gentrification theory does not apply in places like India, because capital is not pumped into disinvested spaces. On the contrary, private property is produced on public land. Thus, beautification processes do not necessarily amount to gentrification.

9 These homes are being built with funds from the Jawaharlal Nehru Urban Renewal Mission (JNNURM), a centrally sponsored scheme for urban infrastructure creation. The tenements at Perumbakkam are estimated to be built at Rs. 6849.39 crores (~$1 billion) (TNSCB n.d.).

10 Field notes, August 4, 2015.

11 In addition to evictions along the Adyar River post the floods, a TNSCB official in an interview said that 15,000 families are to be evicted from along the Cooum River for the river restoration project, and 25,000 families along the Buckingham Canal, "for the same reason."

12 Interview, August 31, 2016.

References

Anwar, T. 2015. Firstpost Investigation: Were the Chennai floods a government-made disaster? *Firstpost*. http://www.firstpost.com/india/firstpost-investigation-were-the- chennai-floods-a-government-made-disaster-2544516.html

Baviskar, A. 2010. Spectacular Events, City Spaces and Citizenship: The Commonwealth Games in Delhi. In J. S. Anjaria and C. McFarlane (eds), *Urban Navigations: Politics, Space and the City in South Asia*, pp. 138–161. London and New York: Routledge.

Baviskar, A. 2003. Between violence and desire: Space, power, and identity in the making of metropolitan Delhi. *International Social Science Journal* 55(175): 89–98.

Chakravartty, A., Venkatesh, S., Sengupta, S. and Pandey, K. 2015. Chennai apart. *Down to Earth*. http://www.downtoearth.org.in/news/chennai-apart-52265

Chatterjee, P. 2004. *The Politics of the Governed: Reflections on Popular Politics in Most of the World*. New York: Columbia University Press.

Coelho, K. 2016. Placing the poor in the flood path: Post-disaster slum resettlement in Chennai. *The Caravan*. http://www.caravanmagazine.in/vantage/placing-the- poor-in-the-flood-pathpost-disaster-slum-resettlement-in-chennai

Coelho, K. and Raman, N.V. 2010. Salvaging and scapegoating: Slum evictions on Chennai's waterways. *Economic and Political Weekly* XLV(21): 19–23.

Curran, W. and Hamilton, T. 2012. Just green enough: Contesting environmental gentrification in Greenpoint, Brooklyn. *Local Environment* 17(9): 1027–1042.

Dooling, S. 2009. Ecological gentrification: A research agenda exploring justice in the City. *International Journal of Urban and Regional Research* 33(3): 621–639.

DTE Staff. 2016. Chennai floods: Panel report highlights encroachments, faulty drainage system. *Down To Earth*. http://www.downtoearth.org.in/news/chennai- floods-panel-report-highlights-encroachments-faulty-drainage-system-55329

ENS Economic Bureau. 2016. Chennai floods in November washed away Rs. 14,000 crore. *The New Indian Express*. http://www.newindianexpress.com/business/2016/mar/31/Chennai-Floods-in-November-Washed-Away-Over-Rs-14000-crore-918382.html

Express News Service. 2016. Chennai's slum-dwellers relive last year's floods. *The New Indian Express*. http://www.newindianexpress.com/cities/chennai/2016/oct/25/chennai39s-slum-dwellers-relive-last-year39s-floods-1531511.html

Ghertner, D.A. 2015. *Rule by Aesthetics: World-Class City Making in Delhi*. Oxford: Oxford University Press.

Ghertner, D.A. 2014. India's urban revolution: geographies of displacement beyond gentrification. *Environment and Planning A* 46: 1554–1571.

Ghertner, D.A. 2012. Nuisance talk and the propriety of property: Middle class discourses of a slum-free Delhi. *Antipode* 44(4): 1161–1187.

Graham, S. and Marvin, S. 2001. *Splintering Urbanism: Networked Infrastructures, Technological Mobilities, and the Urban Condition*. London and New York: Routledge.

Harvey, D. 2004. The "new" imperialism: Accumulation by dispossession. *Socialist Register* 40: 63–87.

Jayaraman, N. 2015a. Chennai floods are not a natural disaster – they've been created by unrestrained construction. *Scroll*. http://scroll.in/article/769928/chennai-floods-are-not-a-natural-disaster-theyve-been-created-by-unrestrained-construction

Jayaraman, N. 2015b. Making of a disaster: Satellite images show how Chennai's new urban jungles caused flooding. *The News Minute*. http://www.thenewsminute.com/article/making-disaster-satellite-images-show-how-chennais-new-urban-jungles-caused-flooding- 36595

Kotteswaran, C.S. 2015. Tamil Nadu: Chennai floods cause a loss of Rs. 50,000-cr. *Deccan Chronicle*. http://www.deccanchronicle.com/151206/nation-current-affairs/article/chennai-floods-caused-loss-50-thousand-crore

Krishnan, R. 2015. Climate experts say El Nino responsible for heavy Chennai rains. *Business Standard*. http://www.business-standard.com/article/current-affairs/climate-experts-say-el-nino-responsible-for-heavy-chennai-rains-115120201026_1.html

Lakshman, N. 2009. Grim Prospects for Kannagi Nagar. *The Hindu*. www.hindu.com/2009/12/07/stories/2009120757970300.htm

LKS. 2014. *Integrated Cooum River Eco-Restoration Plan: Executive Summary of final report*.

Lopez, A.X. 2012. 50% beneficiaries missing from tenements. *The Hindu*. http://www.thehindu.com/news/cities/chennai/50-beneficiaries-missing-from-tenements/article4006818.ece

Narayan, P. 2015. The story of a slum eviction. *OpenDemocracy*. https://www.opendemocracy.net/priti-narayan/story-of-slum-eviction

Pearsall, H. and Pierce, J. 2010. Urban sustainability and environmental justice: evaluating the linkages in public planning / policy discourse. *Local Environment* 15(6): 569–580.

Philip, C.M. 2015. Flood: Chennai corpn learned little from CAG advice. *The Times of India*. http://timesofindia.indiatimes.com/city/chennai/Flood-Chennai-corpn-learned-little-from-CAG-advice/articleshow/49852204.cms

PTI. 2016. TN floods claimed 470 lives, over 3.83 lakh hectare crops damaged. *The Hindu*. http://www.thehindu.com/news/national/tamil-nadu/tn-floods-claimed-470-lives-over-383-lakh-hectare-crops-damaged/article8064739.ece

PTI. 2015a. Tamil Nadu CM J Jayalalithaa announces houses, Rs. 10,000 for flood-hit. *The Economic Times*. http://articles.economictimes.indiatimes.com/2015-12-07/news/68835609_1_flood-relief-immediate-relief-dmk-chief-karunanidhi

PTI. 2015b. Jayalalithaa allots houses for people who lost homes in deluge. *The Hindu*. http://www.thehindu.com/news/cities/chennai/jayalalithaa-allots-houses-for-people-who-lost-homes-in-chennai-floods/article8041904.ece

PTI. 2015c. Army out as worst rain in 100 years batters Chennai. *The Times of India.* http://timesofindia.indiatimes.com/city/chennai/Army-out-as-worst-rain-in-100-years-batters-Chennai/articleshow/50002583.cms

Radhakrishnan, R.K. 2015. "Development" disaster. *Frontline.* http://www.frontline.in/cover-story/development-disaster/article7965568.ece

Ramakrishnan, D.H. 2009. Kannagi Nagar demands its due. *The Hindu.* www.hindu.com/2009/06/15/stories/2009061558030300.htm

Raman, N. 2011. The board and the bank: Changing policies towards slums in Chennai. *Economic and Political Weekly* XLVI(31): 74–80.

Ravi, P. 2015. When the poor have no voice: A brief summary of the hearing at the National Green Tribunal in a case related to the Cooum Restoration. *CAG Blog.* https://www.cag.org.in/blogs/when-poor-have-no-voice-brief-summary-hearing-national-green-tribunal-case-related-cooum

Roy, A. 2009. Why India cannot plan its cities: Informality, insurgence and the idiom of urbanization. *Planning Theory* 8(1): 76–87.

Sample Survey of Losses Sustained During Chennai Floods: With Special Reference to Losses and Damages of Possessions, Loss of Workdays and Damage to Homes. 2016. https://www.cag.org.in/sites/default/files/database/Report%20of%20Survey%20of%20Losses%20Sustained%20during%20Chennai%20Floods_20160113.pdf

Skymet. 2015. Chennai rains rewrite highest rainfall record in December. *Skymet Weather.* http://www.skymetweather.com/content/weather-news-and-analysis/record-breaking-december-for-chennai-rains/

Special Correspondent. 2015. Jayalalithaa orders relief packages. *The Hindu.* http://www.thehindu.com/news/national/tamil-nadu/tn-govt-announces-rs10000-for-flood-victims/article7958436.ece

Special Correspondent. 2011. CCTV network installed in Kannagi Nagar. *The Hindu.* http://www.thehindu.com/news/cities/chennai/cctv-network-installed-in-kannagi-nagar/article2153982.ece

Tejonmayam, U. 2014. Anti-socials rule the roost at Kannagi Nagar. *The New Indian Express.* http://www.newindianexpress.com/cities/chennai/Anti-socials-Rule-the-Roost-at-Kannagi-Nagar/2014/01/30/article2026899.ece

Transparent Cities Network. 2015. *Eviction Mapping: Uncovering Chennai's Invisible Injustice.* https://www.cag.org.in/database/eviction-mapping-uncovering-chennais-invisible-injustice-august-2015-tamil

Unorganized Workers' Federation. 2016. *Report on the Public Hearing on Impact of Recent Floods on Slum and Pavement Dwellers in Chennai city.* http://tnlabour.in/wp-content/uploads/2016/10/Impact-of-Floods-on-Slum-and-Pavement-Dwellers-English.pdf

Upadhyay, V. 2003. Further to the margins by law. *India Together.* http://indiatogether.org/articles/urbanpoor-op-ed

Voinea, A. 2016. India: IFFCO provides relief for flooded Chennai. *Co-operative News.* http://www.thenews.coop/100488/news/agriculture/iffco-co-operative-will-provide-relief-flooded-areas-india/

10

FIXING SUSTAINABILITY: SOCIAL CONTESTATION AND RE-REGULATION IN VANCOUVER'S HOUSING SYSTEM

Noah Quastel

Introduction

The City of Vancouver is situated amongst beautiful scenery (mountains, ocean and temperate forests) and has capitalized on this with carefully cultivated environmental branding. Its first comprehensive city plan, in 1928, borrowed heavily from Frederick Olmsted and the City Beautiful Movement. It created many parks, boulevards, and tree-lined residential neighbourhoods devoted to single family houses, and isolated commercial and industrial spaces into discrete zones (Bartholomew 1928). In the 1970s, the city featured a strong liveability movement, successfully resisting freeways in the central city. Through the 1990s and 2000s, the city and its region became an exemplar of comprehensive planning, leadership on climate action, urban containment boundaries and commitment to walkable complete communities (Hutton 2011). Vancouver has now taken up the mantle of being the "Greenest City in the World" by 2020 (City of Vancouver 2010). While at times voiced in terms of growth through advancing a "green economy," contemporary green city strategies include policies showing a strong moral position on the environment, such as an urban biodiversity strategy and a renewable energy policy calling for zero carbon emissions by 2050.

However, environmental improvement has occurred hand in hand with high home prices. By 2016 there was near consensus concerning a housing crisis. The 2000s saw widespread gentrification in inner city neighbourhoods (Blomley 2004; Calvez and Ilves 2007; Ley and Dobson 2008), but this has given way to concerns about gentrification engulfing not simply the City of Vancouver, but Metro Vancouver as a whole. A small bungalow in the formally working class and immigrant-dominated eastern half of the city now costs over 1.5 million Canadian dollars, and one-bedroom apartments there start at about $300,000. Meanwhile, an "affordable" price for a home – at the metric of three times median gross family income – would be $230,000 for Greater Vancouver. Further flung suburbs are now at similar price levels, and price inflation is also faced by renters, who experience very low vacancy rates (0.6 percent for the city, and 0.8 for the region) and the highest prices in the country. Only two outlying neighbourhoods in the City of Vancouver remain accessible to workers making average wages (Vancity 2016). For the middle classes, this means young people leaving the city or difficulties for businesses in retaining workers (Todd 2016). For the city's poorest, single room occupancy (SRO) rooms in the Downtown Eastside that used to rent for the social assistance rate ($375 a month) are being renovated and re-rented at double to four times that amount, leaving no local options (Colebourn 2016).

As this chapter will discuss, city and provincial governments have initiated new programs and laws that I want to situate in terms of a "sustainability fix" for the city's housing system. The concept of a fix has been used a number of times to describe new urban law and policy that combine environmental improvement and capital accumulation strategies (While et al. 2004; Temenos and McCann 2013; Rosol 2013; Long 2016; Walker 2016). Here, I want to discuss some critiques and offer novel suggestions concerning the fix, drawing on Bob Jessop's state theory and cultural political economy. I hope to highlight the role of compromise and negotiation in the multi-level regulatory framework that now shapes Vancouver housing. This distinct view on fixes can also help show how Vancouver is undergoing a unique, and perhaps less than ideal, kind of "just green enough" strategy (Curran and Hamilton 2012; Wolch et al. 2014). In Vancouver, the twinning of environmental and social sustainability has emerged unevenly and haphazardly, featuring civil society pushback, crisis induced reform, and only limited amelioration to what remains a highly perverse and inegalitarian housing system.

Rethinking the fix

Original theorizations of the sustainability fix (such as While et al. 2004) followed David Harvey, the Regulation Approach, and James O'Connor. Harvey posited a "spatio-temporal fix" by which capital would face crises and barriers until a new strategy could open up new spaces for rounds of investment (Harvey 1982). Regulation Approach theorists focused on the long run decline of profits in the Keynesian welfare state and the search for new strategies for capital accumulation (Peck and Tickel 1994). James O'Connor posited a uniquely capitalist response to environmental problems (O'Connor 1994). Broadly, capital seeks to realize profit through the use of nature, but faces contradictions: While it is in the interest of some firms to degrade nature (through using up forests or polluting the atmosphere, for instance), this can also undermine the "conditions of production" in the long run interest of most firms. The state might then step in to protect and reinvest in such conditions, using fiscal and legal measures to create a "sustainable capitalism" of efficient manufacturing and green technologies. O'Connor's vision has proven somewhat prescient, and especially in the urban context, "sustainability is now at the heart of urban practices and policies such as re-densification, urban compactness, smart growth, green suburbs, healthy communities, and the new urbanism" (Jonas 2015, 121). Naming the so-called "Smart Growth Machine" helped show that utopian ideals of sustainability were in part being realized, but at the same time being tailored to the needs of civic elites (Allred 2015). In many cities such as New York, Austin, Portland, and Vancouver, sustainability policies were used to attract investment or justify new development on brownfield sites. Previously unavailable spaces were now opened up for "environmental" forms of gentrification (Long 2016).

Theorists who use the nomenclature of the "fix" have shown sensitivity to local context and appreciation of the formation of discourse (Temenos and McCann 2012; Long 2016) and civil society contestation (Rosol 2013). However, I want to argue here that the concept of a fix, developed as it was from Harvey's and O'Connor's work, maintains a residual economism and capitalo-centricism. While it seeks to shine the spotlight on how state policy responds to capitalist imperatives, it retains buried assumptions that such imperatives are the sole drivers of state, society and economic restructuring. For O'Connor, "state activity, including every state agency and budgetary item, is concerned with providing capital with access to labor power, nature, or urban space and infrastructure" (O'Connor 1994, 166). This misses the way democratic governments do at times – especially during some crises – listen to, learn from, and accommodate public opinion and civil society organizations, with all the values and ideals of the public interest thereby involved.

A very different concept of a sustainability fix might be developed from Bob Jessop's state theory, cultural political economy, and his neo-Gramscian account of regulation. Following Gramsci's emphasis on discourse and intellectual leadership in the development of "historic blocs," Jessop puts strategic projects and the "imaginaries" they advance at centre stage of how state and economy can be reworked. Some neo-Gramscian approaches lean towards prioritizing discourse (canvassed, in the urban context, in Rosol 2013). Alternatively, Jessop emphasizes that hegemony formation cannot be "arbitrary, rationalistic and willed" (Jessop 1990, 200). He focuses on the way imaginaries are not simply free floating, but provide operating plans for the economy and link together ideology, diverse social forces, and institutions (Sum and Jessop 2013, 199). Moreover, the state must act as a bridge between economic forces (such as developers) and a broad set of social institutions and actors. The state does not represent any kind of unitary capitalist voice – it "cannot just be seen as a regulatory deus ex machina to be lowered on the stage whenever the capital relation needs it" (Jessop 1990, 318). Rather, the state must find some degree of unity, often voiced as the public interest, to resolve economic crises, provide social cohesion and appease and balance the pressures and needs of diverse groups. Thus, a "fix" might be construed as a relatively durable structural coherence created by the ways an overall mode of regulation works together with an economic system (Jessop 2002, 48–51).

Jessop also provides a way to rethink the contradictions and dilemmas that arise given the relationship of capital accumulation to environmental and social systems (see also Quastel 2016). For instance, he focuses on the ways state regulation faces a contradiction between treating objects such as land, knowledge, or labour as exchange value (as resources for firms) and "use value" for society beyond accumulation (Jessop 2002, 42). State law and policy do address the needs of capitalist actors and they are often dominant. But there are also a whole range of persons and institutions with skin in the game – such as education systems, professional bodies, judiciaries, churches, and environmental civil society organizations – each of which bring to the table their own agendas and values. State actors are faced with a difficult task of navigating contending discourses, ethics, and interests. Imaginaries aid this process as they move into policy, become consolidated into law and bureaucracy. They also can face resistance and pushback leading to an ongoing process of revision (Sum and Jessop 2013).

By such an account, a "sustainability fix" can name a relatively stable regulatory compromise that allows capital to "move forward" but, importantly, also reforms or creates new institutions and organizations which may accommodate, or respond to, societal counter-movements against the worst excesses of market-mediated accumulation. The state can hear, learn from, perhaps largely deflect, but also give concessions to, concerned social groups. In the rest of the chapter, I explain how recent events in Vancouver suggest a new form of compromise on housing: Alongside a push for environmental improvement, there is increasing attention to, but certainly not outright fulfillment of, social justice demands.

Vancouver's sustainable housing dilemma

In the 1960s and 1970s, the federal government took the lead on social housing through direct grants and preferential tax treatment for rental housing investment, contracting with the provinces to create public housing, and encouraging non-profit and co-operative housing. This was followed in the 1980s and 1990s by a roll back of these programs – an end to rental subsidies, and a reduction in federal government funds (Pomeroy 2006). The federal government remains influential, but its preferred tools in the 2000s were monetary policy, the setting of interest rates, and underwriting mortgage insurance (Walks and Clifford 2015). In the face of a rollback of federal support, the province continued to administer some social housing. But with its own commitment to low corporate and personal taxes, it became increasingly reliant for funding on capitalizing uplift on lands long-before allocated to social housing.

The City of Vancouver's extensive sustainability planning in the 1990s and 2000s was largely directed around physicalist growth management planning, including zoning to favour a more compact metropolitan region that supported public transit and walkable neighbourhoods. This was meant to address carbon emissions and urban sprawl, and allowed for a congruence of environmental and economic priorities. Planning documents such as CityPlan (1995) allowed growth in neighbourhood centres in the low-density parts of the city. Beyond brownfield sites, CityPlan proved to offer only modest intensification, with rezoning for multi-storey housing often requiring request and city staff review for each individual property (Rosol 2015). Metro Vancouver coordinates land-use planning and population growth forecasting at the regional level. Its Livable Region Strategic Plan (1996) coupled forecasts of ongoing population growth with regional town centres and new housing being built in more dense, walkable and "complete" communities. This vision is continued in the newer regional growth strategy, Metro Vancouver 2040, which directs local municipalities to allow for new housing development in line with forecasted in-migration. It provides a broad vision for the region that follows Smart Growth principles – focusing on densification through urban growth centres and transit-oriented development (Metro Vancouver 2010).

Through most of the 1990s and 2000s, zoning directed density to old industrial sites and some neighbourhood high streets, delaying a broader densification. The city currently has a distinct topography marked by high-rise condominiums in inner city neighbourhoods and near some rapid transit stations, surrounded by a sea of single family neighbourhoods. New housing to absorb population growth now appears increasingly concentrated in high-rise developments in the Eastern suburbs, with transit-oriented development around large shopping mall complexes on the Skytrain line. The largest such agglomeration, at Metrotown in Burnaby, is seeing new high-rises condominiums replace older walk up rental apartments, in what is becoming a new round of gentrification (Jones and Ley 2016).

However, this period saw a diminished emphasis on housing affordability. Not just in Vancouver, but throughout Canada almost no purpose built rental housing was built. Almost all the housing built in the last two decades in the region was through the private sector, with developers catering to new owners by building smaller condominiums. The City relied on an older stock of buildings from the 1960s and 1970s, with homeowners renting out basement suites or condominiums (Mendez and Quastel 2015). The City also retained some minimal programs to ameliorate the worst of private market provisioning: It has had long standing policies of inclusionary zoning, in which a percentage (usually 20 percent) of new developments are set aside for low-income housing, and "rate of change" regulations that specify developers must preserve or replace rental housing (City of Vancouver 2012).

The main conduit for addressing rising housing costs has been increasing density, and expanding housing "choices," such as through legalizing basement suites or laneway houses, or relaxed height and density requirements for developers who promised to provide rental-only towers. Since older industrial sites have largely been redeveloped, new developments are limited to an increasingly small window in a largely outdated zoning system – along some high streets and some institutional sites (such as hospitals and shopping malls). The City of Vancouver had in the past pushed for "EcoDensity" in an effort to increase supply, but this nomenclature fell out of favour with a change in city government (Rosol 2013). Mayor Gregor Robertson and his "Vision Vancouver" party have been in power since 2008. Rather than attempt to update or replace CityPlan (or Ecodensity), they have sought densification through neighbourhood specific area plans, leaving out more than 70 percent of the city. Beyond that, the City appears to rely on site-specific density bonuses when developers initiate rezoning of individual sites (Gurstein and Condon 2015).

Reading the conjuncture

There are a multitude of voices asking what is to be done about Vancouver's housing costs. Most prominent have been those including real estate developers and economists from the region's business schools, but also voices from the left, such as former city mayor and provincial premier Mike Harcourt, who argue more densification is needed (CBC News 2011; Housing Affordability Fund 2016). Sustainability advocates argue for a diversity of urban forms, such as dispersed low-rise apartments rather than the more often seen Corbusier-influenced modernist high-rise towers (Condon 2011). But increased densification as an affordability solution so far remains idealistic. At the time of writing, new condominiums in the City of Vancouver were selling in the range of 800 to 1,000 dollars per square foot (Realtylink 2017).

Moreover, there is strong resistance by neighbourhood groups against new developments and increased building height allowances. One petition against this described the policy as "a response to intense and prolonged pressure from development interests to open up residential neighbourhoods for highly profitable development" (Community Index 2016). In Grandview-Woodlands, initial draft plans showed 35-story apartment towers as part of transit-oriented development plans around the local Skytrain station (Cole 2013). After widespread outrage – including hundreds of people packing neighbourhood meetings – the City resorted to a citizen assembly. The result was lower buildings and more neighbourhood preservation (Citizen Assembly 2015; City of Vancouver 2016). The conflicting pressures of meeting densification targets and allaying neighbourhood fears have rattled the city planning office. The City's chief planner, Brian Jackson, took early retirement after criticism that he pushed towers when residents did not want them (Bula 2015).

It is common to hear derision of the "Eden Complex," whereby residents wish to preserve their paradise and "pull up the drawbridge" (former City of Vancouver Chief Planner Brent Toderian, cited in Luke 2015). Yet opposition to densification also comes from low-income groups concerned about affordability, gentrification, and the lack of social housing and new rental housing. Regional planners estimate that from 2011 to 2014, only about half to two-thirds of the estimated rental housing demand for households earning under $50,000/year was met with new supply (Metro Vancouver 2016). In the run up to the provincial election in 2013, a broad coalition of groups – including the provincial teachers' union, supportive housing providers, neighbourhood resident groups, and student organizations – formed the Social Housing Alliance to demand "Social Housing Now!". They estimate that there are, province-wide, 11,000 visible, street homeless; another 40,000 on the verge (such as couch-surfing or with family on a short-term basis); and a further 65,000 paying over 50 percent of their income on rent. They call for 10,000 units a year to be built with state funds and to remain in public ownership, requiring one percent of the provincial budget (Social Housing Alliance 2016). Housing activists repeatedly point out that the relevant governments are not recognizing the right to housing as established in international law (Gurstein and Young 2013).

Other groups claim the problem is not available housing so much as wages. Business advocates such as the Canada West Foundation and the Business Council of BC come close to restating the environmental gentrification thesis, suggesting the region is already more green than enough and good (but brown) industrial jobs would help people afford to live in the city. As such, the region should accept new industrial projects, such as new pipelines and expanding the port to allow more container shipping and coal exports (Finlayson 2014; Cattaneo 2016). However, the natural resource route to prosperity appears limited – sectors such as film, tourism, computer software development and, needless to say, real estate – are now the leading regional performers (BC Statistics 2014).

Responding to gentrification

City and provincial agencies are increasingly aware of fights over gentrification and seeking ameliorative policies. The City uses, and increasingly relies on, spot zoning to bring revenue to fund social and environmental objectives through Community Amenity Contributions (CACs). This in turn becomes a tool to soften opposition to gentrification. For instance, the planned 26-story "Rise" development in the Mount Pleasant neighbourhood is now being marketed and built as the 19-story "Independent at Main." Opponents argued that it was "a textbook example of gentrification" and "a major precedent for other large-scale projects throughout East Vancouver" (Witt and Antrim 2012). They emphasized issues of social divide, inequality and class antagonism fostered by new frontiers of gentrification: "Renters now pay upwards of 50–80 percent of their income on shelter, whereas home-owners have had their net worth more than double in ten years" (Witt and Antrim 2012). The final approval did not squarely address gentrification and affordability concerns, but did try to appease local residents with lowered building heights and arts organization funding; the developers gave 1.5 million dollars to the nearby "Western Front," a well-known (and "hip") exhibition space for contemporary arts, which allowed it to buy its heritage building (Barrett 2016).

A financially hampered welfare state now relies on leveraging uplift, coupling densification and gentrification with the promise of more housing elsewhere. For instance, at the Little Mountain site (2.5 km south of the Rise development), a low-rise social housing project with 224 units was sold to developers and bulldozed to create a higher density, mixed-use community (1,400 market condos and repla-cement for the social housing). While most residents were relocated to other social housing across the city, others refused to leave in protest before the buildings were raised in 2009. Rosol (2015) notes how "the tenants of Little Mountain were not protesting against redevelopment or higher density per se, but against the degree of densification, their displacement, the lack of a consultation process before relocation and demolition started, and the privatization of public land meant for social housing" (157). The province claimed the redevelopment would add 300 million dollars to its supportive housing budget (BC Housing 2017).

Area plans recognize threats of gentrification and respond with housing pre-servation and the language of "social mix." From 2009 to 2014 the City engaged in area planning for the Downtown Eastside – home to the city's poorest people, with approximately 50 per cent of residents living on income assistance or disability pensions, and a large number with mental health and addiction problems (City of Vancouver 2014). Activists have long resisted gentrification in the area (Blomley 2004) and engaged in a new round of protests and drawing up of alternatives (CCAP 2009). The final area plan clearly allows for many new condominiums and higher-income renters (City of Vancouver 2014, 201), and "The vision for the DTES is to be a vibrant hub of social innovation requiring housing for all income levels and in a diverse community" (91). Activists decry "deconcentration," fearing that poor people and services aimed at them are to be gradually dispersed from the area (Crompton et al. 2014). On the other hand, the "Single Room Accom-modation Bylaw" makes it difficult for landlords to demolish or convert SROs (but not to increase rents when old tenants leave). Over 30 years, 4,400 new "social housing" units are planned for the area, coupled with 3,350 to be built in other parts of the city. This definition allows much of a building to be market rental if it is owned by a nonprofit or government agency and at least 30 percent of the units are at low-income rates. Funding will be primarily through partnership funding agreements with provincial authorities. One sub-district, "Oppenheimer," has a "60/40" requirement whereby new buildings need to be 60 percent social housing and the other 40 percent is market rental. Overall, the plan privileges social mix with some minimal attention to social justice needs.

Towards re-regulation

While city planning has led to significant supply problems, the City has for a number of years been building up its own housing policy, largely oriented to ensuring some level of basic needs to address homelessness and supportive housing, and so taking on some residual social welfare functions. Mayor Robertson's 2008 Vision party platform – aimed at holding the centre of the political spectrum – called for building a more livable and affordable city for all (Rolfsen 2008). While falling well short of recognizing human rights commitments, the City adopted a Housing and Homeless Strategy subtitled "A Home for Everyone" (City of Vancouver 2011). The City has rolled out a series of initiatives—acting on its own to build homeless shelters (long thought to be a provincial government role) and programs such as the Secured Market Rental Housing Policy (City of Vancouver 2012b) which creates a suite of incentives (such as waiving developer fees) for purpose-built rental buildings. The City also has some of its own land and has earmarked $125 million for a new Affordable Housing Agency that can deliver new housing (City of Vancouver 2015). It owns some supportive housing and has found funding (mostly from the provincial government's sale of Little Mountain) for 1500 supportive housing units on 14 city-owned sites.

The Vision platform now openly acknowledges "Housing affordability is the biggest challenge we face in Vancouver" and that "Vancouver should remain a city that people of all ages, backgrounds, and income levels can afford to call home" (Vision 2016). Yet the City remains hampered by limited funds from higher levels of government and is unwilling to dramatically change tax structures to finance welfare-state level public housing. The regional government's recently adopted Affordable Housing Strategy (2016) is much in line with the City's approach: It recognizes there are severe housing problems but argues "local governments' chief role lies in ensuring an adequate supply of residential land to meet housing demand through the land use planning and regulatory process" (Metro Vancouver 2016, 4). The strategy doubles down on transit-oriented development as a solution but adds a suite of potential interventions – much like the City of Vancouver has initiated – to offer modest subsidies for affordable rental housing and to open up surplus sites for new publicly-owned housing.

Speculative investment

Finally, there has been increasing concern about market foundations and the role of speculative investment, and this has emerged as a major new area of regulation. Geographers and urban planners have observed a strong influence of foreign investment on Vancouver property prices, particularly from Hong Kong and China (Ley 2011; Moos and Skaburskis 2010). Others have emphasized loose credit and backdoor state support for financial speculation in Canadian real estate (Walks 2014; Walks and Clifford 2015). In June 2015, mayor Robertson formally asked the province for (but was not granted) new legislation, including an increased property transfer tax on the most expensive residential properties with the proceeds invested back into creating more affordable housing (Robertson 2015; Bailey 2015).

Through 2015 and 2016 there was an upsurge of concern as prices rose. New, more middle-class activists emerged, such as Eveline Xia, who used the social media handle "#donthave1million" to decry the inaccessibility of home ownership and organize rallies (Fumano 2015). Vancouver area candidates in the 2015 federal election reported that housing was the key political issue (Culbert 2015), and in 2016 one global index proclaimed Vancouver the "worst housing bubble in the world" (UBS 2016). By the summer of 2016, the Organization of Economic Cooperation and Development and others began to flag housing in Vancouver and Toronto – and the possibilities of a "correction" – as major economic risks to the country (Reuters 2016).

The summer of 2016 saw significant policy reversal. In June, the provincial government announced a suite of measures to "keep home ownership an attainable dream for the middle class," including a reconstituted Real Estate Council with stronger powers to impose penalties (BC Government 2016a), and the collection and release of data on foreign real estate transactions (BC Government 2016b). After more than a year of refusing to do so, the provincial government also gave the City of Vancouver powers to tax vacant homes (BC Government 2016c). Most unexpected was the new property transfer tax – a 15 percent tax on purchases of residential property in metro Vancouver by foreign nationals. In September, the government announced that the housing boom had created unexpected tax revenues, and $500 million would be redirected towards affordable rental housing (BC Housing 2016). At the federal level, the new liberal government has promised (but not yet delivered) a new National Housing Strategy. By early October 2016 some new measures were introduced, including closing a loophole on capital gains that allowed non-residents to buy homes in Canada and claim them as a principal residence, and tightening mortgage requirements through a new "stress test" of potential borrowers (Evans 2016). By January 2017 monthly sale volumes for detached houses, condos, and townhouses had fallen by close to 40 percent compared to January 2016, with benchmark prices slipping down 3.7 percent since the July peak (Jang 2017).

Assessing a new hegemony

What appears to be emerging is a shift beyond physical planning of housing, to create a more embedded liberal rule with social sustainability characteristics – what might be termed a more "inclusive neoliberalism" (Bakker 2015, 447). On top of environmental regulation, there is some limited attention to social housing, efforts to facilitate new rental housing, modest investment controls, and some regulation of the real estate industry. This process has involved a rescaling of housing regulation, with cities moving from spatial planning and zoning to environmental and (limited) social welfare roles. This also depends on coordinating with other levels of government and non-profit "partners." The province, through new forms of market regulation, is participating in a system of multi-scalar governance.

The state, at diverse levels, is responding to civil society pushback as it seeks to maintain legitimacy. Opposition to gentrification and the push for housing in Vancouver and the wider province is at times voiced in economic language, focused on stabilizing markets to avoid corrections and crashes, or guaranteeing homes for workers in Vancouver's growing high tech industries. But the city and province cannot simply ignore moral arguments – just as "the environment" includes broad concerns about ecosystems and biodiversity, much of the housing debate is fuelled by concerns about distributive justice, fairness, basic needs, and human well-being. That said, readings of the conjuncture and future imaginaries – and the policies that match them – fit within the ambit of the private sector-led market economy. Interventions to address speculative investment focus on access to middle-class ownership and market stability, not distributive justice per se. New social housing initiatives now rely, for the most part, on a short-term strategy of selling off state-owned lands. The current balance of social forces in Vancouver includes many distraught residents and established channels of housing activism, but also prosperous real estate and development industries – and tens of thousands of newly wealthy house owners. In Vancouver, we are seeing a very modest amelioration of what has become a region-wide gentrification problem in what appears a new round of fixes. But they are only partly successful and mark only a subtle offset of what remains a cruel housing situation.

References

Allred, D. 2015. Development governances and the new regionalism: 'Sustainable Development' and restructured metropolitan space, in Wilson, D. (ed.) *The Politics of the Urban Sustainability Concept.* Champaign, Illinois: Common Ground Publishing, pp. 8–35.

Bailey, I. 2015. Mayor aims to moderate housing prices: Gregor Robertson asks province to increase transfer tax on expensive properties to fund affordable homes. *Globe and Mail,* June 4, 2015: S.1.

Bakker, K. 2015. Neoliberalization of nature, in Perrault, T., Bridge, G., and McCarthy, T. (eds.) *The Routledge Handbook of Political Ecology.* New York: Routledge, pp. 446–456.

Barrett, J. 2016. Developer dollars enable Western Front to buy building. *The Vancouver Courier,* January 11, 2016. www.vancourier.com/opinion/developer-dollars-enable-western-front-to-buy-building-1.2148463

Bartholomew, H. 1928. *A Plan for the City of Vancouver, British Columbia.* Vancouver: City of Vancouver.

Blomley, N. 2004. *Unsettling the City: Urban Land and the Politics of Property.* London: Routledge.

British Columbia (BC) Government. 2016a. Government ends self-regulation, strengthens consumer protection in real estate industry 29 June 2016. news.gov.bc.ca/releases/2016PREM0074–001180

British Columbia (BC) Government. 2016b. Government releases real estate transaction data. The province released the first set of data resulting from new measures to track the extent of foreign real estate transactions. news.gov.bc.ca/releases/2016FIN0028–001239

British Columbia (BC) Government. 2016c. Government to introduce legislation to enable Vancouver vacant homes tax and protect consumers. http://housingaffordability.gov.bc.ca/tile/housing-affordability-actions/

BC Housing. 2016. B.C. makes largest housing investment ever in province's history. www.bchousing.org/Media/NR/2016/09/19/12228_1609191320-706

BC Housing. 2017. Little Mountain website. https://www.bchousing.org/partner-servces/major-projects/little-mountain

BC Statistics. 2014. *Profile of the British Columbia High Technology Sector: 2013 Edition.* Victoria, BC.

Bula, F. 2015. Planning chief resigns over criticism: Brian Jackson is retiring after three years on the job, citing opposition from former staff over high-density development. *Globe and Mail,* July 27, 2015: S1.

Calvez, K. and Ilves, E. 2007. *Cultural Divide: A Neighbourhood Study of Immigrant Rental Housing in Vancouver.* Vancouver: Pivot Legal Society.

Canadian Broadcasting Corporation (CBC News). 2011. Vancouver aims to be world's greenest city by 2020: Former premier calls for end to single-family zoning. *CBC News,* July 15, 2011. www.cbc.ca/news/canada/british-columbia/vancouver-aims-to-be-world-s-greenest-city-by-2020-1.980278

Carnegie Community Action Project (CCAP). 2009. *Seeing it Our Way: Vision of the Downtown Eastside.* https://ccapvancouver.files.wordpress.com/2009/12/seeingitourway.pdf

Cattaneo, C. 2016. When NIMBYs move in; Vancouver port's struggles highlight increase in activism. *National Post*, July 9, 2016: FP1.

Citizen Assembly on the Grandview-Woodlands Community Plan. 2015. *Final Report*. http://www.grandview-woodland.ca/download/final-report-citizens-assembly%E2%80%A8on-the-grandview-woodland-community-plan-low-resolution-2/

City of Vancouver. 2010. *Vancouver 2020: A Bright Green Future: An Action Plan for Becoming the World's Greenest City by 2020*. http://vancouver.ca/greenestcity/PDF/Vancouver2020-ABrightGreenFuture.pdf

City of Vancouver. 2011. *Housing and Homelessness Strategy 2012–2021: A Home for Everyone*. http://vancouver.ca/files/cov/Housing-and-Homeless-Strategy-2012–2021pdf.pdf

City of Vancouver. 2012. *Bold Ideas Towards an Affordable City: Report of the Mayor's Task Force on Housing Affordability*. http://vancouver.ca/files/cov/Staff_report_to_Council_re_task_force_report.pdf

City of Vancouver. 2012b. *Secured Market Rental Housing Policy*. http://vancouver.ca/files/cov/secure_market_rental_policy.pdf

City of Vancouver. 2014. *Downtown Eastside Area Plan*. vancouver.ca/files/cov/downtown-eastside-plan.pdf

City of Vancouver. 2015. *2014 Housing and Homelessness Strategy Report Card*. Administration report, 26 May 2014, RTS No. 10831, Van RIMS No. 08-2000-20.

City of Vancouver. 2016. *Grandview-Woodlands Community Plan*. vancouver.ca/files/cov/grandview-woodland-community-plan.pdf

Cole, Y. 2013. Critics decry Grandview-Woodland development plan. *The Georgia Straight*, July 3, 2013. http://www.straight.com/news/397091/critics-decry-grandview-woodland-development-plan

Colebourn, J. 2016. Low-income rental units drying up in Vancouver's Downtown Eastside. *Vancouver Sun*, March 21, 2016: A5.

Community Index. 2016. *The Affordable Home Ownership (AHO) Policy & Program*. http://communityindex.ca

Condon, P. 2011. *A Convenience Truth: A Sustainable Vancouver by 2050*. Vancouver: School of Architecture and Landscape Architecture & the School of Community and Regional Planning of the University of British Columbia.

Crompton, N., Markle, T. and Wallstam, M. 2014. Vancouver City Hall approves "dispersal" plan for Downtown Eastside's most vulnerable. March 20, 2014. http://rabble.ca/blogs/bloggers/mainlander/2014/03/vancouver-city-hall-approves-dispersal-plan-downtown-eastsides-mos

Culbert, L. 2015. Real estate dominates voter concerns. *The Vancouver Sun*, October 2, 2015: A8.

Curran, W. and Hamilton, T. 2012. Just green enough: Contesting environmental gentrification in Greenpoint, Brooklyn. *Local Environment* 17(9): 1027–1042.

Evans, P. 2016. Ottawa tightens mortgage requirements and targets foreign money. *CBC News*, October 03, 2016. www.cbc.ca/news/business/ottawa-housing-tax-real-estate-1.3788725

Finlayson, J. 2014. Vancouver's incomes low, but costs are high; Trailing nation. *The Vancouver Sun*, August 8, 2014: B6.

Fumano, D. 2015. Protest over housing draws hundreds; Unaffordable city. *The Province*, May 25, 2015: A8.

Gurstein, P. and Young, M. 2013. Housing justice: A human rights approach. *World Academy of Science and Technology* 76: 74–80.

Gurstein, P. and Condon, P. 2015. Entire city requires a framework to grow upon; Piecemeal problem. *The Vancouver Sun*, November 24, 2015: B6.

Harvey, D. 1982. *The Limits to Capital*. Oxford: Blackwell.

Housing Affordability Fund. 2016. Website. www.housingaffordability.org

Hutton, T. 2011. Thinking Metropolis: From the "livable region" to the "sustainable metropolis" in Vancouver. *International Planning Studies* 16(3): 237–255.

Jang, B. 2017. Signs of a housing market shift. *The Globe and Mail*, February 3, 2017: B1.

Jessop, B. 1990. *State Theory*. Pittsburgh: Pennsylvania State University Press.

Jessop, B. 2002. *Future of the Capitalist State*. Cambridge: Polity Press.

Jonas, A. 2015. Beyond the urban "sustainability fix": Looking for new spaces and discourses of sustainability in the city, in Wilson, D. (ed.) *The Politics of the Urban Sustainability Concept*. Champaign, Illinois: Common Ground Publishing, pp. 117–135.

Jones, C. and Ley, D. 2016. Transit-oriented development and gentrification along Metro Vancouver's low-income SkyTrain corridor. *The Canadian Geographer* 60(1): 9–22.

Ley, D. 2011. *Millionaire Migrants: Transpacific Life Lines*. Hoboken, NJ: Wiley-Blackwell.

Ley, D. and Dobson, C. 2008. Are there limits to gentrification? The contexts of impeded gentrification in Vancouver. *Urban Studies* 45(2): 2471–2498.

Livable Region Strategic Plan. 1996. Greater Vancouver Regional District. http://www.metrovancouver.org/services/regional-planning/PlanningPublications/LRSP.pdf

Long, J. 2016. Constructing the narrative of the sustainability fix: Sustainability, social justice and representation in Austin, TX. *Urban Studies* 53(1): 149–172.

Luke, P. 2015. Just how fast is Metro Vancouver growing? Prediction that region will be home to one million more people by 2040 could be far off the mark, say experts. *The Province*, June 14, 2015: A10.

Mendez, P. and Quastel, N. 2015. Subterranean commodification: Informal housing and the legalization of basement suites in Vancouver from 1928 to 2009. *International Journal of Urban and Regional Research* 39(6): 1155–1171.

Metro Vancouver. 2010. *Metro Vancouver 2040: Shaping Our Future*. Regional Growth Strategy Bylaw No.1136.

Metro Vancouver. 2016. *Regional Affordable Housing Strategy*. www.metrovancouver.org/services/regional-planning/PlanningPublications/RegionalAffordableHousingStrategy2016.pdf

Moos, M. and Skaburskis, A. 2010. The globalization of urban housing markets: Immigration and changing housing demand in Vancouver. *Urban Geography* 31(6): 724–749.

O'Connor, J. 1994. Is sustainable capitalism possible? in O'Connor, M. (ed.) *Is Capitalism Sustainable? Political Economy and the Politics of Ecology*. New York: Guilford Press.

Peck, J. and Tickell, A. 1994. Searching for a new institutional fix: The after-Fordist crisis and the global-local disorder, in Amin, A. (ed.) *Post-Fordism: A Reader*. Oxford: Blackwell, pp. 280–315.

Pomeroy, S. 2006. *Was Chicken Little right? Case studies on the impact of expiring social housing operating agreements*. Ottawa: Canadian Housing and Renewal Association.

Quastel, N. 2016. Ecological political economy: Towards a strategic-relational approach. *Review of Political Economy* 28(3): 336–353.

Realtylink. 2017. Online master database of multiple listing service listings in Greater Vancouver. www.realtylink.org/

Reuters. 2016. OECD flags housing correction as Canada's biggest risk and urges tighter rules. *Financial Post*, June 13, 2016. business.financialpost.com/news/economy/oecd-flags-housing-correction-as-canadas-biggest-risk-and-urges-tighter-rules

Robertson, G. 2015. Give Vancouver the tools to level the playing field in housing market. *Huffington Post*. www.huffingtonpost.ca/gregor-robertson/vancouver-housing-tax-mayor_b_7512556.html

Rosol, M. 2013. Vancouver's "EcoDensity" Planning Initiative: A struggle over hegemony? *Urban Studies* 50(11): 2238–2255.

Rolfsen, C. 2008. Robertson vows a safer, greener city; Vision Vancouver to unveil party's new 57-point platform. *The Vancouver Sun*, 27 Oct, 2008: A1.

Rosol, M. 2015. Social mixing through densification? The struggle over the Little Mountain public housing complex in Vancouver. *Die Erde* 146(2–3): 151–164.

Social Housing Alliance. 2016. Social housing now!www.socialhousingbc.com

Sum, N. and Jessop, B. 2013. *Towards a Cultural Political Economy: Putting Culture in its Place in Political Economy*. Cheltenham, UK: Edward Elgar.

Temenos, C. and McCann, E. 2013. The local politics of policy mobility: Learning, persuasion, and the production of a municipal sustainability fix. *Environment & Planning A* 44(6): 1389–1406.

Todd, D. 2016. Is foreign homebuyers tax the 15 per cent solution? *The Vancouver Sun*, October 22, 2016: A8.

UBS. 2016. UBS global real estate bubble index. www.ubs.com/global/en/wealth_mana gement/chief-investment-office/investment-views/global-bubble-index.html

Vancity. 2016. Rent Race: The growing unaffordability of rent in Metro Vancouver. https:// www.slideshare.net/VancityCU/rent-race-the-growing-unaffordability-rent-in-metro- vancouver/1

Vancouver (BC) Planning Department. 1995. *CityPlan: Directions for Vancouver*. City of Vancouver.

Vision. 2016. Vote Vision. http://www.votevision.ca/inclusive_city

Walks, A. 2014. Canada's housing bubble story: Mortgage securitization, the state, and the global financial crisis. *International Journal of Urban and Regional Research* 38(1): 256–284.

Walks, A. and Clifford, B. 2015. The political economy of mortgage securitization and the neoliberalization of housing policy in Canada. *Environment and Planning A* 47: 1624–1642.

Walker, S. 2016. Urban agriculture and the sustainability fix in Vancouver and Detroit. *Urban Geography* 37(2): 163–182.

Witt, A. and Antrim, S. 2012. Gentrification of Mount Pleasant: Developers, displacement and real-estate's new frontier. *The Mainlander*, January 23, 2012. themainlander.com/ 2012/01/23/gentrification-of-mount-pleasant-developers-displacement-and-real-esta tes-new-frontier/

While, A., Jonas, A. and Gibbs, D. 2004. The environment and the entrepreneurial city: Searching for the urban "sustainability fix" in Manchester and Leeds. *International Journal of Urban and Regional Research* 28(3): 549–569.

Wolch, J., Byrne, J. and Newell, J. 2014. Urban green space, public health, and environmental justice: The challenge of making cities "just green enough." *Landscape and Urban Planning* 125: 234–244.

PART IV

Mobilizing and planning for just, green futures

11

MOBILIZING COMMUNITY IDENTITY TO IMAGINE JUST GREEN ENOUGH FUTURES: A CHICAGO CASE STUDY

Leslie Kern

In early 2012, Midwest Generation announced that two of its notoriously polluting coal-fired power plants within Chicago's city limits would be permanently retired ahead of the city-imposed deadline to either shut down or perform environmental upgrades (Wernau 2012a). Their closure in August 2012 was hailed as a major victory for environmental justice organizing in the two Latinx neighborhoods – Pilsen and Little Village – that had been home to these plants (Lyderson 2014; Wernau 2012b). The Fisk (Pilsen) and Crawford (Little Village) plants were among Illinois' largest emitters of toxins, and a Harvard School of Public Health report suggested that pollution from the two plants was responsible for 2800 asthma attacks, 550 emergency room visits, and 41 premature deaths per year (Levy and Spengler 2001). The shutdown was, however, only one dimension of the long-term struggle for environmental, social, and economic sustainability in these low-income minority communities. As the city's focus shifts from closing the plants to the economic development opportunities offered by these now-vacant industrial sites, Pilsen and Little Village face a second set of challenges: *redevelopment of brownfield sites has rarely been shown to provide tangible benefits to existing communities* (Lee and Mohai 2012; Byrne and Scattone 2001). Furthermore, cleanup and closure of industries can spark gentrification and displacement. As previously undesirable neighborhoods are deemed "healthy," they may become much more attractive to middle class home-buyers and capital investment. Labelled "environmental gentrification" by researchers, this process can drive up real estate prices and lead to the displacement of working class and minority residents (Curran and Hamilton 2012; Dale and Newman 2005; Dooling 2009; Essoka 2010). Pilsen is already gentrifying due to city-led redevelopment and the expansion of the University of Illinois Chicago campus (Anderson and Sternberg 2013; Betancur and Kim 2016). Little Village is just beginning to antici-pate this kind of pressure. In both areas, celebration of environmental improvements is tempered by well-founded concerns about displacement.

Midwest Generation filed for bankruptcy and the sites were taken over by NRG Energy in March 2014 (Wernau 2014). Despite projected total remediation costs of about $100 million, development proposals have been received, although several years of consultations have not resulted in any official plan for the sites. It is clear that community organizations are advocating for a "just green enough" future along the river, with living wage jobs and public green space identified as the highest priorities for redevelopment (PERRO 2012; Fisk and Crawford Reuse Task Force 2012; Pilsen Alliance 2013). Curran and Hamilton (2012, 1028) suggest that just green enough "makes room for continued industrial use and blue-collar work, where cleanup does not automatically or exclusively lead to the 'parks, cafes, and a riverwalk' model of a green city." New development must serve the needs of the existing working class residents, rather than the perceived desires of newcomers. But what kinds of just green enough visions can gain hold? Powerful and competing discourses about history and identity can emerge to shape the contours of what might be imagined for a just green enough future. In Pilsen and Little Village, a strong sense of pride in the areas' industrial heritage is linked to the notion that these are historically "port of entry" neighborhoods, where successive waves of immigrants first settled in order to take advantage of industrial jobs. While pride in working class history and industrial heritage lends support to the idea of a just green enough future, the naturalization of the notion of "waves of immigrants" suggests that the Latinx presence in these communities may not be seen as an essential part of that future. This may legitimate a just green enough future where desirable and trendy industry can still exist – for example, craft brewing – but current immigrant communities will "naturally" be displaced as wealthier young professionals arrive. A counter-discourse arising from grassroots activism asserts that a just green enough future will also need to be "Latinx enough," i.e. cultural displacement is unacceptable, and brownfield redevelopment must serve and respect the cultural heritage of the Midwest's largest Mexican population.

In this chapter, I draw on interviews with community organizers, fieldwork in Pilsen and Little Village, a variety of recent and historical news items, and archival research on the history of these areas. This research illustrates both the tenacity of historical narratives about place and the shifts in discourse that occur as different immigrant groups re-shape place. Discourse produces what Foucault (1977) calls "truth effects," which structure what can be said, and done, about a particular problem. Interacting with and co-producing material, structural forces and effects, dominant narratives and counter-narratives work and re-work the limits of what might be imagined for Pilsen and Little Village. In order to assert a right to a say in redevelopment that will benefit existing residents, community organizations must denaturalize the "port of entry" narrative, as well as the notion that change – specifically, gentrification – is an inevitable aspect of the port of entry story. This case study offers an opportunity to enhance just green enough strategies through understanding the role of identity, and powerful discourses about identity, in shaping visions for just and sustainable redevelopment.

Working class identity and industrial pride in a "port of entry" area

The Lower West Side, which includes Pilsen, is considered Chicago's oldest working class neighbourhood (Pugh 1987). Beginning in the 1830s, massive public infrastructure projects like canals and railroads attracted European labourers to the area, particularly eastern Europeans, including Czechs, Poles, Slavs, Lithuanians, and Slovenians (Fernández 2012). By the 1870s there was a large concentration of Czech workers and Pilsen took its name from the Bohemian city (Pugh 1987). At that time, Little Village, adjacent to the southwestern edges of Pilsen, was known as South Lawndale/Crawford, and had been envisioned as an Anglo bourgeois suburb and farming community (Magallon 2010). Industry soon came along the canals and railroads, and eastern Europeans would eventually dominate that area as well. In both areas, thousands of people were employed in the leading industrial concerns of the day, including Commonwealth Edison (operating since 1903) and Western Electric Hawthorne (since 1924), the power plants that eventually became known as Fisk and Crawford. Other major industries included lumber yards, brewing, farm equipment manufacturing, and the garment industry.

This nexus of America's industrial growth was, unsurprisingly, the site of some of the earliest and most heated working class activism in the country. In 1877, the "Great Upheaval" nationwide railroad strike led to the infamous Battle of Halsted Street Viaduct, where nearly 30 workers were killed by police (Adelman 1983). The notorious Haymarket Square protests were organized at a rally in Pilsen after attacks on workers at the McCormick Reaper Plant (Adelman 1983). A massive 1910 garment industry strike occurred here as well, uniting women and immigrant workers (Pero 2011; Pugh 1987). As Pero (2011, 8) notes in his history of Pilsen, "Pilsen is all about work." Archival materials reveal that the news media often drew on similar tropes when discussing Pilsen: "Pilsen has always been a working man's [sic] neighborhood" (Kay 1964); or "industry has always been the lifeblood of Pilsen" (Casuso 1981). One hundred and fifty years later, it is not too much to suggest that a radical working class consciousness is embedded in the West Side. Planted and nourished by the socialist and free-thinking eastern Europeans, it has been continued and strengthened by the Latinx immigrant labouring communities over the past 70 years. As community organizers note, the long history of activism – hunger strikes, sit-ins, walkouts etc. – in the West Side has helped maintain working class communities for many decades.

In the 1950s and 60s Mexican laborers, who had begun arriving in Chicago during World War 1, and whose presence increased during and after World War 2, began to migrate to Pilsen and Little Village (Anderson and Sternberg 2013; Magallon 2010). Many were forcibly displaced from the Near West Side by urban renewal and slum clearance projects, including the expropriation of lands for expressways and a new Chicago campus for the University of Illinois. Others arrived from Mexico, Texas, and the southwest. Puerto Ricans also made up a small number of the migrants, although most moved to Humboldt Park and West Town (Fernández 2012). Pilsen sits just south of the Near West Side, and with its location close to key industries, was a logical settling place for those displaced and a port of entry for those newly arrived. South Lawndale/Little Village was considered a step above Pilsen for middle-class families (Pugh 1987; Fernández 2012). By this time, European families had begun leaving both of these crowded areas for more suburban locations. Dramatic racial succession occurred through the 1970s, and by 1980 about three quarters of both Little Village and Pilsen were identified as Mexican/Spanish-speaking (Fernández 2012). This marked change allowed for the notion of "waves of immigrants" through a "port of entry" area to take hold. To many, it seemed like a straightforward case of Chicago School-style neighborhood transition. The absence of any notable public conflicts between these waves also allowed the news media to consistently portray this succession as a peaceful evolutionary process. For example: "They have stayed in the old homes, and joined forces with new residents in a sudden upsurge of neighborhood pride" (Kay 1964). However, local tensions existed and Latinx residents felt the sting of racism. One community organizer recalled that when her Mexican parents first moved to Pilsen, some businesses had signs that read "no dogs or Mexicans."

The expanding Latinx community brought their own working class consciousness to the existing political milieu. Organizations focused on workers' and immigrants' rights were founded, as well as groups advocating for women's rights and for new schools in the area. Based on their recent experiences with the Near West Side, this consciousness included a sharply honed focus on the possibility of displacement, as well as concerns with the overcrowded and neglected conditions of the barrio: "the newcomers know only the unemployment and overcrowding – and the fear of displacement" (Casuso 1981). The spectre of gentrification (before it was labelled as such) could be discerned in the early 1960s, where fear of creating a "chic monster" like the gentrified Old Town neighborhood "haunts the Pilsenites" (Kay 1964). These material concerns articulated with the rising Chicano/a movement, which provided inspiration for local activists who wanted to nurture "a sense of pride in oneself, one's history, and one's indigenous roots" (Fernández 2012, 209). Pilsen was the centre for an emerging cultural nationalism and the embrace of a distinctively Mexican identity (Pugh 1987).

Concern for the working class nature of Pilsen and its industrial heritage could be seen in the late 1960s and 1970s, as the development of artists' lofts and studio spaces in older buildings led to fears that there would be a clash of industry versus artists. As a former Pilsen resident, John Podmajersky, set out to purposefully develop an artists' colony at the east end of Pilsen, some were wary: "Because he brings essentially middle-class people into a poor neighborhood, Podmajersky is seen as something of a threat by some of the organizations in the predominantly Latino neighborhood" (O'Hara 1979). In 1986, the former Schoenhofen Brewery site was given National Historic District Status (Wilke 1986), prompting worries that the site would be converted into artists' lofts, while many other industrial sites struggled to stay open and provide jobs. There were also fears of urban renewal projects coming to Pilsen: "Urban renewal is a dirty word to those who saw nearby Greek and Italian neighbors evicted from their homes to make room for the

University of Illinois," but "young intellectuals who like low rents and who want to be on the ground floor of exciting change ... are beginning to move in" (Kay 1964). These worries continued for decades, through the transition from eastern Europeans to Latinx populations: "Most of the Latinos moved to Pilsen because we could identify with the community. This time we will fight to stay" (Casuso 1981); and into the 1990s: "The university displaced the Latinos. Now, people are saying they were moved once and they're not going to be moved again" (Feely 1990).

Despite this recognition that the Lower West Side was concerned about displacement and urban renewal, the theme of "thriving on change" was also prevalent in the media. For example: "Gritty Pilsen, on the Near Southwest Side, has been a port-of-entry neighborhood for more than a century" (DeBat and Meyers 1989); "Pilsen for a century has been a gateway to America for immigrants" (Mabley 1977); and, "Pilsen is a vibrant neighborhood that revels in its own heritage. It pulses with the rhythm of change as it breathes history" (Midwest Generation 2003). In Little Village, similar demographic changes led to several name changes, from Lawndale-Crawford, to South Lawndale, and then Little Village. The latter was prompted as the adjacent North Lawndale, an African-American neighborhood, became nationally infamous as a devastated urban ghetto facing high unemployment, disinvestment, and crime (Magallon 2010). Locals now refer to Little Village as *La Vilita*, in homage to the dominant Spanish-speaking population. Like Pilsen, Little Village is viewed as an area where demographic change and racial succession is natural and simply part of its history.

The past identities of Little Village and Pilsen are never far away as both of these neighborhoods, albeit at different stages, grapple with gentrification in general, and the specific concerns that come with environmental cleanup (e.g. making the best use of brownfield sites). Pilsen has already experienced gentrification, with home values rising, influxes of white residents, and the loss of thousands of Latinx residents (Betancur and Kim 2016). Little Village is still zoned for heavy industry, but according to community organizers, there is lots of planning activity taking place at the city level – a sign that the city is paying attention to the neighbourhood and its potential. There has been some development and real estate pressure close to the Pink Line CTA stations here, as this route can take commuters into the Loop. A recent news story detailed the protests of seven families facing eviction from a Cermak Road apartment building that has been purchased by a developer (Serrato 2016). A resident noted: "I feel like we're going to go through the same changes that Pilsen is going through.... Compared to Pilsen, Little Village is affordable, but still, people can't afford to pay the rent. They're still struggling" (Huggins 2016).

Although gentrification is a present threat for both neighborhoods, residents hold tight to a working class identity. For example, former Pilsen Alliance leader Nelson Soza asserts: "Pilsen has been a historic immigrant and working class community, and many residents have been instrumental in the struggle for cleaner air, better schools and access to transportation" (Lulay 2015). Remarking on a piece of graffiti that read "memories are sacred," a journalist notes: "So many people, from

[Alderman] Danny Solis to [Pilsen Alliance leader] Byron Sigcho to whoever requested historical status for the warehouse in question, echo this graffiti's sentiment: that Pilsen's recent past, as a working-class, predominantly Latino area, is sacred and worth preserving" (Rice 2016). Efforts to "pump the brakes" on gentrification, as one community organizer put it, have focused on affordable housing initiatives in both areas designed to keep working class families in their homes (Cromidas 2016; Lulay 2015). In Pilsen, groups were successful in creating a zoning advisory committee in 2005, and they continue to pressure the Alderman and the city to "downzone" the area to limit high-rise, high-density development (Curran and Hague 2006).

But even as residents and leaders express concerns about gentrification, the "port of entry, thriving on change" trope threads through the discourse on gentrification. "Everyone agrees Chicago's Pilsen neighborhood is changing. Some embrace it while others dread it" (Torres 2016), suggests one report, echoing others that set up the gentrification debate as between those who fear change and those who welcome it. Repeatedly targeted with anti-gentrification graffiti, the Bow Truss coffee shop in Pilsen has become a symbol of this debate. The latest batch of graffiti included the phrase "white people out of Pilsen," prompting the media to seek comment on the inflammatory rhetoric. Narratives of naturalized change arise throughout, often focusing on the historical waves of immigrants: "Alderman Solis says, 'Pilsen has always been a community that's accepted different groups, different ethnic groups, different racial groups.' He's right. It began as an enclave for German and Irish immigrants, then became mostly Czech, Lithuanian and Polish. Latinos are the most recent newcomers" (Parker 2015). Other examples note that another transition is currently taking place: "Pilsen has been subject of gentrification concerns as demographics have shifted in recent years from a primary Mexican immigrant population. Folks have pondered the negative and positive effects on the community" (Selvam and Gerzina 2015); and, "Pilsen is known as a community with Mexican roots that's been changing in recent years" (Selvam 2015). A similar dynamic exists in Little Village, where fears of "spillover" gentrification from Pilsen lead residents to worry about rising rents, but also to speak about embracing change: "'I noticed that little by little, Asians, African-Americans and white people have been joining our community,' [resident Jesus] Zamudio said. 'I like that, because I don't want to be a part of only Mexicans, but I want to see other cultures around here'" (Huggins 2016). Community organizers in both neighborhoods are acutely aware of the tensions embedded in these processes: while being open to increased diversity, and acknowledging histories of demographic change, they need to assert the right to place of the working class Latinx communities that have defined these areas for three generations. Many mentioned the fear that the cultural appeal of Pilsen and Little Village as Mexican neighborhoods will be commodified. As one organizer put it, they do not want to see a Mexican neighborhood without Mexicans, a "place where white people can get drunk and wear a sombrero made in China." Over the last few months, these fears have been exacerbated by racist and sexist graffiti (e.g. "Rape Mexico") appearing repeatedly on a local church (Lulay 2016).

This discussion of the historical and continuing narratives about the character and identity of these two neighborhoods reveals a deep-rooted tension for those looking to just green enough strategies for redevelopment of the coal plant sites and other brownfields. While there is pride in the role of industry, a vibrant labour movement, and working class community building, the invocation of change as an equally important part of this history means that a desire to preserve and build on a working class heritage is not necessarily linked to preserving the Mexican and now broader Latinx working class community. When residents have been consulted about their desires for brownfield redevelopment, options such as green manufacturing, youth training sites, green energy production, waterfront access, recreation, and community space emerge as just green enough priorities. Environmental justice issues are key; heightened consciousness about environmental racism means that Pilsen and Little Village are not prepared to allow continued toxic exposures for the already-vulnerable populations here. However, Little Village community organizer Kim Wasserman-Nieto asserts, "Folks who fought for these things should be able to stay in the neighborhood and enjoy them" (Greenfield 2016).

Counter-discourses: De-naturalizing gentrification

With powerful narratives about the history and the inevitability of change in Pilsen and Little Village, those advocating for just green enough brownfield development are wary of the potential for displacement. In this case, class and race intersect as working class displacement would mean Latinx displacement. Neighborhood organizations are deeply conscious that the fight for affordability, jobs, and working class families is simultaneously a fight to preserve Latinx presence. This requires the articulation of a counter-discourse that denaturalizes "change," and in particular, the changes brought by gentrification. It also involves highlighting the intersection of gentrification with environmental racism. Two grassroots organizations, the Pilsen Alliance and the Little Village Environmental Justice Organization (LVEJO), have been highly active in environmental justice and anti-gentrification struggles. Not only were they instrumental in pushing for the coal plant closures, they are also leading the struggle to redefine the story of Pilsen and Little Village. Although each organization has its own philosophy and tactics, they are both determined to preserve the Latinx presence in the Southwest Side, and to achieve brownfield redevelopment plans that will explicitly serve this community.

Pilsen Alliance is a bilingual social justice organization that focuses on housing, public education, city government accountability, and health. Their strategies include "innovative community education tools and programs, direct action organizing campaigns and advocacy initiatives reflecting the popular education philosophy of building social consciousness for personal and social collective transformation" (Pilsen Alliance n.d.). Pilsen Alliance embraces the radical labour history of the Lower West Side, and respects the continuing presence of manufacturing industries. However, they have been concerned about the continued presence of polluting facilities and the toxic legacies of past industry in the area, and have made efforts to educate the community about the risks of toxins such as lead and heavy metals (Hawthorne 2015). Thus, their social and economic justice actions incorporate environmental concerns and the recognition that good jobs in Pilsen cannot come at the cost of human and environmental health.

One of their major missions is to raise awareness of what they call "planned gentrification" in an effort to counter the "change is inevitable" narrative. They argue that since the 1980s and 90s, transition has not been about waves of new immigrants finding homes in the West Side – it's about forcible displacement through the various machinations of aldermen, city hall, corporations, and universities that have long had redevelopment aspirations for this Loop-adjacent area. Pilsen Alliance works to challenge the idea that this kind of change is natural by making visible the plans, decisions, processes, and the exercise of agency and power involved. By contesting planning decisions, conducting research with local academics (Hague, Curran, and Pilsen Alliance 2008), and frequently challenging the pro-development alderman Danny Solis, they continue to "pump the brakes" on gentrification by pushing developers and decision makers to justify their plans to the community. Pilsen Alliance has also developed detailed Affordability Plans that offer a concrete alternative vision for the future of the neighbourhood, one where housing speculation is curtailed. This work is supported by consciousness-raising efforts such as door-to-door campaigns that seek to educate families about their rights as homeowners and tenants to challenge evictions and property tax increases. The slogans *"Pilsen no se vende"* ("Pilsen is not for sale") and *"no desplazamiento"* ("no gentrification/displacement") reflect Pilsen Alliance's commitment to the right to stay put.

Pilsen Alliance's role in fighting for the closure of the plants was to bring an explicit anti-gentrification ethic to the campaign. An Alliance leader noted that while the plant closure was massively important for the health of the area, keeping the focus on the smokestack is problematic. "What happens when it closes? How do you keep the same neighbors?" These are the more critical questions, because "Pilsen is a sanctuary neighbourhood" and displaced families will not find this community anywhere else. Engaging in long-term planning and analysis is necessary, especially given concerns expressed about ongoing corporate influence, the mayor's attempts to co-opt the environmental justice struggle and claim responsibility for the shut down, and the notorious lack of transparency in Chicago politics (Rice 2016). To this end, Pilsen Alliance negotiated a Community Benefits Plan with Midwest Generation designed to keep community concerns and needs at the forefront in a just green enough approach. One leader reminded me that the plants had played a huge role in the growth of the city, bringing electrification to much of the Southwest Side. Over time, they became associated with illness and death; now, they have an opportunity to play a new role as places of life and employment.

LVEJO brought issues of environmental racism into public consciousness with their campaign to clean up or close the coal plants (Lyderson 2014). Citing research and gathering community-based evidence for the disproportionate effects of air and water pollution on the racialized, low-income population of Little Village (Levy and Spengler 2001), LVEJO made it impossible for Chicago politicians to ignore the coal plants. They also conduct "Toxic Tours" of the area to educate locals and visitors about the different environmental and health concerns in their neighbourhood. The closure was a major campaign for LVEJO, though they simultaneously worked to convert a former EPA Superfund site into the area's only real park (La Vilita Park). LVEJO was also instrumental in developing the Paseo – a walking and biking trail connecting Pilsen and Little Village along disused train tracks that has itself raised controversy as a potential site of environmental gentrification, with examples such as Chicago's 606 trail and New York's High Line park serving as warning about the effects of property value increases near popular green trails. Although their primary framework is one of environmental justice, LVEJO is extremely aware of what one organizer called the "hidden costs of green space," as well as the potential for co-optation or greenwashing by politicians. These hidden costs include the possibility of gentrification, as Little Village may become perceived as more liveable. LVEJO's leaders anticipate that tax reappraisals will occur, and property values will rise. As former LVEJO Executive Director Kim Wasserman-Nieto has suggested, movements for economic and environmental justice cannot be segregated (Curran and Breitbach 2010). While the looming presence of the Cook County Jail and regular reports of gun violence in the area may counter gentrification pressures, activists remain vigilant about the danger that cleaning up the environment will lead to calls for other kinds of "cleanup," given the experiences of other Latinx communities in Humboldt Park (Wilson and Grammenos 2005; see also Betancur 2002; Wilson and Sternberg 2012).

To this end, LVEJO deploys a powerful discourse advocating for the right to stay and enjoy a cleaner neighborhood for those who fought for environmental cleanup after bearing the brunt of toxic exposures. One of their tactics is to use the language of sustainability in order to promote an anti-gentrification agenda. One organizer described their sustainability plans as actual "community rootedness plans" promoted under the guise of sustainability. The LVEJO 2015–2020 Strategic Plan (LVEJO 2014) focuses on issues such as climate adaptation and energy resiliency but insists that there must be a "just transition" away from the industrial economy that includes building on existing community strengths. The plan foregrounds neighbourhood self-determination principles, and focuses on better paying jobs, political representation, the existing local economy (formal and informal), and culture. This includes the community's own ideas for the redevelopment of brownfields such as the Crawford plant site, which might include a youth training campus and workforce development. Like Pilsen Alliance, LVEJO actively seeks to counter pernicious racialized narratives about change; for example, the idea that because Chicago is a global city, soft notions of diversity and racial mix should guide ideas about neighborhood change. Instead, LVEJO points out the ways in which these narratives justify the displacement of some groups of people. Here, as in Pilsen, a just green enough strategy must push back against subtle and not-so-subtle racialization tactics that position some groups as healthy and desirable, and others as disposable.

Conclusions: Contested just green enough futures

Hamilton and Curran (2013) discuss the role of "place-framing" as a potential catalyst for social movements. The construction of a collective neighbourhood identity can draw people into shared struggles such as urban environmental activism. The power of historical narratives to shape a sense of place is an important factor in how these struggles play out and in shaping the outcomes that are envisioned. Of course, collective identities are always contested. This Chicago case study offers a detailed look at how stories about the past can become stories about the future, and the ways in which these stories must be interrupted to broaden the scope of just and sustainable environmental redevelopment. Just green enough futures are bound up with a neighborhood's sense of where it has come from, and the ways that activists choose to draw on (or re-envision) this past has implications for determining the priorities of a just green enough brownfield strategy.

In the case of Little Village and Pilsen, pride in working class identity and an industrial heritage provide an effective avenue for promoting continued blue-collar work in a less toxic environment. But the framing of these areas as existing in a state of continual ethnic and demographic change can generate indifference to the possibility of displacement. Here, awareness of the environmental racism of the industrial era is mobilized to generate a counter-narrative around *no desplazamiento*: the right to stay put. Activists insist that any just green enough future needs to be "Latinx enough." So what lessons might emerge from this case study for those studying and strategizing around just green enough ideals?

The existing literature on environmental gentrification notes that in some cases, "strategic alliances" (Hamilton and Curran 2013) across class, and among long-time residents and newcomers/gentrifiers, are effective in generating enough momentum to push for environmental cleanup while remaining sensitive to the economic concerns of working class communities (Curran and Hamilton 2012; Pearsall 2013). Hamilton and Curran (2013) suggest the category of "gentrifier enhanced environmental activism" to capture the nature of this alliance. In Pilsen, gentrification is widely recognized as an ongoing process and in Little Village, as a slowly encroaching threat (Wilson, Beck, and Bailey 2009). Should organizations such as Pilsen Alliance and LVEJO cultivate these strategic alliances to meet their environmental justice goals? Here, it is critical to consider the intersections of race and class with respect to environmental gentrification. Checker's (2011, 216) research in Harlem highlights the long history of neighborhoods' "simultaneous greening and whitening" and warns about the danger of co-optation of oppositional anti-racism groups into "less threatening" political movements such as environmentalism. Essoka (2010) found that racial minority groups were more likely to experience displacement after brownfield redevelopment. The rhetoric of "cleanup" is also problematically implicated in racialized policing and incarceration practices related to the war on drugs and zero tolerance policies. Wilson and Grammenos (2005) illustrate how this discourse facilitated Latinx displacement in Chicago's Humboldt Park, lessons that Pilsen and Little Village activists take to heart.

The uneven vulnerability to displacement across race and ethnicity suggests that any such strategic alliances should be led by people of color and must prioritize the claim that environmental gentrification is itself a kind of environmental racism. Efforts must be made to guard against the uncritical romanticization of an industrial era that fails to recognize the racist consequences of the by-products of industrial activity, or to advocate for racial justice as central to just green enough visions. As this Chicago case study illustrates, neighborhood identity shaped through historical narratives is a powerful force in normalizing a just green enough future, but identities are inherently exclusionary. Care must be taken to ensure that, just as environmental claims cannot wipe out economic need, economic need cannot wipe out racial justice.

References

Adelman, W.J. 1983. *Pilsen and the West Side: A Tour Guide*. Chicago: Illinois Labor History Society.

Anderson, M.B., and C. Sternberg. 2013. "Non-White" Gentrification in Chicago's Bronzeville and Pilsen: Racial Economy and the Intraurban Contingency of Urban Redevelopment. *Urban Affairs Review* 49(3): 435–467.

Betancur, J. 2002. The Politics of Gentrification: The Case of West Town in Chicago. *Urban Affairs Review* 37(6): 780–814.

Betancur, J. and Y. Kim. 2016. *The Trajectory and Impact of Ongoing Gentrification in Pilsen*. Report of the University of Illinois Planning and Policy Department. Chicago: University of Illinois Planning and Policy Department.

Byrne, J., and R. Scattone. 2001. Community Participation Is Key to Environmental Justice in Brownfields. *Race, Poverty and the Environment* 3(1): 6–7.

Casuso, J. 1981. Pilsen – Port of Entry for Newest Americans. *Chicago Sun-Times*, October 2. Chicago History Museum Research Center Archives (Chicago Communities, Lower West Side, Pilsen).

Checker, M. 2011. Wiped Out by the "Greenwave": Environmental Gentrification and the Paradoxical Politics of Urban Sustainability. *City & Society* 23(2): 210–229.

Cromidas, R. 2016. Pilsen is getting 45 new affordable housing units. *Chicagoist*, February 11. http://chicagoist.com/2016/02/11/pilsen_is_getting_45_new_affordable.php

Curran, W., and C. Breitbach. 2010. Notes on Women in the Global City: Chicago. *Gender, Place and Culture* 17(3): 393–399.

Curran, W., and E. Hague. 2006. *The Pilsen Building Inventory Project*. Chicago: DePaul University Department of Geography.

Curran, W., and T. Hamilton. 2012. Just Green Enough: Contesting Environmental Gentrification in Greenpoint, Brooklyn. *Local Environment* 17(9): 1027–1042.

Dale, A., and L.L. Newman. 2009. Sustainable Development for Some: Green Urban Development and Affordability. *Local Environment* 14(7): 669–681.

DeBat, D. and G.S. Meyers. 1989. Gritty Pilsen Excels as Neighborhood That's "Port of Entry." *Chicago Sun-Times*, July 21. Chicago History Museum Research Center Archives (Chicago Communities, Lower West Side, Pilsen).

Dooling, S. 2009. Ecological Gentrification: A Research Agenda Exploring Justice in the City. *International Journal of Urban and Regional Research* 33(3): 621–639.

Midwest Generation. 2003. El Mosaico Pilsen: The Voice of Pilsen's Heritage. Chicago History Museum Research Center Archives (Chicago Communities, Lower West Side, Pilsen).

Essoka, J. D. 2010. The Gentrifying Effects of Brownfields Redevelopment. *The Western Journal of Black Studies* 34(3): 299–316.

Feely, M. 1990. The Richness is the Entire Neighborhood. *Chicago Tribune*, June 1. [News clipping]. Chicago History Museum Research Center Archives (Chicago Communities, Lower West Side, Pilsen).

Fernández, L. 2012. *Brown in the Windy City: Mexicans and Puerto Ricans in Postwar Chicago*. Chicago: University of Chicago Press.

Fisk and Crawford Reuse Task Force. 2012. *Final Report*. Prepared by the City of Chicago's Mayor's Fisk and Crawford Reuse Task Force. Delta Institute.

Foucault, M. 1977. *Discipline and Punish: The Birth of the Prison*. 1st American ed. New York: Pantheon Books.

Greenfield, J. 2016. Little Village Residents Hope Paseo Won't Be a Path to Gentrification. *Chicago Reader*, March 23. http://www.chicagoreader.com/chicago/little-village-pilsen-paseo-displacement-fears/Content?oid=21527919

Hague, E., W. Curran, and Pilsen Alliance. 2008. Contested Chicago: Pilsen and Gentrification/ Pilsen y el aburguesamiento: Una lucha para conservar nuestra comunidad. Newberry Library Chicago Archives.

Hamilton, T., and W. Curran. 2013. From "Five Angry Women" to "Kick-Ass Community": Gentrification and Environmental Activism in Brooklyn and Beyond. *Urban Studies* 50(8): 1557–1574.

Hawthorne, M. 2015. Pilsen Residents Kept Waiting for Cleanup of Toxic Lead Contamination. *Chicago Tribune*, October 6. http://www.chicagotribune.com/news/local/breaking/ct-pilsen-epa-lead-cleanup-20151006-story.html

Huggins, H. 2016. Little Village Residents Welcome Diversity, Fear Rising Rents. *Medill Reports Chicago*, January 27. http://news.medill.northwestern.edu/chicago/little-village-residents-welcome-diversity-fear-rising-rents/

Kay, V. 1964. Pilsen's Fighting to Hold the Fort. *American*, February 2. [News clipping]. Chicago History Museum Research Center Archives (Chicago Communities, Lower West Side, Pilsen).

Lee, S., and P. Mohai. 2012. Environmental Justice Implications of Brownfield Redevelopment in the United States. *Society & Natural Resources* 25(6): 602–609.

Levy, J., and J.D. Spengler. 2001. Estimated Public Health Impacts of Criteria Pollutant Air Emissions from Nine Fossil-Fueled Power Plants in Illinois. Harvard School of Public Health Report, prepared for Clean Air Task Force. http://www.catf.us/fossil/problems/power_plants//

Lyderson, K. 2014. Closing the Cloud Factories: Lessons from the Fight to Shut Down Chicago's Coal Plants. *Midwest Energy News* [Chicago, IL]. https://midwestenergynews.atavist.com/closingthecloudfactories

Lulay, S. 2015. As Gentrification Continues, Pilsen Alliance Plans Meeting on Housing. *DNA Info Chicago*, November 12. https://www.dnainfo.com/chicago/20151112/pilsen/as-gentrification-continues-pilsen-alliance-plans-meeting-on-housing

Lulay, S. 2016. "Rape Mexico," Swastika Scrawled on Pilsen Church Window, Pastor Says. *DNA Info Chicago*, March 30. https://www.dnainfo.com/chicago/20160330/pilsen/rape-mexico-swastika-scrawled-on-pilsen-church- window-pastor-says

Little Village Environmental Justice Organization (LVEJO). 2014. *LVEJO 2015–2020 Strategic Plan*. Chicago: LVEJO.

Mabley, J. 1977. Pilsen. *Today*, April 22. [News clipping]. Chicago History Museum Research Center Archives. (Chicago Communities, Lower West Side, Pilsen).

Magallon, F.S. 2010. *Images of America: Chicago's Little Village – Lawndale-Crawford*. Charleston, SC: Arcadia Publishing.

O'Hara, D. 1979. Pilsen's Low Cost Lofts Draw Artists. [News clipping]. Chicago History Museum Research Center Archives. (Chicago Communities, Lower West Side, Pilsen).

Parker, M. 2015. Pilsen Coffee Shop Hit Again by Anti-Gentrification Graffiti. *CBS Chicago*, October 27. http://chicago.cbslocal.com/2015/10/27/pilsen-coffee-shop-hit-again-by-anti-gentrification-graffiti/

Pearsall, H. 2013. Superfund Me: A Study of Resistance to Gentrification in New York City. *Urban Studies* 50(11): 2293–2310.

Pero, P.N. 2011. *Images of America: Chicago's Pilsen Neighborhood*. Charleston SC: Arcadia Publishing.

P.E.R.R.O. 2012. Fisk Power Plant Remediation and Redevelopment. Report prepared by Architecture for Humanity. Chicago: Architecture for Humanity.

Pilsen Alliance. n.d. About Us. http://www.thepilsenalliance.org/about-us/

Pilsen Alliance. 2013. Mission. http://www.thepilsenalliance.org/about-us/

Pugh, R. 1987. Pilsen/Little Village. *Chicago History Magazine* XXVI(1), Spring.

Rice, M. 2016. Can Anyone Stop Pilsen From Gentrifying? *Chicagoist*, June 28. http://chicagoist.com/2016/06/28/can_anyone_stop_pilsen_from_gentrif.php

Selvam, A. 2015. Bow Truss in Pilsen Again Roasted with Anti-Gentrification Graffiti. *Chicago Eater*, October 26. http://chicago.eater.com/2015/10/26/9616294/bow-truss-pilsen-more-gentrification-graffiti.

Selvam, A. and D. Gerzina. 2015. UPDATED: Bow Truss Pilsen's Windows Covered with Anti-Gentrification Signs. *Chicago Eater*, January 23. http://chicago.eater.com/2015/1/23/7879503/bow-truss-pilsen-with-signs-gentrification

Serrato, J.. 2016. Little Village Tenants Protest Evictions: "We Will Not Be Gentrified!" DNI Info Chicago, August 17. https://www.dnainfo.com/chicago/20160817/little-village/little-village-tenants-protest-evictions-we-will-not-be-gentrified

Sternberg, C., and M.B. Anderson. 2014. Contestation and the Local Trajectories of Neoliberal Urban Governance in Chicago's Bronzeville and Pilsen. *Urban Studies* 51(15): 3198–3214.

Torres, S. 2016. Rising Housing Prices Leading to Demographics Shift in Pilsen. *CBS Chicago*, April 13. http://chicago.cbslocal.com/2016/04/13/rising-housing-prices-leading-to-demographics-shift-in-pilsen/

Wernau, J. 2012a. Midwest Generation to Close 2 Chicago Coal Plants Early. *Chicago Tribune*, May 2. http://articles.chicagotribune.com/2012-05-02/news/chi-midwest-generation-to-close-2-chicago-coal-plants-20120502_1_fisk-and-crawford-coal-plants-environmental-groups

Wernau, J. 2012b. Closure of Chicago's Crawford, Fisk Electric Plants Ends Coal Era. *Chicago Tribune*, August 30. http://articles.chicagotribune.com/2012-08-30/business/chi-closure-of-chicagos-crawford-fisk-electric-plants-ends-coal-era-20120830_1_fisk-and-crawford-midwest-generation-coal-plants

Wernau, J.. 2014. Redevelopment Ahead for Chicago's Two Coal Plant Sites. *Chicago Tribune*, December 1. http://www.chicagotribune.com/business/ct-crawford-fisk-sites-1130-biz-20141126-story.html

Wilke, D.E. 1986. Pilsen Neighborhood Thrives on Change Over the Years. *Chicago Tribune*, June 8. [News clipping]. Chicago History Museum Research Center Archives. (Chicago Communities, Lower West Side, Pilsen).

Wilson, D., and D. Grammenos. 2005. Gentrification, Discourse, and the Body: Chicago's Humboldt Park. *Environment and Planning D: Society and Space* 23: 295–312.

Wilson, D., D. Beck, and A. Bailey. 2009. Neoliberal-Parasitic Economies and Space Building: Chicago's Southwest Side. *Annals of the Association of American Geographers* 99(3): 604–626.

Wilson, D., and C. Sternberg. 2012. Changing Realities: The New Racialized Redevelopment Rhetoric in Chicago. *Urban Geography* 33(7): 979–999.

12

BRING ON THE YUPPIES AND THE GUPPIES! GREEN GENTRIFICATION, ENVIRONMENTAL JUSTICE, AND THE POLITICS OF PLACE IN FROGTOWN, L.A.

Esther G. Kim

Introduction

What does "just green enough" look like in a neighborhood confronted with a future of large-scale greening? How do the politics of place, identity, and environmental justice factor into community resistance to green gentrification? This chapter addresses these questions by presenting the story of urban environmental change and community activism in Elysian Valley, a small neighborhood in Los Angeles. Caught between deindustrialization of the Northeast Los Angeles area and the ambitious undertaking of restoring the Los Angeles River, the neighborhood must contend with the uncertainty of shifting socio-ecological conditions. As the growing critical literature on eco-/environmental gentrification and urban sustainability demonstrates, the reframing of gentrification as inner-city "revitalization" or "regeneration," combined with the hegemonic status of "sustainability" as an indisputable urban policy agenda results in ignoring or obfuscating the ways in which vulnerable populations are displaced, marginalized, and rendered invisible, as well as depoliticizing the ways in which these unjust sociospatial relations are reinforced (Checker 2011; Slater 2011).

In this chapter, I show how these processes threaten the neighborhood of Elysian Valley, but also illustrate how members of the community respond to the environmental changes they see transpiring in the spaces of their everyday lives. Rather than passively accept these changes as the natural outcomes of urban policy or ecologically sound scientific practice, residents and stakeholders actively work to improve their neighborhood conditions by practicing a place-based politics that attempt to re-politicize the formation of place, *their* place. This politics of place involves construction of a collective identity grounded in histories and memories of neighborhood transformation. In this way, the Elysian Valley community practices a political activism based around mobilizing allies, appealing to policymakers, and increasing visibility, but also promulgating particular narratives of place that highlight previous injustices inflicted upon them. As occupants of a place that has historically been saddled with spatial injustices, residents and stakeholders present the identity of a community that has long been disregarded, devalued, and given little power to control their environmental conditions. Strategically utilizing this place-based identity can and does challenge environmental injustices as well as the depoliticizing effects of sustainability discourses that present gentrification as natural outcomes of "green" urban policies.

This chapter is based on two years of ethnographic fieldwork in Los Angeles, during which I interviewed residents, community stakeholders, policymakers, environmental activists, and agency representatives, all of whom were involved in the politics of the L.A. River as well as the neighborhood. I also attended meetings hosted by both community groups and government offices, participated in various neighborhood events, and photo-documented the neighborhood landscape. In addition, I analyzed numerous policy reports, planning documents, news articles, and other texts relating to Elysian Valley, Los Angeles, and the L.A. River. As a result, this chapter is a deeply ethnographic account of how green gentrification unfolds and is resisted in one particular place.

Greening Frogtown: Deindustrialization, restoration, and gentrification

The neighborhood of Elysian Valley is located within the northeast portion of the city of Los Angeles, approximately five miles northwest of downtown. It is bounded by two major freeways and also lies adjacent to the channelized Los Angeles River. Though the neighborhood is formally named Elysian Valley, it is more commonly known as Frogtown, due to past events of frogs swarming the neighborhood (McMillan 1987). The population is racially, ethnically, and socioeconomically diverse, and is home to many intergenerational families. Annexed into the city in 1910, the area was historically settled by a mix of White and Mexican residents; recent census data shows a majority Latinx population with considerable numbers of Whites and Asians.[1] Though frequently characterized as a working class community, Frogtown hosts a range of income levels and professions, as there are high percentages of both low-income and higher-income households (Mapping LA n.d.). A variety of professional and blue-collar workers, as well as an active informal economy in food service, carpentry, and automobile repair, all contribute to the diverse class makeup (Leung and Lamadrid 2015). Industrial development significantly shaped land use patterns in Northeast Los Angeles (NELA), as railroad tracks, railyards, manufacturing, and processing facilities claimed the cheap, plentiful riverfront properties. NELA's industrial activity encompassed "ceramic and pottery manufacturing, clothing manufacturing, furniture manufacture, food processing, wholesale baking, metal working, and engine repair" (Historic Resources Survey Report 2012), and industries such as wholesale bakeries provided employment for hundreds of local residents (Hamilton 1987). In Elysian Valley, which the city's planning department describes as "most characterized by the decades-long co-existence of its equally viable and abutting residential and industrial uses," the majority of land is zoned residential, while industrially zoned tracts are found concentrated along the river in the northern half of the neighborhood (Los Angeles Department of City Planning 2004, I-4).

Over the past thirty years, a variety of economic, political, and cultural forces – operating at multiple scales – have reshaped Frogtown's landscape and demographics. Regional economic restructuring in a post-Fordist economy led to decentralization of industrial production in Los Angeles. In Elysian Valley, restructuring manifests in ongoing deindustrialization, as manufacturing and rail activity move out of the area, leaving behind unused facilities (Gordon 1985; Meltzer 2014). Entrepreneurial urban regimes seek to recapture the value of these obsolete industrial facilities by reinserting the immobile capital sunk into these fixed structures into new rounds of accumulation (Harvey 1985). This revalorization is encouraged and facilitated by local state intervention, in the form of land use policies, zoning changes, and other "adaptive reuse" measures that convert former industrial spaces into newly viable commercial and residential ones in hopes of attracting an urbane, "creative class" demographic (Ley 2003; Lloyd 2010; Zukin

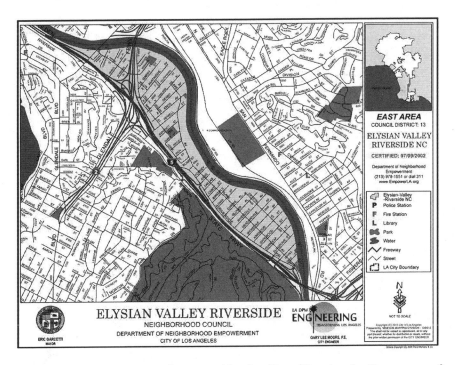

FIGURE 12.1 Map of Elysian Valley created by the City of Los Angeles Department of Public Works, Bureau of Engineering
Source: City of Los Angeles Department of Neighborhood Empowerment

1989). Among the adaptive reuse policies passed in Los Angeles, one enacted in 2004 specifically targeted manufacturing-zoned land in Elysian Valley, reclassifying land designated for "traditional industrial uses" into "modern," hybrid commercial-residential-light-manufacturing zones (Los Angeles City Planning Department 2007).[2] Meanwhile, neoliberal growth policies and urban regeneration strategies in L.A. spurred intense revitalization and redevelopment of downtown and arts districts, rebranding these neighborhoods as vibrant, culturally authentic, and livable (Marguardt and Fuller 2012; Molotch 1996; Vincent 2013). While these downtown arts districts underwent gentrification, NELA neighborhoods grew in locational appeal as they offered both proximity to important industry clusters (Hollywood, Wilshire Corridor, Downtown) and, due to historical patterns of disinvestment, relatively affordable housing prices (Lin 2015).

Due to its advantageous location, lower housing costs, and repurposed post-industrial spaces, Elysian Valley is positioned as an attractive neighborhood for displaced artists, young professionals, and small-scale craft producers seeking affordable yet creatively-viable places to live and work. One brewery owner explained that he moved into the neighborhood because "the area was also full of the kinds of creative spaces we like: old warehouses at affordable prices" (Sagahan and Saillant 2014). Other artists, designers, and architects echoed this appeal. The recent influx of younger, middle-class, and creative professionals does not go unnoticed among existing residents. One longtime homeowner elucidated the potential downside to the neighborhood's rising desirability among artists:

> Anytime there has been… an artist enclave[,] that's a death wish right there. Because that means your neighborhood is going to be flipped over, and prices are going to go up…. When they flipped downtown – where are those people going to go? They needed big spaces to work; we were a little rundown community. When [manufacturing] had to leave… they moved out of the area, leaving big factories open and that's why the artists came here.
>
> *(Interview, 7/26/13)*

Another resident, who had lived in the neighborhood for over 30 years, remarked upon the demographic change he observed:

> Today's renters are a whole different group. It's no longer the Hispanic family or it's no longer the Asian family. It's the Anglo up-and-coming hipster…. This is a more educated group who can afford to come in and pay greater rent than others might.
>
> *(Interview, 7/16/13)*

Though many of the residents I spoke with did not explicitly use the term "gentrification," what they described in regards to land use change, desirability, and the shifting racial/socioeconomic status of newcomers all allude to Elysian Valley becoming gentrified.

Then, there is the Los Angeles River. Long regarded as an important feature in the neighborhood, its recently elevated status as a sustainability initiative undertaken by local, state, and federal agencies signals the intensified addition of an ecological component to Elysian Valley's gentrification (Bryson 2013; Dooling 2009; Quastel 2009). Improvement projects along the river, such as parks, bike paths, and artwork, began to be built in the mid-1990s, with many more planned/proposed. These enhancements position the river as a highly desirable urban amenity, particularly within those NELA neighborhoods (including Elysian Valley) located along a less-channelized and therefore more aesthetically/ecologically vibrant stretch of the river. Moreover, in September 2013, the U.S. Army Corps of Engineers released its Ecosystem Restoration Feasibility Study, a seven-year study undertaken by both the federal flood control agency and the city of Los Angeles to investigate opportunities to restore riparian ecosystems along eleven miles of the L.A. River. In 2014, L.A.'s mayor and Congress adopted Alternative 20 of the study, which is the most extensive restoration alternative laid out in the report (Sagahun 2014). If approved, this restoration program dedicates over $1 billion in federal and city funds to construct greening and development projects along the river.

Since the announcement of the adoption of Alternative 20, a flurry of riverside real estate transactions have occurred in Frogtown. The promise of over a billion dollars of public investment dedicated to restoring the L.A. River appears to increase the rent gap of riverside land, prompting developers to buy up properties in order to capitalize on this future value (Smith 1996). Data from the Los Angeles County Office of the Assessor shows that "between October 2011 and December

FIGURE 12.2 Rendering of restored reach of Los Angeles River at Taylor Yard
Source: U.S. Army Corps of Engineers Ecosystem Restoration Feasibility Study Draft Report

2014, 39 commercial/industrial properties have changed ownership in Elysian Valley. Of these 39 properties, 10 are river adjacent. Five of those acquisitions of river-adjacent properties took place in 2014" (Leung and Lamadrid 2015, 17). An architecture firm reported that "15 out of 30 riverfront properties have been sold in [2013–2014]"; meanwhile, another real estate firm reports that "more properties along the river have changed hands than any year since 2001" (Lubbell 2014). New construction projects and development proposals have materialized with greater frequency. In the northern half of the neighborhood, construction for a residential complex of 56 condominiums is already underway, while a project involving the conversion of industrial storage buildings into 40 live/work units and 15,000 feet of commercial space is undergoing environmental impact reviews (Eastsider 2014a; Jao 2015). Meanwhile, both former bakery facilities are under redevelopment. One facility, vacated in 2004, was recently purchased by a real estate developer who proposed converting it into a multi-use complex that includes 117 residential units (Los Angeles City Planning Department April 2015). Another major facility was purchased in 2014 by the owners of a high-end interior design company hoping to adapt the building into commercial/retail space (Eastsider 2014b).

The greening of the Los Angeles River is not regarded by all in Frogtown as an uncontested good. The recent real estate transactions around riverfront properties have heightened residents' concerns, as they regard environmental improvements to the river as an accelerant to the gentrifying patterns already taking place. Confronted with the current reality – and future prospect – of rising land values, residents foresee an increase in displacement of lower-income residents and renters. According to one homeowner, who had lived in Elysian Valley his whole life:

> You have gentrification in full force, and that has its good things and that has its bad things.... The downside is you do lose a sense of the old community, because people are priced out.... We do see that we have lost people who have historically been here for many years, generations at times, because they simply could not afford to live here any longer. And I think that's one of the tragedies of that.
>
> *(Interview, 7/16/13)*

Other residents described future restoration projects as likely to spur displacement of the more vulnerable subset of the neighborhood population. One concluded that there is "just no question that [gentrification's] gonna happen here in this neighborhood," which would primarily impact "the rents for the low-income apartments here" (Interview, 7/23/13). Residents are not alone in voicing these concerns. Environmentalists and activists describe the recent real estate activities as constituting "a land grab," a "land boom," and "enormous speculation" (Sagahun and Sailant 2014; Zahniser 2015). Since 2013, there has been a noticeable upsurge in media coverage of the threat of gentrification related to river restoration (Hayden 2014). Certain city bureaucrats and agency representatives I spoke with acknowledged that river improvements could – and do – contribute to resident displacement. Even the Army Corps study recognizes that restoration would be harmful to certain groups, reporting that while projects could "act as a catalyst for the renewal and redevelopment/beautification of adjacent commercial, industrial, business, and residential properties," "minority renters would be negatively impacted due to rent increases, which could potentially displace minority and special interest group residents" (USACE 2013, 107–108). Therefore, there is acute awareness of the possibility that restoration of the L.A. River could further compound the gentrifying forces that make Elysian Valley less livable for the most vulnerable.

Nevertheless, restoring the L.A. River is touted as a win-win situation for Los Angeles. Planning reports and soundbites from elected officials draw upon and reinforce discourses of urban sustainable development, with their claims of achieving ecological health, economic growth, and social equity through targeted measures and projects. Planning reports such as the Army Corps study or the city's 2007 revitalization master plan lay out how river restoration not only creates/restores valuable ecological habitat/function and promotes community development, but also creates thousands of jobs, increases property values, and stimulates other economic activity. However, "urban sustainability" often means the execution of environmental agendas through market-driven growth strategies, which are ultimately laden with contradictions and unable to adequately address the uneven development perpetrated by capitalist urbanization (Isenhour et al. 2015; Krueger and Gibbs 2007; While et al. 2004). Yet the unjust outcomes of these agendas are obscured or ignored through the pernicious depoliticization of urban processes carried out under the mantle of achieving "sustainability," that absolute and incontrovertible good (Swyngedouw 2009). Indeed, environmental gentrification, one such unjust outcome, remains so threatening because it:

> operates through a discourse of sustainability which simultaneously describes a vision of ecologically and socially responsible urban planning, a "green" lifestyle which appeals to affluent, eco-conscious residents, and a technocratic, politically neutral approach to solving environmental problems.
>
> *(Checker 2011, 212)*

Environmental policymaking around the L.A. River reflects a reliance on market-based strategies of achieving urban sustainability (Browne and Keil 2000). This sanitizing and depoliticizing of green gentrification is demonstrated in a statement by L.A.'s mayor, who promised to "capture what's good" with revitalization while working to "mitigate what is the bad side of gentrification" (Jao 2014). For those in Elysian Valley threatened with displacement, however, there is little of "what's good" to be found.

Community activism and place-based identity: Re-politicizing environmental change

Confronted with urban environmental change, the residents of Elysian Valley respond by engaging in a form of activism that strategically uses histories of place and place-based identity. According to Pulido, "place-based identities are not static or unitary, but are multiple and changing", and the formation of particular place identities are "acts of resistance on the part of the subordinated" (1997, 19–20). These processes of place-making and identity formation can play significant roles in communities' resistance to and mobilization against various forms of marginalization (Anguelovski 2014; Martin 2003; Pena 2003) In Elysian Valley, residents engage in resistance against environmental injustices by forming and performing a particular place-based identity that invokes specific narratives of neighborhood transformation. These narratives, which chronicle histories of spatial injustice and infrastructural neglect,[3] are employed in the construction of a collective identity, a Frogtown "community" that has long been politically disempowered and excluded from decision-making and planning processes at all levels. By deploying this community identity, residents strive to politicize their place, an endeavor which I argue is crucial to challenging the naturalizing and stultifying rhetoric of environmental gentrification.

In Elysian Valley, community identity is informed by a collective history of place, in particular the narratives of spatial injustices experienced by the neighborhood. These injustices came in the form of large-scale, state-sponsored infrastructural projects that displaced households, demolished community spaces, and disrupted residents' day-to-day lives. The channelization of the Los Angeles River in the 1930s by county and federal agencies, executed under the banner of flood control, caused massive ecological destruction, removed huge swathes of potential public greenspace, and established a watershed management regime that prohibited access to the river, effectively criminalizing the historically established interactions between riverside resources and communities (Davis 1998). Another case of spatial injustice is the demolition of Chavez Ravine, a once close-knit Mexican-American community, in the mid-1950s (Masters 2012). Designated by the city as the site, first, for new public housing and then later for Dodger Stadium, residents of Chavez Ravine were forcibly removed from their homes and displaced from their neighborhood, many without the replacement housing promised by the city (Laslett 2015). Reportedly, a large number of displaced Chavez Ravine residents moved into nearby Elysian Valley, thus forging a racialized historical-spatial connection between the two neighborhoods, as the history of Chavez Ravine is partially absorbed into the history of Elysian Valley (Simpson 2014). In addition, the place history of Elysian Valley is shaped by the collective memory held by residents of freeway construction in the 1950s and 1960s. The Interstate 5 freeway runs through Elysian Valley alongside Riverside Drive, one of the neighborhood's main arterial roads. Residents claim that freeway construction displaced homeowners, divided family/community networks, crippled local commercial businesses, and further physically isolated a neighborhood already bounded by a flood control channel and another freeway (Interview, 7/11/12). To many, the freeways symbolize the government's blatant disregard for their well-being, a deep-seated sentiment shared by other communities decimated by freeway construction (Avila 2014). The place history of Frogtown is explicitly raced and classed, and the community's rootedness to that place politicizes their everyday lived experiences.

The clearest illustration of how place identity is performed and strategically utilized in community activism is the neighborhood's ongoing conflict with the Metrolink Central Maintenance Facility (CMF). Built in 1992 at the former Southern Pacific railyard site on the east side of the L.A. River, the CMF is a maintenance railyard owned and operated by Metrolink, a regional commuter rail system. While, in 2001, residents began to voice concerns over plumes of smoke, harsh smells, and disruptive, late-night noises coming from the CMF, it was not until 2011 that considerable mobilization against Metrolink arose. Community members argued that diesel particulate matter from train engine emissions contributed to higher rates and risk of asthma and pulmonary illnesses. They demanded that Metrolink adopt cleaner practices while also funding a community health risk assessment, that regulatory agencies enforce stricter air quality standards and monitoring practices, and that there be greater community involvement in decision making over CMF operations. Mobilization took the form of residents appealing to elected officials, hosting community meetings, setting up a website, reaching out to media outlets, and partnering with environmental organizations (Northeast LA Residents for Clean Air). Through these targeted actions, community members reiterated the environmentally unjust nature of the CMF, a facility sited without proper environmental review among nonwhite, immigrant, and lower-income/working class neighborhoods (Jao 2013). Through interviews, website updates, and statements at public meetings, neighborhood activists brought up past injustices in order to stress several claims: that a clear pattern of disregard and disrespect has historically been imposed upon the community, that these projects intentionally targeted politically disempowered neighborhoods, and that residents are already impacted by the environmental burden of emissions from two major freeways. The siting of the CMF was a continuation of the injustices imposed upon them and their place.

The conflict with Metrolink demonstrates how a collective place-based identity is integral to community activism against environmental injustice in Frogtown. Residents and stakeholders reveal the bitter and brutal politics entangled in the formation of their place in order to expose the unequal power relations and exclusionary planning practices that they believe have long dictated the production of their everyday environments. By uncovering the highly politicized processes that go into shaping their neighborhood – and highlighting the gross spatial injustices that resulted from them – community activists demand greater inclusion in determining how those planning processes should proceed. Therefore, what community members in Frogtown push for is environmental justice that extends beyond the equitable distribution of environmental burdens and goods to also encompass greater participatory access to decision making, based on the recognition that underlying political-economic processes produce places inflicted with multiple forms of denigration (Walker 2009). Demands for recognition and participation represent a politics of place that merge identity, territory, and lived experience, and further provide opportunities for challenging other forms of environmental injustice, such as environmental gentrification.

Substantive community resistance to environmental gentrification remains in early stages in Elysian Valley, yet there is potential for strategic deployment of place-based identity in order to re-politicize processes of neighborhood change. The neighborhood's struggle against the Metrolink CMF offers valuable lessons on engaging in effective activism, including the necessity of alliances between older and newer residents, and countering assumptions that urban policies are politically neutral. Mobilization was successful partly due to the combined capabilities of older residents, who embodied the experience and knowledge of living with pollution, and newer residents, who possessed the higher social capital, access to resources, and English language skills to bring political attention to the problem (Jao 2013). Through concerted efforts, older residents carrying the lived memory of past injustices were able to access the right avenues for voicing their experiences, while newer residents were allowed to lay claim to narratives of historical injustice in Frogtown by virtue of inhabiting that place and adopting its place-based identity. This dynamic was seen during one meeting where a newer resident connected the construction of the I-5 Freeway to the siting of the CMF to claim that his community was continually targeted.

Cooperation between newer and older residents is therefore critical to resisting the encroachment of environmental gentrification in Elysian Valley. According to Curran and Hamilton (2012, 1028), strategic alliances/partnerships among longtime residents and newcomers can be potentially effective in opening up "new spaces of politics for sustainability" that resist the "model of a green city" that "quite literally 'naturalizes' the disappearance of working-class communities". Newer residents, those perceived as "gentrifiers," need to ally themselves with their working class neighbors. In the past several years, the social infrastructure able to facilitate these alliances has undergone promising growth, arguably assisted by the anti-CMF activism. The Elysian Valley Neighborhood Watch (EVNW) hosts regular meetings that allow community members to interact with one another through the shared concern of neighborhood safety and cooperation with police. Events such as the monthly "neighborhood beautification" days hosted by the EVNW provide opportunities for residents to feel involved with the community through improvement projects such as cleanups and plantings. Another notable organization, the Elysian Valley Arts Collective, likewise strives to establish a sense of community by hosting meetings and social events for longtime and newly moved-in artists. The Arts Collective began hosting the Frogtown Artwalk, an annual neighborhood art festival, in an attempt to build community ties between artists and residents. Now a popular NELA event, the Artwalk celebrates and advertises Frogtown's creative and colorful character, thus representing ongoing efforts by many toward establishing an artist community and shaping neighborhood identity.

There is also the official neighborhood council – Elysian Valley Riverside Neighborhood Council (EVRNC) – that has in recent years intensified their role in overseeing neighborhood affairs, liaising between the community and state offices,

FIGURE 12.3 Advertising for the Frogtown Artwalk. Created by Shawn Freeman for the Elysian Valley Arts Collective

and facilitating outreach and interaction among diverse residents. The EVRNC, composed of an eclectic mix of residents and other stakeholders, exemplifies how both old and new community members can begin to mobilize around the heightening threat of environmental gentrification. In 2012, the council formed their Environment and Land Use Committee, a group dedicated to monitoring and actively participating in land use changes. Along with investigations into environmental nuisances, this committee closely monitors new development projects slated for various riverfront properties. The neighborhood council then formed an ad hoc displacement committee in 2015, largely in response to the growing concerns that river restoration could possibly displace low-income residents and renters. Most notably, in 2014 the EVRNC proposed modifying zoning regulations in order to stymie rampant riverfront development. In partnership with their district councilmember, the EVRNC hopes to pass an ordinance that would tighten building/design restrictions (known as "Q Conditions") in certain industrially zoned lands adjacent to the L.A. River. Specifically, existing Q Conditions would be updated to reduce the maximum permissible building height, require new buildings to occupy no more than 50% of the lot area, reduce the amount of standard residential development, and reduce building density by lowering the floor-area-ratio (Los Angeles Department of City Planning, August 2015). Despite performing varied tasks, the council's central objective is greater participation in the environmental planning of the neighborhood. The committee and councilmembers work toward fostering strong relationships with elected officials, public agencies, and other planning entities in order to cultivate a well-informed, policy-literate neighborhood constituency, and to acquire increased access to decision-making procedures. During meetings and workshops, residents repeatedly emphasized the critical need to be informed and included by agencies, given the neighborhood's history of enduring decades of disrespect and disregard by them.

These arguments – namely, that increased community control over planning and policymaking is crucial to avoid repeating past injurious experiences – directly and indirectly draw upon Frogtown's place history and the identity of its community members as embodying those experiences. Residents attempt to incorporate Frogtown's history of spatial injustice into the emerging narrative of gentrification's encroachment upon riverside neighborhoods to justify their fears of displacement, and justify their desire for restricting riverfront development. In recent news articles examining the rising land values and development pressures along the L.A. River, Elysian Valley residents refer to freeway construction and the history of Chavez Ravine as reasons for their community's fear of displacement; one interviewed resident declares that with restoration projects, "people who live here won't be able to afford it anymore" which is "particularly sad considering so many of the people here are the ghosts of Chavez Ravine" (Sagahun and Saillant 2014; Simpson 2014). Similar statements are shared in meetings and events. In 2014, two stakeholders commissioned a neighborhood design firm (LA Más) to gather information on present and future issues related to river restoration and land development in Elysian Valley. Through data collected from a series of public meetings, interviews, and community workshops, LA Más produced a report (*Futuro de Frogtown*) documenting residents' major concerns and presenting recommendations on how future planning in Frogtown could ameliorate those concerns. The report found that among many longtime and lower-income residents, there was genuine fear of displacement due to gentrification. In meetings among community members and conversations with planning department representatives, these residents invoked the painful, politicized place history of Elysian Valley, fraught with incidents of spatial injustice, in arguments against gentrification and market-based riverside development. In particular:

> Long time residents expressed concerns about yet another predominantly low-income Latino neighborhood being neglected... Those who had moved to Elysian Valley after the tragic events of Chavez Ravine, when families were displaced by eminent domain in the 1950's... especially felt the sentiment. *The events of Chavez Ravine serve as a reason as to why developers should not be allowed to shape their neighborhood....* Many residents believe the process of constructing new housing stock in the neighborhood could lead to displacement similar to that of Chavez Ravine.
>
> (Leung and Lamadrid 2014, 27, emphasis added)

Fearful of displacement and distrustful of government agencies, these residents rally behind the place-based identity of being a community long experienced with forcible removal, government disregard, and unjust development practices. In doing so, they reinsert the highly fraught politics of place formation into dialogues around

FIGURE 12.4 Murals of frogs in Elysian Valley, along the Los Angeles River

urban greening and disrupt the naturalizing and neutralizing discourses embedded in environmental gentrification. Re-politicizing place is crucial. While efforts to use "smart growth" as a strategic urban planning tool to counter the glut of large-scale development complexes that could crop up alongside the river have brought subsets of the community together around a common cause, the discussion around gentrification and the L.A. River cannot stray too far from the concerns of the most vulnerable populations.

Conclusion

The case of Elysian Valley illustrates how residents form and utilize a place-based identity that highlights the environmental and spatial injustices held in collective memory, and further helps to re-politicize their lived environments so that they remain "just green enough." Through collective action, residents of Frogtown carry out a just green enough strategy that involves fighting air pollution and demanding cleaner industrial land uses while still resisting rampant redevelopment carried out in the name of sustainability. For those who live and work in Elysian Valley, just green enough does not mean limiting the actual greening of their place, as residents have long appreciated, used, and formed attachments to the Los Angeles River and express desires for it to become ecologically healthy once more. To them, a just green enough strategy involves receiving more information, being included in planning processes, and finding the means to exert control over the environmental conditions in which they live, work, and play. The formation of a community identity that is informed by, among other things, place-based histories of injustice and exclusion can strategically challenge the depoliticized discourse of urban sustainability and green gentrification. As there is still uncertainty about how the neighborhood will be reshaped by pressures brought about by the L.A. River restoration, challenging depoliticization is vital. More work is needed toward building alliances between newer, middle-class professionals and older, working class families, and expanding community resistance to gentrification through demands for more affordable housing. All members of the Frogtown community must embrace a strategy of just green enough that entails challenging what could become yet another moment of spatial injustice – this time in the form of environmental gentrification – from occupying a place in their neighborhood history.

Notes

1 By 1980, the census reported that Elysian Valley's population was 59% Latino, 22% Asian, 18% White, and 1% Black (McMillan 1987). According to 2000 census data, the racial breakdown was reported as 61% Latino, 25.6% Asian, 9.7% White, 1.1% Black, and 2.6% as Other (Mapping LA n.d.). In 2009, data reports that the northern half of the neighborhood is 68% Latino and 7% White, while the southern half is 46% Latino, 12% White, and 34% Asian (USACE 2013).

2 Some key policies include: a 1981 Artist-in-Residency ordinance that allowed live/work units in existing industrial/commercial buildings in areas zoned for manufacturing, a 1999 Adaptive Reuse Ordinance that "relaxed zoning code requirements for the conversion of pre-1974 existing commercial and industrial buildings into residential uses" first for downtown districts, and then for the rest of the city (Los Angeles Department of City Planning 2009, 3), and a 2010 amendment ordinance re-classified the zoning of adaptive reuse spaces from commercial to residential (Los Angeles City Ordinance 18113).

3 Residents frequently pointed out the lack of adequate infrastructure throughout the neighborhood, such as street lighting, sidewalks, and adequate sewer lines.

References

Anguelovski, I. 2014. *Neighborhood as Refuge: Community Reconstruction, Place Remaking, and Environmental Justice in the City.* Cambridge: MIT Press.

Avila, E. 2014. L.A.'s Invisible Freeway Revolt: The Cultural Politics of Fighting Freeways. *Journal of Urban History* 40(5): 831–842.

Browne, D.R. and R. Keil. 2000. Planning Ecology: The Discourse of Environmental Policy Making in Los Angeles. *Organization & Environment* 13(2): 158–205.

Bryson, J. 2013. The Nature of Gentrification. *Geography Compass* 7(8): 578–587.

Checker, M. 2011. Wiped Out by the "Greenwave": Environmental Gentrification and the Paradoxical Politics of Urban Sustainability. *City & Society* 23(2): 210–229.

Isenhour, C., G. McDonogh, and M. Checker (eds). 2015. *Sustainability in the Global City: Myth and Practice.* New York: Cambridge University Press.

Curran, W. and T. Hamliton. 2012. Just green enough: Contesting environmental gentrification in Greenpoint, Brooklyn. *Local Environment* 17(9): 1027–1042.

Davis, M. 1998. *Ecology of Fear: Los Angeles and the Imagination of Disaster.* New York: Metropolitan Books.

Dooling, S. 2009. Ecological Gentrification: A Research Agenda Exploring Justice in the City. *International Journal of Urban and Regional Research* 33(3): 621–639.

The Eastsider. January 7, 2014a. Riverside development taking shape in Elysian Valley. http://www.theeastsiderla.com/2014/01/riverside-development-taking-shape-in-elysian-valley/.

The Eastsider. February 3, 2014b. Modernica furniture owners take over former Twinkies bakery. https://www.theeastsiderla.com/2014/02/modernica-furniture-owners-takeover-former-twinkies-bakery/.

Gordon, Larry. November 17, 1985. Economy, Modernization Quiet Rail Yard. *Los Angeles Times*, pg. SG8.

Hamilton, D. 1987. Business Just Keeps Rising for L.A.'s Bakeries. *Los Angeles Times*, May 3, WS6.

Harvey, D. 1985. *The Urbanization of Capital: Studies in History and Theory of Capitalist Urbanization, Vol. 2*. Oxford: Blackwell.

Hayden, T. June 11, 2014. Will the Trickle Become the L.A. River? And for Whom? KCET. http://www.kcet.org/socal/departures/columns/green-justice/will-the-trickle-become-the-la-river-and-for-whom-tom-hayden-peace-and-justice-resource-center.html.

Historic Resources Survey Report: Northeast Los Angeles River Revitalization Area. June 2012. Prepared by Historic Resources Group and Galvin Preservation Associates for City of Los Angeles Community Redevelopment Agency.

Jao, C. February 5, 2013. Elysian Valley Residents Speak Out About a Silent Threat. *KCET*. http://www.kcet.org/socal/departures/lariver/confluence/rivernotes/elysianvalleyr esidents speakoutaboutasilentthreat.html.

Jao, C. June 2, 2014. Mayor Garcetti Addresses Gentrification Concerns Along L.A. River. *KCET*. https://www.kcet.org/confluence/mayor-garcetti-addresses-gentrification-concerns-along-la-river.

Jao, C. February 18, 2015. Riverfront "creative campus" coming to Elysian Valley. KCET. https://www.kcet.org/earth-focus/riverfront-creative-campus-coming-to-elysian-valley.

Krueger, R. and D. Gibbs (eds.) 2007. *The Sustainable Development Paradox: Urban Political Economy in the United States and Europe*. New York and London: Guildford Press.

Laslett, J.H.M. 2015. *Shameful Victory: The Los Angeles Dodgers, the Red Scare, and the Hidden History of Chavez Ravine*. Tucson: University of Arizona Press.

Leung, H. and M. Lamadrid. 2015. Futuro de Frogtown Report. *LA Mas*. http://www.mas.la/futuro.

Ley, D. 2003. Artists, Aestheticisation and the Field of Gentrification. *Urban Studies* 40(12): 2527–2544.

Lin, J. 2015. Gentrification, Boulevard Revitalization, and Authentic Urbanism in Northeast Los Angeles. Paper presented at the Annual Meeting of the American Sociological Association. Chicago, IL.

Lloyd, R. 2010. *Neo-Bohemia: Art and Commerce in the Postindustrial City*. London: Routledge.

Los Angeles City Planning Department. 2007. *Recommendation Report for the City Planning Commission, LA River Lofts*.

Los Angeles City Planning Department. April 23, 2015. *Initial Study/Mitigated Negative Declaration for Blake Avenue Riverfront Project*. Prepared by Parker Environmental Consultants.

Los Angeles Department of City Planning. July 9, 2009. *Recommendation Report*. City of Los Angeles. http://cityplanning.lacity.org/StaffRpt/InitialRpts/CPC-2009-1771.pdf.

Los Angeles City Ordinance 18113. Council File No. 9–1845. Adopted April 1, 2010.

Los Angeles Department of City Planning. 2004. *Silver Lake-Echo Park-Elysian Valley Community Plan*. City of Los Angeles. http://planning.lacity.org/PdisCaseInfo/Home/Get GeneralPlanningDocument/MTE20.

Los AngelesDepartment of City Planning. August 13, 2015. *Recommendation Report for the City Planning Commission on Q Conditions*.

Lubbell, S. November 14, 2014. Growing Pains: Some Worry as Development Explodes along the Los Angeles River. *The Architect's Newspaper*. http://www.archpaper.com/news/articles.asp?id=7661#.VS4mUfnF_hk.

Mapping LA. n.d. *Los Angeles Times*. http://maps.latimes.com/neighborhoods/neighbor hood/elysian-valley/.

Marguardt, N. and H. Fuller. 2012. Spillover of the Private City: BIDs as a Pivot of Social Control in Downtown Los Angeles. *European Urban and Regional Studies* 19(2): 153–166.

Martin, D.G. 2003. "Place-Framing" as Place-Making: Constituting a Neighborhood for Organizing and Activism. *Annals of the Association of American Geographers* 93(3): 730–750

Masters, N. September 13, 2012. Chavez Ravine: Community to Controversial Real Estate. *KCET*. https://www.kcet.org/shows/lost-la/chavez-ravine-community-to-controversial-real-estate.

McMillan, Penelope. March 8, 1987. Elysian Valley: Frogtown Holds Bucolic "Secret" Minutes from Downtown L.A. *Los Angeles Times*.

Meltzer, J. February 2, 2014. Viewpoints: What Is Next in Frogtown's Future? *The Eastsider*. https://www.theeastsiderla.com/2014/02/viewpointsisfrogtownnextinlinetobegentrified/.

Molotch, H. 1996. LA as Design Product: How Art Works in a Regional Economy. In Scott, A.J. and E.W. Soja (eds). *The City: Los Angeles and Urban Theory at the End of the Twentieth Century*. Berkeley: University of California Press.

Pena, D.G. 2003. Identity, Place and Communities of Resistance. In Agyeman, J., Bullard, R.D., and B. Evans (eds). *Just Sustainabilities: Development in an Unequal World*. Cambridge: MIT Press.

Pulido, L. 1997. Community, Place, and Identity. In Jones, J.P., H.J. Nast, and S.M. Roberts (eds). *Thresholds in Feminist Geography: Difference, Methodology, Representation*. Lanham: Rowman and Littlefield.

Quastel, N. 2009. Political Ecologies of Gentrification. *Urban Geography* 30(7): 694–735.

Sagahun, L. May 28, 2014. Army Corps to Recommend $1-Billion L.A. River Project. *Los Angeles Times*.

Sagahan, L. and C. Saillant. May 24, 2014. Big Plan, and Concerns, Surround L.A. River's Revitalization. *Los Angeles Times*.

Simpson, I. August 20, 2014. L.A.'s Hottest New Neighborhood, Frogtown, Doesn't Want the Title. *LA Weekly*.

Slater, T. 2011. Missing Marcuse: On Gentrification and Displacement. *City* 13(2–3): 292–311.

Smith, N. 1996. *The New Urban Frontier: Gentrification and the Revanchist City*. London and New York: Routledge.

Swyngedouw, E. 2009. The Antinomies of the Postpolitical City: In Search of a Democratic Politics of Environmental Production. *International Journal of Urban and Regional Research* 33(3): 601–620.

USACE (United States Army Corps of Engineers). 2013. *Ecosystem Restoration Feasibility Study Report, August 2013. Appendix B: Economics*.

Vincent, Roger. 2013. Commercial Real Estate Quarterly Report; Gaining Traction; Trendy shops, eateries, and offices transform downtown L.A.'s arts district. *Los Angeles Times*, January 20, B1.

Walker, G. 2009. Beyond Distribution and Proximity: Exploring the Multiple Spatialities of Environmental Justice. *Antipode* 41(4): 614–636.

While, A., A.E. Jonas, and D. Gibbs. 2004. The Environment and the Entrepreneurial City: Searching for the Urban "Sustainability Fix" in Manchester and Leeds. *International Journal of Urban and Regional Research* 28(3): 549–569.

Zahniser, D. March 26, 2015. Remaking a Landscape; Costs Flood in for River Revamp: L.A.'s tab for restoration could reach $1.2 billion, but officials hope to share burden with U.S. more evenly. *Los Angeles Times*.

Zukin, S. 1989. *Loft Living: Culture and Capital in Urban Change*. New Brunswick: Rutgers University Press.

13

THE CONTESTED FUTURE OF PHILADELPHIA'S READING VIADUCT: BLIGHT, NEIGHBORHOOD AMENITY, OR GLOBAL ATTRACTION?

Hamil Pearsall

Introduction

This chapter tells the story of Philadelphia's Reading Viaduct, a dilapidated, contaminated, and defunct rail line at the northern border of the city's gentrifying center. Proposed to become a linear park similar to the High Line in New York City, this vision has been supported and contested by multiple actors over the last decade. Advocates argue that the park will help repopulate an abandoned, industrial neighborhood, provide a cost-effective reuse of the rail infrastructure, add much-needed green space to the neighborhood, and put Philadelphia on the map of cities with an elevated park, while opponents see the rail to park conversion as inconsistent with local needs. Opponents and skeptics raise concerns about investing such attention and resources into a "park in the sky" aimed at a middle- to upper-class, largely white audience without addressing what they see as more pressing needs on the ground, such as blight, safety, and affordable housing, or acknowledging the greening projects that longtime residents have done, including ongoing neighborhood cleanups, neighborhood park creation, and extensive tree planting campaigns. This debate reveals a controversy about what it means to be "just green enough" in a place with different and often competing notions of a safe, livable, and attractive neighborhood.

Though previous research has examined resistance to environmental gentrification through activism and large-scale acts of resistance (Pearsall 2013; Hamilton and Curran 2013; Checker 2011; Anguelovski 2015), as well as smaller-scale everyday actions to resist the negative impacts of gentrification (Pearsall 2012; Sandberg 2014; Lugo 2015), "just green enough" describes a process through which coalitions of neighborhood activists and gentrifiers find common ground in discussions of environmental remediation and greening and attempt to create a just process of neighborhood change (Curran and Hamilton 2012; Wolch, Byrne, and Newell 2014). A just green enough process inspires hope for alternatives to classic cases of environmental gentrification observed in neighborhoods in New York, Austin, Philadelphia, Boston, and Toronto (Checker 2011; Essoka 2010; Dooling 2009; Pearsall 2010; Bunce 2009; Kern 2015), and Curran and Hamilton (2012) observed this collaborative activism in their study of the remediation of the industrial waterfront in Greenpoint, New York.

This study questions what just green enough is in a neighborhood with diverse needs and associated visions of neighborhood change. In Philadelphia, advocates of the rail park envision it as part of an exciting initiative to catalyze positive change and revitalization across the neighborhood. Opponents of the park see this piecemeal approach to redevelopment as a harbinger of widespread gentrification driven by speculative development. Park opponents exercised their opposition by defeating a key bill proposed to City Council that would tax current residents to generate funding for park and neighborhood maintenance. This successful challenge, which came together over fears of gentrification as opposed to environmental awareness, is significant because it highlights the potential of vulnerable residents with little political power – particularly within the neoliberal context – to have an impact, reveals the pervasive inequities associated with the privatization of public space and parks (Madden 2010; Loughran 2014; Reichl 2016), and highlights the importance of an inclusive and comprehensive approach for a just green enough process. This chapter relies on a content analysis of 65 newspaper articles published about the proposed rail park in local (e.g. The Philadelphia Inquirer) and national news-papers (e.g. The New York Times) from 2000 to 2015 to capture dominant discourses of neighborhood change and the potential of the park to revitalize the neighborhood, as well as six interviews with key stakeholders conducted in summer and fall 2015 to include the direct experiences of those leading the coali-tion to create the park and the counternarratives from those questioning its role in the neighborhood.

A proposal for an elevated linear park in Philadelphia

The Reading Viaduct opened in 1893 and saw its final commuter train cross the tracks in 1984 (Center City District 2015). The viaduct, north of Philadelphia's bustling commercial center known as Center City, became overgrown with vegetation. The neighborhood around the viaduct has historically been industrial, surrounded by coal yards and iron foundries, among other industries. As Philadelphia experi-enced its industrial decline through the 1970s, the Reading Company divested of some of its properties in Philadelphia, invested in a California entertainment firm, and moved its offices out of Philadelphia in 2000. In the 1990s, there was discussion of demolishing the viaduct to remove the source of blight in the neighborhood and reclaim oddly shaped lots that abutted the elevated rail for housing and commercial redevelopment, an initiative that the Chinatown community strongly supported as they sought to expand their geographic boundaries into the area with extensive vacant land (Interview 5). The decision to purchase the viaduct was postponed during an administrative change, and Reading continued to hold the land that remained unused, overgrown, and contaminated with PCBs and lead.

While the viaduct conversation stalled in City Hall, community dynamics continued to evolve. The neighborhood around the viaduct has had three different names, concurrently in use by different organizations, companies, and communities: the Loft District (preferred at one time by real estate professionals), Callowhill (preferred by residents in the neighborhood who tended to be aligned with the viaduct park conversion), and Chinatown North (preferred by those with connections to Philadelphia's Chinatown community). The Chinatown North designation emerged in the 1990s as Chinatown, located to the south of the area surrounding the viaduct, grew. Several years later, the Callowhill designation was created when residents living in generally the same area decided to organize to oppose a proposal to place a baseball stadium in the neighborhood.

In 2004, two artists living near the viaduct, Sarah McEneaney and John Struble, created a non-profit organization called the Reading Viaduct Project to begin the process of converting the railway to an elevated park. The artists, who moved to the neighborhood decades ago in search of studio space, became motivated by elevated parks in other global cities, such as the Promenade Plantée in Paris and New York City's High Line. The founders of the Reading Viaduct Project stated that the park would help to attract more residents to the neighborhood and could become an attraction for all Philadelphians. The local paper, the *Philadelphia Inquirer*, invoked frontier language to describe the efforts of these residents to colonize and repopulate the area: "The Loft District's urban pioneers, who have been busy with their own reclamation of the area's abandoned factories, want to build on nature's work" (Saffron 2004). The park advocates described the challenges to creating the park, including extensive environmental remediation of the viaduct, gaining government support and funding, and acquiring the property from the Reading Company. Despite these challenges, they received support from the Friends of the High Line and piqued the interest of other groups and residents across Philadelphia (Interview 4).

Over the next five years, the nascent idea to convert the elevated line to a park quickly gained traction among city officials, businesses, and certain Philadelphians. The success of the High Line in New York City provided compelling evidence for the potential of economic revitalization, particularly to city officials who watched Philadelphia lose over a quarter of its population since 1950 and continue to suffer from persistently high unemployment and poverty (an estimated 15.1% and 26.5%, respectively, based on the 2013 American Community Survey data). The *New York Times* reported that the High Line, though costing $153 million to build, "generated an estimated $2 billion in new developments. In the five years since construction started on the High Line, 29 new projects have been built or are under way in the neighborhood, according to the New York City Department of City Planning. More than 2,500 new residential units, 1,000 hotel rooms and over 500,000 square feet of office and art gallery space have gone up" (Shevory 2011). The president of Philadelphia's Center City Business Improvement District announced to the local paper that he became an ardent supporter of the proposed rail park after seeing the High Line: "It was a complete turnaround for me" (Taylor 2010). The potential for the proposed park to stimulate economic development in a neighborhood with an estimated 32% vacancy rate as of the 2010s (according to the Center City District) motivated city officials who had been grappling with Philadelphia's financial woes for decades.

Voices of opposition

Voices of skepticism and opposition became stronger in 2009, particularly from those who stood to lose the most from the development. The Philadelphia Chinatown Development Corporation's (PCDC) executive director published an editorial in the local paper expressing his concern about the park given the neighborhood's other more pressing needs: "The city has a desperate and growing need for affordable housing, not only for seniors and families with children, but also for young people starting their careers. Is an elevated park and its resulting costs to maintain and clean an adequate response to this need?" (Chin 2009). In response to this editorial, an architectural critic published an article in the paper that compared the Chinatown neighborhood association to aggressive New York City developers. The critic lamented the potential loss of neighborhood character as a detractor for future development (Saffon 2009).

This depiction of PCDC's development vision is ironic given that the primary redevelopment interests of the Chinatown community was affordable housing. According to one board member of PCDC, they feared the potential division the neighborhood along class lines should the park be built: "What we don't want in Chinatown is these, um, financially well-off folks up top the rail park looking down on [a] low-income immigrant community" (Interview 5). The interviewee also pointed out the different needs of residents in the neighborhood, and the challenges that each group had in understanding the other's needs. He suggested that those with financial means may not understand the need for affordable housing, while those living under the poverty line may not prioritize the creation of a novel elevated linear park, though he mentioned several other neighborhood greening projects, including tree plantings, a local park and new green plaza that PCDC had spearheaded.

This lack of understanding played out in a few different ways, reinforcing the divide between park advocates and opponents and challenging the potential for a collaborative process. For instance, one interviewee, a former board member of PCDC, discussed the ways in which the Chinese community was overlooked in the planning process: "I found out they were having a charrette and was like, 'Oh, well, you are meeting over at PCDC to talk to them about what's going on'... 'Oh, we didn't think of them.' I am like, really? You are only talking to the people who live in the Callowhill, this small area, that want to see this thing become a park but not to... So of course they didn't, it was an afterthought, the Asian community. The Chinese community was an afterthought" (Interview 6). That the Chinatown community felt excluded from these early discussions is concerning. According to the 2010 Census, the neighborhood was comprised of 40% White, 35% Black, and 20% Asian residents (2010 US Census). Yet, park advocates who have been closely involved with the park's creation clearly state their commitment to community partnerships. For instance, one advocate listed six community partners that were actively involved (Interview 1). Further, several advocates enthusiastically reported that there were no opponents to the park proposal, citing the concerns of the Chinatown community only after some reflection.

The term "opponents" is potentially misleading, as many people who raised concerns about the park also saw room for compromise. For instance, although PCDC initially advocated for the demolition of the viaduct to allow for commercial and affordable residential development (Interview 5), others in the Chinatown community were receptive to the idea of incorporating the park – even portions of the viaduct – into a neighborhood plan that made space for affordable housing. In other words, they were supportive of a plan that integrated the visions of different perspectives in the neighborhood. Yet, as one interviewee recalled, over time it became apparent that the advocates of the park were not interested in pursuing the neighborhood plan:

> The folks, the original people, didn't really care. They said that's [affordable housing] not our issue, we are only concerned about the viaduct. We don't want to get involved in that conversation. We only want to develop a park. So, yeah, that's fine, but you can't do it in a vacuum. You know, that was like, I kept saying that, but they didn't... they weren't hearing that. And that's, you know, when we saw the brochure, and it said nothing about the properties around the viaduct – "Oh we want to develop this beautiful park up the in air" – and I'm going, you didn't get it, you really didn't get what we were saying. You could have addressed that up front, we would, I would have been supporting what they were doing.
>
> *(Interview 6)*

This reference to the park development happening in a vacuum is interesting and may well summarize the demise of the version of "just green enough" captured by the neighborhood plan.

The narrow focus on the rail park was confirmed in interviews with park advocates who reinforced that their goal was the development of the park, as opposed to the redevelopment of the neighborhood. They supported equitable development in general, yet did not think it was the responsibility of the park developers to play an active role in the neighborhood development (Interview 1). Another park advocate indicated that she didn't have expertise in affordable housing and therefore did not see it as her responsibility. However, all park advocates interviewed for the study agreed that the park's creation would necessarily have an impact on the surrounding neighborhood. Representatives from the Chinatown community found it exceedingly frustrating that the advocates of the park would not include some plans for the redevelopment of nearby sites that would include affordable housing. This disconnect between the Chinatown community and the park advocates continued to play out during subsequent discussions.

From idea to endorsed plan

The year 2010 marked a pivotal year for the proposed park. Paul Levy, president of the Center City District, started to work with Philadelphia's Commerce Department and the Department of Parks and Recreation to assess possible redevelopment opportunities. The consulting team reviewed options for demolition, renovation, and redevelopment alternatives, including an economic impact assessment on the surrounding community. The report posted on the Center City District's website indicates that demolition would be more expensive than renovation due to the extensive environmental remediation required of the viaduct (Center City District 2015). Capping the contamination on site and converting it into a park could save millions of dollars. The price tag of demolition was an estimated $50 million, yet park retrofitting was a mere $36 million. Further, it was estimated that real estate near the park would appreciate at a higher rate with the park's presence (Saffron 2011). Yet, as one interviewee with experience working with the City of Philadelphia and PCDC noted, the estimate does not include the potential financial benefits of the developable land that would be created through demolition, which could also include a park on the ground. According to the interviewee, this cost-estimate simply became "part of the narrative" to support the elevated park's construction.

The City of Philadelphia announced its support of the park in 2010 by referencing it in the city's new comprehensive plan (Philadelphia City Planning Commission 2016). The City sent representatives to Los Angeles, California, to negotiate purchase from the Reading Company (Saffron 2011) and engaged in a conversation with Philadelphia's regional transit authority about acquiring other portions of the viaduct for the park (Russ 2011f). While the demolition/environmental remediation approach appeared too costly for the City, the plans for the park fit squarely within their sustainability plan, released in 2009. This plan called for an increase of green space across the city and additional green infrastructure for stormwater management. Green2015, the roadmap for adding 500 acres of new publicly accessible green space by 2015, explicitly included the Reading Viaduct as a potential new park (Saffron 2010). While the goal of Green2015 was to increase greenspace, the city lacked funding to purchase 500 acres of privately owned land. Instead, the city planned to green government-owned land and to reclaim railroad right of ways. Though the goal of adding to add parks to underserved neighborhoods was not controversial, the local paper published an editorial that raised some concerns about the financial feasibility of long-term maintenance of the new sites: "While there's little regular maintenance needed for asphalt-paved playgrounds, every tract of grass, shrubs, and trees must be tended – as is all too evident in sometimes neglected parts of Fairmount Park. Even in thinking small about adding parkland, making the plans to look after those new green spaces will be a big deal" (Anonymous 2010). The issue of ongoing maintenance became a pivotal issue in the proposed rail park.

Voices of dissent became stronger in 2011. Witold Rybczynski from the University of Pennsylvania's School of Design articulated his concern in an editorial about the commercial and development potential of Philadelphia's Rail Park, seeing some key differences between the Reading Viaduct and the High Line: "The High Line may be a landscaping project, but a good part of its success is due to its architectural setting, which, like the 12th Arrondissement, is crowded with interesting old and new buildings. The park courses through the meatpacking district and Chelsea, heavily populated, high-energy residential neighborhoods. Very few American cities – and Manhattan is the densest urban area in the country – can offer the same combination of history and density" (Rybczynski 2011). Rybczynski compares the enthusiasm for elevated linear parks to other – failed – efforts to revitalize economically depressed urban areas like downtown shopping malls.

Several months later, the local paper published one of the first articles documenting local concerns about the rail park (Russ 2011d), conveying PCDC's concern about the elevated park creating the same types of community impacts as the High Line, namely, gentrification. The executive director of PCDC is quoted as reiterating the need for affordable housing, which the proposed rail park would likely not provide: "This puts pressure on low-income people... It creates gentrification for Chinatown." While advocates of the park agree that gentrification is happening in the neighborhood, they see it as a product of multiple factors: "I think the rail park will be blamed just like the High Line is blamed for Chelsea which is equally not true. But these things don't happen in a vacuum and, you know, the development, I mean it's those damned artists, they've moved into what is now Callowhill for 30 years and, um, development often follows artists" (Interview 2). It should be noted that this interviewee was not pro-gentrification of the neighborhood and supported an equitable development approach.

Local media reported that real estate developers targeted the "Loft District" because they saw the proposed rail park as an attraction: "Even in this depressed market, developers Mike and Matt Pestronk were drawn to the Loft District because of the viaduct. They are busy converting the former Goldtex building on 12th Street to 162 rental apartments. To promote the development, they plan to project video images of the viaduct on the building's south side, starting this weekend" (Saffron 2011). Further, one interviewee, an active advocate of the park, noted that he observed real estate professionals including references to the rail park in their marketing materials for residential properties for sale (Interview 1). This developer advocacy of the park illustrates the stark divide between what PCDC sees as community need – affordable housing and jobs – and what new residents see as a key goal of the park – attracting residents to the neighborhood to live and play in a renowned park.

Resistance to the rail park gains traction

Until this point in the discussion of the rail park, local community concerns seemed limited in their potential to have a meaningful impact on the outcome of the park. An editorial here and an article there, all subject to critique and ridicule by the ever-growing chorus of park advocates. The power dynamic between the voices of dissent – largely a low-income immigrant community – and park advocates – city officials, real estate developers, and residents with connections and means – seemed to point towards the inevitability of the park's development. Yet, a proposal to deal with the issue of long-term maintenance revealed the power of a neighborhood alliance to rein in the gentrifying potential of the park's development.

Like the High Line in New York, the proposed rail park would also be served by a "friends" group that would contribute to the cost of ongoing maintenance and programming beyond what the City's Department of Parks and Recreation is able to provide. Advocates of the park see this additional support as critical to the success of the park (Interviews 1 & 2). In April 2011, Councilman Frank DiCicco proposed the Callowhill Neighborhood Improvement District (NID) as a means to raise money, approximately $240,000 per year, by adding to the property taxes of residents living in the neighborhood surrounding the park. DiCicco claimed that the funds would not support the park's construction, but could potentially fund the park's ongoing maintenance. Proposals for NIDs or BIDs (business improvement districts) had been passed with minimal contention in 14 other neighborhoods in Philadelphia by 2011, and supporters of the Callowhill NID assumed that it would pass.

The contention surrounding the NID proposal highlights the importance of an inclusive process and comprehensive vision to truly be "just green enough." While DiCicco spent several months speaking with residents and generating support for the NID, many community members raised concerns about the tax burden and lack of notification and transparency regarding the process. As one concerned community member raised in an editorial: "The NID's tax applies to property owners who have already been hit with a 10 percent tax increase approved by City Council in May 2010 and a 3.85 percent tax increase approved in June 2011. What neighborhood can afford a 20.35 percent real estate tax increase during this recession?" (Anonymous 2011). Many other residents, from artists to local business owners, echoed this concern about the burden of another tax levied on their properties.

Additionally, many residents indicated that their interests were insufficiently represented by the tax. For instance, PCDC commented that Chinese-speaking residents were not consulted in the proposal for the NID (Russ 2011d). Another resident spoke out against City Council giving a small group of people the right to tax their fellow neighbors (Graham 2011). The local paper reported on the delayed notification of the proposal – many residents commented that they learned about it just one month before the hearing (Russ 2011e) – and concerns about the lack of transparency in the proposal: "There is tension over accusations that organizers haven't been clear about the purpose of the NID and how proceeds from a proposed 7 percent additional property-tax assessment for that neighborhood would be used" (Russ 2011b). One interviewee conveyed the sense of distrust about the NID: "'Oh, it has nothing to do with the viaduct,' but it always had to do with the viaduct. It was always about funding the maintenance of the viaduct and that was really the purpose, and they really should have said that" (Interviewee 6). The opponents of the NID felt misled by the process and the potential impact.

The NID is defeated

The contested identity of the neighborhood also played out in the debates over the NID and the proposed park. As one report summarized the divisions, residents that referred to the neighborhood as Callowhill generally supported the NID and those that opposed the NID referred to the area as Chinatown North (Russ 2011b). However, these divisions were oversimplified, and the debate sparked new alliances among long-time residents and new divides among older and newer residents. One resident, who opposed the NID, described the resulting tensions in terms of inclusion and exclusion in community decision making: "The conflict in our neighborhood began when a tiny group of loft-dwelling elitists decided to treat longtime residents and Asian business owners as though they were guests in their own neighborhood" (Russ 2011a). These new alliances, created through gentrification concerns as opposed to environmental ones, led to a powerful response to the proposal.

Upon learning of the strong opposition to the NID, DiCicco attempted to modify the proposal by removing two predominately Chinese blocks from the zone that would be taxed and reiterating that the funds would not necessarily be used for the park maintenance. However, these efforts did not adequately respond to the concerns. Media coverage described the efforts of a couple in the neighborhood, John and Maria Yuen, who rallied significant local political support to successfully defeat the NID following the September 2011 hearing. They partnered with PCDC to create the North of Vine Association to better represent all of the residents who opposed the NID: "The Yuens reached out beyond the Asian-American community – to help break down the perception that 'this was about the Chinese against the whites'" (Russ 2012). As reported, the couple knocked on doors and called landowners to discuss the NID and to see if more support for their cause existed. They found that the majority did support them. According to one resident in the area, owners of 57% of the taxable properties opposed the NID and filed letters of objection (Russ 2011c).

This defeat of the NID is significant for three key reasons. First, it marks an unprecedented moment of local community members rallying together to oppose a neighborhood tax advocated by a pro-development council person (Russ 2012). Second, it demonstrates the power of a minority voice to assert itself in a city-wide debate through official political channels, as the Mayor of Philadelphia vetoed the bill once the votes were tallied. The ability of this couple to forge new alliances in a highly divided neighborhood to oppose what they saw as a threat to their everyday wellbeing is powerful: "In the realms of politics and power in Philadelphia, unknowns like Maria and John Yuen aren't expected to win a stare-down against longtime former City Councilman Frank DiCicco and Paul Levy" (Russ 2012).

Third, it marks the point at which "just green enough" is realized in a highly contested environmental debate. While the defeat did not stop the park proposal, it eliminated a local tax on residents that posed a direct threat to some residents' ability to remain in the neighborhood. Additionally, the contested NID sent a strong message to city officials and advocates regarding the position and needs of certain community members, and the need for an inclusive planning process that accurately represents the needs and visions of all residents. This statement is important, as many advocates of the park assumed that most of the community supported it. This defeat made it clear that dissenting voices will influence the future development of the park.

Conclusion

This case study shows a complicated version of "just green enough," a scenario in which the power dynamic associated with the park's development is thwarted, just enough, to restrain what vulnerable residents see as a growing threat to the affordability of their neighborhood and to demonstrate the power of this alliance to influence the park's planning process. Yet, why was this planning process particularly contested and what reinforced the conflicts? Certainly, the competing visions of neighborhood change created a challenging setting for dialogue. On the one hand, the Chinatown community seeks affordable housing and commercial development to support the growth of the established Chinatown community. On the other hand, the Callowhill residents would like to reinvigorate the abandoned industrial neighborhood with amenities and people, and they see the rail park as a way to make it attractive to more Philadelphians. These different visions are not necessarily mutually exclusive, and it is interesting to consider why they became particularly at odds with each other.

One factor driving the conflict was the planning process. That residents in the Chinatown community felt excluded from certain conversations is certainly important, but also that the overarching plan to redevelop the neighborhood was different between the two groups. Advocates of the rail park aimed to create the park first and to let the neighborhood develop around the park. Park skeptics and opponents found this approach to be the critical problem, and one that could lead to unchecked gentrification. Instead, they advocated for designating certain parcels for particular land uses – specifically affordable housing and a commercial uses – so that development that followed the park's creation was part of a comprehensive neighborhood plan, rather than being dictated by real estate developers' vision for a profitable investment. While there had been some discussion with the Center City District about designating parcels adjacent to the viaduct for particular land uses, according to some interviewees, these ideas became lost in the rush to realize the park's vision. Further, certain advocates of the park commented that they didn't know about affordable housing or how to implement it (Interview 4). Park advocates were reluctant to commit to additional development that might slow the creation of the park. While this may seem hasty, it reflects Philadelphia's financial constraints and the limited funding available. For instance, although the Friends of the Rail Park envision, ultimately, converting several miles of rail into a park, they have only successfully acquired the land, support, and capital to cover one-fourth of a mile of park, called "Phase I." The estimated cost of Phase I is approximately $10 million, and advocates of the longer, linear park regard Phase I as a proof of concept and the knuckle to connect the future stretches of the park (Interview 2).

This piecemeal approach to neighborhood development, where the Friends of the Rail Park does "park development" and PCDC does "affordable housing," seems far more likely to generate conflict than a comprehensive neighborhood planning approach, and perhaps this is a lesson for "just green enough" solution in other contexts. As this case study shows, an environmental initiative that pays minimal attention to its social and economic impacts is likely to create strife, particularly in a neighborhood with diverse resident interests and perspectives on the future of the neighborhood. Unfortunately for Philadelphia, the political and economic climate has not been conducive to comprehensive neighborhood development approaches, despite formal efforts to generate plans, and contested areas like the Callowhill/Chinatown North community, as some diplomatically call it, demonstrate these challenges. The question remains as to whether the alliance that defeated the NID can be used to advance an alternative proposal for neighborhood development, or whether planning for the Rail Park will proceed with increasing support from those living outside its boundaries and occasionally shaped and impacted by residents seeking to reduce the negative impacts of the park's development.

References

Anguelovski, I. 2015. Alternative food provision conflicts in cities: Contesting food privilege, injustice, and whiteness in Jamaica Plain, Boston. *Geoforum* 58: 184–194.

Anonymous. 2010. Editorial: A bit of green is golden. *Philadelphia Inquirer*, 8 Dec.

Anonymous. 2011. Letters: In Chinatown, 2 nays for the Neighborhood Improvement District. *Philadelphia Inquirer*, 8 Nov.

Bunce, S. 2009. Developing sustainability: Sustainability policy and gentrification on Toronto's waterfront. *Local Environment* 14(7): 651–667.

Center City District. 2015. *The Viaduct Rail Park Project: Background & Overview 2015* [cited 26 Oct 2015]. https://www.centercityphila.org/about/viaduct.php.

Checker, M. 2011. Wiped out by the "greenwave": Environmental gentrification and the paradoxical politics of urban sustainability. *City & Society* 23(2): 210–229.

Chin, J. 2009. Letters to the editor. *The Philadelphia Inquirer*, 28 Jul.

Curran, W., and T. Hamilton. 2012. Just green enough: Contesting environmental gentrification in Greenpoint, Brooklyn. *Local Environment* 17(9): 1027–1042.

Dooling, S. 2009. Ecological gentrification: A research agenda exploring justice in the city. *International Journal of Urban and Regional Research* 33(3): 621–639.

Essoka, J.D. 2010. The gentrifying effects of brownfields redevelopment. *Western Journal of Black Studies* 34(3): 299.

Graham, T. 2011. Neighbors in evolving Callowhill section debate proposed tax. *Philadelphia Inquirer*, 21 Sept.

Hamilton, T., and W. Curran. 2013. From "five angry women" to "kick-ass community": Gentrification and environmental activism in Brooklyn and beyond. *Urban Studies* 50(8): 1557–1574.

Kern, L. 2015. From toxic wreck to crunchy chic: Environmental gentrification through the body. *Environment and Planning D: Society and Space* 33: 67–83.

Loughran, K. 2014. Parks for profit: The high line, growth machines, and the uneven development of urban public spaces. *City & Community* 13(1): 49–68.

Lugo, A. 2015. Can human infrastructure combat green gentrification? Ethnographic research on bicycling in Los Angeles and Seattle. In *Sustainability in the Global City*, edited by C. Isenhour, G. McDonogh, and M. Checker. New York: Cambridge University Press.

Madden, D.J. 2010. Revisiting the end of public space: Assembling the public in an urban park. *City & Community* 9(2): 187–207.

Pearsall, H. 2010. From brown to green? Assessing social vulnerability to environmental gentrification in New York City. *Environment and Planning C, Government & Policy* 28(5): 872.

Pearsall, H. 2012. Moving out or moving in? Resilience to environmental gentrification in New York City. *Local Environment* 17(9): 1013–1026.

Pearsall, H. 2013. Superfund me: A study of resistance to gentrification in New York City. *Urban Studies* 50(11): 2293–2310.

Philadelphia City Planning Commission. 2016. *Philadelphia 2035*. Philadelphia: City of Philadelphia.

Reichl, A.J. 2016. The High Line and the ideal of democratic public space. *Urban Geography* 37(6):904–925.

Russ, V. 2011a. Council OKs viaduct improvement district. *The Philadelphia Daily News*, p. 16, 18 Oct.

Russ, V. 2011b. Council to debate Callowhill clean-up plan. *The Philadelphia Daily News*, 20 Sept.

Russ, V. 2011c. Opponents claim backing to stop viaduct plan. *The Philadelphia Daily News*, 14 Dec.

Russ, V. 2011d. Some in Chinatown favor demolishing part of viaduct. *The Philadelphia Daily News*, 29 Aug.

Russ, V. 2011e. Viaduct clean-up plan taxing residents' patience. *The Philadelphia Daily News*, 21 Sept.

Russ, V. 2011f. Viaduct revival. *The Philadelphia Daily News*, 29 Aug.

Russ, V. 2012. Democracy 101: Callowhill NID foes went up against powerful forces… and won. *The Philadelphia Daily News*, 6 Feb.

Rybczynski, W. 2011. Bringing the High Line back to earth. *The New York Times*, 15 May.

Saffon, I. 2009. Changing Skyline: Reinventing a railroad; New York's abandoned High Line is being transformed into an elevated park that offers a new way to experience the city. *Philadelphia Inquirer*, 17 Jul.

Saffron, I. 2004. Making an old viaduct viable again; One possible use for the strone structure: An elevated park with fine views of the city. *Philadelphia Inquirer*, 20 Feb.

Saffron, I. 2010. City plans proliferation of small parks. *Philadelphia Inquirer*, 6 Dec.

Saffron, I. 2011. Changing Skyline: A park on high; The extension of New York's vibrant High Line sparks excitement for our own Reading Viaduct – what could be "a linear version of Rittenhouse Square." *Philadelphia Inquirer*.

Sandberg, L.A. 2014. Environmental gentrification in a post-industrial landscape: The case of the Limhamn quarry, Malmö, Sweden. *Local Environment* 19(10):1068–1085.

Shevory, K. 2011. After the High Line, old tracks get another look. *The New York Times*, 3 Aug.

Taylor, K. 2010. The High Line, a pioneer aloft, inspires other cities to look up. *The New York Times*, 15 Jul.

Wolch, J.R., J. Byrne, and J.P. Newell. 2014. Urban green space, public health, and environmental justice: The challenge of making cities "just green enough". *Landscape and Urban Planning* 125: 234–244.

14

INFORMAL URBAN GREEN SPACE AS ANTI-GENTRIFICATION STRATEGY?

Christoph D. D. Rupprecht and Jason A. Byrne

Introduction

Urban greening initiatives are underway in many cities internationally, intended to address issues associated with global environmental change (Brink et al. 2016). Urban greening has diverse drivers, scaling-up from the local to the global, including climate change, food security, mass migration, and rapid urbanization (Wolch et al. 2014). Urban greening activities also respond to revitalization initiatives (to attract new investment) and sometimes to community demands for better greenspace access. Greenspace accessibility is seldom uniform across urban areas and is typically socio-spatially differentiated (Rutt and Gulsrud 2016).

Histories of discrimination and unfair land use planning and land development practices can produce urban landscapes bereft of formal greenspace (Byrne and Wolch 2009). Over the past two decades, international research has found inequalities in the socio-spatial distribution of parks, recreation areas and urban forests (Anguelovski 2016). Levels of maintenance, facilities provision, variety of programming, crowding levels, and policing are often differentiated by socio-demographic characteristics (e.g. race, ethnicity, class, gender and (dis)ability) (Sister et al. 2010). Marginalized and disadvantaged communities tend to have lower levels of facilities provision and less access to formal greenspaces (e.g. parks, greenways, botanic gardens, etc). Researchers have also identified psychological barriers to greenspace access, which can negatively impact diverse communities (Shackleton and Blair 2013). Urban greening has become an environmental justice concern.

Recently, some researchers have observed that urban greening can trigger "environmental gentrification," further entrenching environmental inequalities (Checker 2011; Eckerd 2011; Kern 2015; Pearsall 2010). Environmental gentrification occurs when the conversion of brownfields to greenspace, provision of new greenspace, or redevelopment of existing greenspace drives up property values, because a location becomes more attractive to investors and/or more desirable for residents (Millington 2015; Quastel 2009). Increased desirability is partly attributable to the multiple ecosystem services and functions of greenspace (e.g. heat attenuation, stormwater interception, pollution reduction) and concomitant benefits that urban greening can confer upon urban residents (e.g. increased physical activity, improved mental health, improved property values) (Rutt and Gulsrud 2016). This begs the question: "What actions might be undertaken to redress the environmental-gentrification that accompanies greenspace provision?" Commentators have suggested interventions such as rent control, additional park provision or even environmental offsets (e.g. green roofs) (Wolch et al. 2014), but less attention has been given to the possibility of activating other urban spaces in what might be thought of as a "just green enough" strategy (Curran and Hamilton 2012). Informal greenspace is an example.

Informal urban greenspaces (IGS) such as vacant lots, street or railway verges, brownfields, and powerline corridors (Figure 14.1), are receiving renewed attention from researchers and greenspace planners alike (Rupprecht and Byrne 2014a; Rupprecht and Byrne 2014b; Rupprecht et al. 2015a; Rupprecht et al. 2015b; Rupprecht et al. 2016). In contrast to formal greenspaces, informal greenspaces have not been intentionally designed for parks, open space, recreation or community agriculture; rather the opposite. Informal greenspaces occur where a landowner's ambivalence or neglect has been exploited by (non)human agents, for instance where spontaneous vegetation (e.g. weeds) colonizes a site and attracts animals and people. Arguably, informal urban greenspace might better answer the needs of some urban residents, because it does not embody a particular cultural politics of nature. Scholars have noted that parks and gardens often instantiate philosophies of nature that undergird and legitimize particular socio-cultural projects (e.g. moral uplift, citizen fitness) (Byrne 2012). Indeed, Nohl (1990, 65) has asserted that informal greenspace provides the potential for a "provisional arrangement" that leaves room for both emancipated greenspace users and nonhumans because "it disciplines neither people in their actions nor nature in its development."

In this chapter, we draw upon political ecology and environmental justice perspectives to examine whether informal urban greenspaces (IGS) such as vacant lots, street or railway verges, brownfields, and power line corridors could meet residents' greenspace needs without triggering gentrification. Taking a cue from (Curran and Hamilton 2012, 1030), we ask how might alternative greenspace and/or green infrastructure "complicate gentrification and neoliberalisation"? Based on fieldwork in Japan and Australia we examine the location of IGS, its use by residents, and its potential impact on property values. We conclude that the IGS we have assessed does not exhibit the same patterns of socio-spatial (dis)advantage reported for many public parks. IGS appears to fulfill the needs of different types of urban residents while avoiding the financial demands of formal greenspace, which may require a "return on investment" (e.g. via property (re)development), thus potentially avoiding environmental gentrification.

FIGURE 14.1 Photographs of informal greenspace types following the IGS typology devised by Rupprecht and Byrne (2014a): (a) Street verge, covered in spontaneous herbal vegetation (Brisbane, Australia); (b) Lot, formerly residential with perfunctory access restriction (Tokyo, Japan), (c) Gap, space between three buildings with spontaneous herbal vegetation used by birds (Sapporo, Japan); (d) Railway, annual grass verge between rail track and street; (e) Brownfield, spontaneous vegetated industrial space around abandoned factory (Brisbane); (f) Waterside, spontaneous vegetation on banks and deposits in highly modified river (Nagoya, Japan); (g) Structural, spontaneous vegetation growing out of vertical, porous retaining wall (Tokyo); (h) Microsite, grass growing spontaneously out of crack in the pavement (Nagoya); (i) Powerline, vegetated right of way underneath high voltage powerline (Brisbane)

Political ecology(ies) of just urban greenspace

Urban greening can improve cities by meeting residents diverse recreational needs (Lin et al. 2015), cooling ambient temperatures (Byrne et al. 2016), intercepting urban stormwater (Fitzgerald and Laufer 2016) and providing spaces for locally-grown food (Lafontaine-Messier et al. 2016). While urban greening offers manifold benefits, some scholars contend that we need "more democratic, diverse and just" greenspaces in cities (Curran and Hamilton 2012, 1039). Formal greenspace acquisition and management can create administrative challenges (e.g. safety concerns, increased crime, property impacts, maintenance burdens, etc.) (Sreetheran and van den Bosch 2014). And greenspace planning may perpetuate existing environmental inequalities and create new ones (Anguelovski 2016).

Marginalized and vulnerable people tend to be disproportionately exposed to environmental harm in cities and typically have less access to environmental benefits, including greenspaces (Checker 2011). But efforts to re-green cities, especially in low-income and so-called minority neighborhoods can have paradoxical consequences. For instance, researchers have shown that the development of parks and other greenspaces can increase property values (Eckerd 2011). Unless efforts are taken to manage this effect, it can eventually result in the displacement of marginalized and vulnerable people (Pearsall 2012). Are there alternatives?

A political ecology perspective suggests that the potential of informal greenspace to provide an alternative model to the gentrifying effects of parks and other greenspaces is likely influenced by multiple factors (e.g., social, political, cultural, environmental) (Miller 2016). Three factors are salient: (i) the amount of accessible recreation area potentially provided by informal greenspace; (ii) whether informal greenspace is socio-spatially differentiated (e.g. by (dis)advantage); and (iii) whether multiple axes of difference such as income and education circumscribe residents' access to, use of, and perceived benefits from the space. The first factor is particularly important.

If IGS is not proximate, residents may be prevented from using it by the same mechanisms that can limit park visitation. If IGS is locally available, but physical barriers, land tenure or management make access difficult, then its potential benefits are unlikely to be realized. Even if IGS is generally accessible, patterns of socio-spatial disadvantage may still circumscribe benefits available to marginalized and vulnerable communities. Axes of difference such as gender, age, (dis)ability, income or education can affect both actual and perceived accessibility, and may render some sites "off limits."

Methods: Assessing informal greenspace distribution and accessibility

To examine IGS amount, and interactions between patterns of socio-spatial disadvantage, and its appreciation and use by low-income residents, we draw upon results from a recent cross-national IGS study in Brisbane, Australia and Sapporo, Japan (Rupprecht and Byrne 2014a; Rupprecht et al. 2016). As we have described elsewhere (Rupprecht and Byrne 2014a), these two cities have similarities and differences that lend them well to comparison (Table 14.1). They provide excellent opportunities for cross-cultural research. Both cities are relatively young (being founded in the 19th century) and they saw most of their growth during the 20th century, especially in the post-second world-war period. Their close geographical size is complemented by a similar urban morphology. They are built around a dense central business district, are situated proximate the coast and upland regions, and are bisected by a central river. These similarities contrast with differences in population density, population growth forecasts, and available greenspace.

TABLE 14.1 Comparison of cities containing the survey areas

Characteristics	City of Brisbane (LGA)	Sapporo
Founded	1824, city status 1902	1868, city status 1922
Population	1,089,743 (2011) (2031: 1.27 million)	1,936,189 (2013) (2030: 1.87 million)
Area	1,338 km^2	1,121.12 km^2
Pop. density	814/km^2	1,699/km^2
Peak density	>5,000/km^2	>8,000/km^2
Climate	Humid subtropical (Cfa)	Humid continental (Dfa)
Industry	Tourism, resources, retail, financial services, agriculture hub, education	Tourism, retail, IT, agriculture hub, resources, education
Greenspace	Local parks: 3,290 ha (32m^2/capita)	Parks: 2,345 ha (12.3m^2/capita)
	All parks: 11840ha (115m^2/capita)	All greenspace: 5,508 ha (28.9 m^2/capita)
Park area planned	40m^2/capita, minimum 20m^2/capita	"No greenspace loss, park renovation"

Source: Rupprecht and Byrne (2014a)

While Sapporo has seen rapid growth throughout the second half of the 20th century and currently has a population of about 1.9 million, its population is now stagnating and is predicted to decline in the future. In contrast, Brisbane has a population of around 1 million but is still growing relatively quickly (Table 14.1). In both cities, formal greenspace consists of networks of over 2,000 public parks, many of them small local parks. Brisbane has 3,290 ha of local parkland (32 m^2/capita), whereas Sapporo has 2,345 ha (12.3 m^2/capita) (Table 14.1). All parks in Brisbane comprise an area of 11,840 ha (115 m^2/capita), while those in Sapporo combine to form an area of 5,508 ha (28.9 m^2/capita). These greenspaces include forested hillsides in the southwest of both cities, providing residents with additional recreation space. However, access to these spaces can be restricted due to bushfires in Brisbane (Queensland Government 2012) and bear sightings in Sapporo (Sapporo Kankyōkyoku Midori No Suishinbu 2013).

Amount of accessible IGS in Brisbane and Sapporo

To assess the amount of IGS in the dense centers of the two cities, the first author systematically surveyed a 10x10 km grid containing 121 sampling sites of 2,500 m^2 per city, drawing upon data recorded in the field and aerial photography. IGS was classified by type (see Figure 14.1). Accessibility of IGS was classified using a three-level scale, based on the amount of physical or psychological effort necessary to overcome access barriers (Rupprecht and Byrne 2014a).

Findings: Informal greenspace distribution in Australia and Japan

Our results show that IGS in both cities accounts for a significant area of accessible urban greenspace, about 14% of total greenspace in the survey areas. Further, informal greenspace is widely distributed throughout both cities (Figure 14.2), and in both cities over 80% of IGS appears to be accessible or partly accessible. This suggests IGS may provide a valuable contribution as an alternative greening strategy to limit environmental gentrification.

IGS accessibility

The surveyed area in Brisbane consisted of 6.3% IGS, while the surveyed area in Sapporo consisted of IGS to 4.8%. Street verges made up over 80% of IGS in the Brisbane survey area, while vacant lots (42.2%) and gaps (19.2%) were the two largest IGS types in the Sapporo survey area (Rupprecht and Byrne 2014a). In comparison to formal greenspace (e.g. parks, sports, recreation, and conservation areas) and private greenspace (gardens, shared greenspace, community land, and commercial and industrial greenspace), IGS in Brisbane contributed more than half as much (6.3%) as formal greenspace (11.6%) and more than one-fifth as much IGS than private greenspace (27.4%). In Sapporo, the IGS area (4.8%) was almost a third of formal greenspace area (15.4%) and private greenspace (15.0%). We found IGS was present in most of the sampling sites in both cities (Figure 14.2), with the obvious exceptions of sites located in areas with large-scale land use types (e.g. Brisbane river, Mt. Moiwa in the southwest of Sapporo). In Brisbane, 78% of IGS area was fully accessible, 7% partially accessible and 15% not accessible. In Sapporo, the accessible IGS area (68%) and not accessible area (10%) was smaller, offset by a larger partially accessible IGS area (21%) (Rupprecht and Byrne 2014a).

IGS occurrence and socio-economic (dis)advantage

To analyze the socio-spatial effects of IGS, we drew upon the results of the IGS survey in Brisbane (Rupprecht et al. 2016), testing for interrelationships between IGS distribution and socio-economic disadvantage. We used the Index of Relative Socio-economic Advantage and Disadvantage (IRSAD), calculated based on the Australian Bureau of Statistics 2011 Census of Population and Housing (Pink 2013). The IRSAD summarizes variables (related for example to income, education, employment, occupation, housing) that indicate either relative advantage or disadvantage, to rank areas on a continuum from most disadvantaged to most advantaged (Pink 2013). We calculated the IRSAD percentile for each IGS survey site in Brisbane based on the IRSAD percentile of their statistical area (Level 1, Pink 2013). For sites located on two or more statistical areas with different IRSAD percentiles, we adjusted the IRSAD percentile for IGS sites by weighting the contribution of each statistical area percentile by the area it contributed to the IGS site. For example, an IGS site consisting of 50% each of

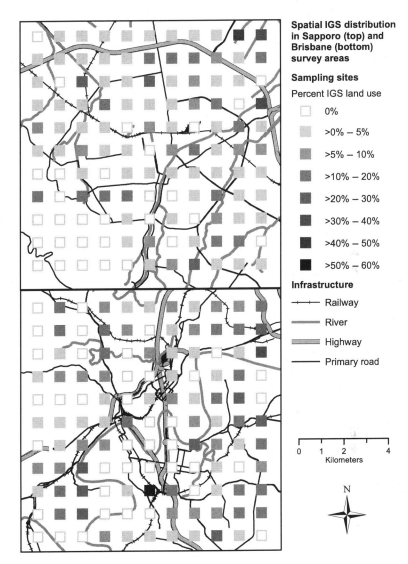

Spatial IGS distribution in Sapporo (top) and Brisbane (bottom) survey areas

Sampling sites

Percent IGS land use

- 0%
- >0% – 5%
- >5% – 10%
- >10% – 20%
- >20% – 30%
- >30% – 40%
- >40% – 50%
- >50% – 60%

Infrastructure

- Railway
- River
- Highway
- Primary road

0 1 2 4
Kilometers

N

FIGURE 14.2 Spatial IGS distribution: Percentage of IGS per sampling site in Sapporo (top) and Brisbane (bottom)

two statistical areas with percentiles of 50 and 100, the IGS site was given an IRSAD percentile of 75. We then performed non-parametric Spearman's rho tests in SPSS (v. 22, OSX) to analyze whether IRSAD percentile was correlated with the percentage of total IGS land use or with the percentage of a particular IGS type on the Brisbane sites.

Our results showed no significant ($p > 0.05$) correlations between IRSAD percentile and total IGS land use, nor did we find a significant correlation between the

IRSAD percentile and any of the different IGS types. This means that IGS was equally distributed between socio-economically advantaged and disadvantaged areas in our survey sites. In contrast, researchers have shown that formal greenspace in Brisbane and other Australian countries is significantly scarcer in low-income areas (Astell-Burt et al. 2014). While our result is limited to the 121 sites we surveyed for IGS, it could suggest that IGS is more evenly distributed than formal greenspace. IGS could thus make a valuable contribution to limiting environmental gentrification.

IGS use and appreciation – influence of education and income

To consider how residents view the role of IGS in the local context, we have drawn upon an exploratory letterbox-drop, reply-paid mail-back survey of 1,910 households in Brisbane (valid responses 123; response rate 6.4%) and 1,980 in Sapporo (valid responses 163; response rate 8.2%) about IGS (Rupprecht et al. 2015b). Questionnaires were only distributed at sites where IGS was located within the 400m radius, to maximize potential respondents IGS interaction. The 121 sampling sites were placed on the intersecting lines of a 10km by 10km grid, centered on the city centers.

In the questionnaire, residents were asked about their IGS perception, evaluation, and use, employing multiple-choice questions and one open comment question. We also included socio-demographic questions (e.g., household income, housing type, respondent age). To analyze the quantitative data, we used SPSS (v. 21, OS X) to perform descriptive and inferential statistical analyses. Initial analyses indicated that the sample data was not normally distributed (P-P plots, skewness and kurtosis tests). We used Kruskal-Wallis and Fisher's Exact tests to analyze a possible influence of respondents' income and level of education on their appreciation and use of IGS. For the qualitative data, derived from respondents' comments in the open response questions, we used content analysis and coding to identify themes present in the text (Sproule 2006). Respondents were assigned pseudonyms chosen from popular names during their time of birth in their respective cultures, to protect anonymity.

Our results show that respondent income and level of education had no significant influence (p>0.05) on their evaluation of IGS in Brisbane or Sapporo (Rupprecht et al. 2015b). Respondent income and level of education also had no significant influence on their reported IGS use or frequency as adults or during their childhood or teen age. In contrast, the literature has reported an association between lower respondent income and higher constraints to formal greenspace use, including social barriers (e.g. fear of crime), physical barriers (e.g. lack of transport or cost of transport), and motivational barriers (reduced interest) (Mowen, Payne, and Scott 2005).

Respondents also highlighted the difference between formal and informal greenspace in their open-ended comments. They criticized the rigidity of parks, valuing the flexibility afforded by IGS. For example:

[IGS]'s informality allows more people to use the space in more and different ways. Its informality echoes the informality of our society in our youth and formative years.

(Giorgos, 60, male, Brisbane)

A neutral zone that belongs to nobody is necessary: left-over room, margins, interstices, space. A life like in the city, where man-made objects are surrounded by nothing but artificial greenspace, is suffocating.

(Satoshi, 45, male, Sapporo)

These comments prompt us to consider whether designing and planning greenspace is always desirable and whether it actually caters to residents' needs. They also challenge the notion that planning produces superior outcomes to residents' informal management. Survey respondents recognized that access to greenspace has environmental and intergenerational justice dimensions too:

Near railway lines people often grow vegetables and flowers and so on. You can see it a lot when riding the train. I think they grow it there because they have no other space.

(Yumiko, 60, female, Sapporo)

I think that there is a clear link between growing up in an area where children can 'interact' with their environment, and environmental awareness/compassion, as an adult. I have travelled extensively and I have seen areas where children grow up in high rise apartments, with only infrequent access to a sterile (i.e. unchanging) park, and these have been the areas of the most unnecessary (and widespread) environmental damage.

(Thomas, 41, male, Brisbane)

Today, there's no place for young teenagers to go other than hanging out in front of convenience stores. Even in Doraemon [a famous Japanese cartoon] the children play in vacant lots every day. And parks are so over-maintained there's nothing except a few ants.

(Akiko, 42, female, Sapporo)

Respondents' observations suggest that IGS could provide a valuable greenspace resource to residents who are deprived of formal greenspace. While our study results are limited to the respondents from Brisbane and Sapporo, they suggest that IGS could have the capacity to avoid issues associated with environmental gentrification, such as displacement.

Other studies have found similar results. In his account of the Brooklyn Eastern District Terminal in New York, Campo (2013) for instance, noted how land use planners' efforts to formalize informal greenspaces can alienate their users. Similarly, QvistrÖm (2012) has shown how residents in Gyllin's Garden, Sweden, were opposed to the way the traditional planning processes diminished their enjoyment and use of that previously informal space. So what are the alternatives to formalizing liminal and "derelict" sites such as these?

Problems and possibilities in IGS provision and use: Insights from Japan

To conclude the chapter, we draw upon insights from three Japanese examples. These examples show how different land tenure arrangements can produce divergent outcomes for residents. The sites were assessed as part of the first author's fieldwork.

IGS gardening in Sapporo and Nagoya

Site 1 is located behind the embankment of Tenpaku River close to its estuary, in the south of Minami Ward, Nagoya, Japan (Figure 14.3). It is a mixed-use locality of residential and industrial land. Alongside a small road with little traffic, what was originally a storm drain gutter has been filled with soil to form a narrow roadside verge (nature strip). Almost the complete length is used by residents for informal gardening. Plantings include decorative flowerbeds (next to a small factory building), fruit trees, and a variety of vegetable gardens (e.g., onions, cabbage, carrots, broccoli). Vegetable gardens show different intensities of use. While some feature casual cultivation, many have improvised fences, raised beds, dry stonewalls, and water collection basins (see Figure 14.3).

Use of this IGS site is characterized by uncertainty. Site signage shows the space is contested. According to one user, inhabitants of the street have been cultivating this roadside verge for many years (personal communication). Asked about tenure, he said the city is the formal owner of the land, and he noted the informal nature of the residents' activities. He commented that he would have to give up his lot if the city asked him to, but stated that under the circumstances, residents were doing their best with the land. The site also shows evidence of vegetable theft. Some lots have hand-made signs that read "don't take anything" or "somebody is watching." One even featured a commercial "surveillance camera" sign.

Site 2 is located on the artificial raised riverbanks of Motsukisamu River in Toyohira Ward, Sapporo, Japan. It is flanked on both sides by medium to high-density residential land use (Figure 14.4). The site measures about one kilometer in length, and the width varies between two to five meters wide. While spontaneous vegetation covers some parts, most of the area is informally gardened. Plantings include a variety of flowerbeds (e.g., tulips, sunflowers) and vegetables (e.g. onions, pumpkins, tomatoes), but also grape vines, which require long-term care and investment. In contrast to the first site, here lots are not demarcated by fences. Because the riverbanks are located about two to three meters below street and housing level, users have installed their own ladders to provide access. Whereas users of site 1 rely on basins to catch rainwater, gardeners at the second site use a wall drainage system to collect water, via an improvised irrigation system.

FIGURE 14.3 Photographs of site one, informal roadside IGS garden lots (Minami Ward, Nagoya): (a) View from Tenpaku River embankment over roadside gardens in industrial area; (b) High level of site modification with improvised fences and repurposed entrance door; (c) "Don't take them" – sign to admonish potential vegetable thieves; (d) "Security camera installed" – sign to deter potential vegetable thieves; (e) Planted tree and rainwater collection tools; (f) Fenced lot with dry stonewall

FIGURE 14.4 Photographs of site two, informal riverbank IGS gardening (Toyohira Ward, Sapporo): (a) Grape vine using the existing fence next to a variety of vegetable patches; (b) Gardening-prohibited sign placed by city government inside vegetable patches; (c) Ladder providing easy access to riverbank site; (d) Vegetable patches continuing along the side of Motsukisamu River; (e) Riverbank garden used as extension to private garden, with ladder for easy access

This second site is characterized by an ongoing conflict with the city as the official property owner. Not only is there no official use agreement in place to guarantee long-term site access, the city government considers any use of the river banks for agriculture to be a violation of the river law (*kasenhō*). The city has demanded that the residents return the river banks to their former condition, but how the city government intends to enforce this remains unclear. Because the artificial river banks were created to prevent flooding, which the Motsukisamu river was prone to do before its modification (Wikipedia, "望月寒川" (motsuki-samugawa) 2014), flash floods may be a matter of concern for city officials, and could be dangerous for IGS users.

Site 3 is located in a power transmission corridor in Minami Ward, Nagoya, Japan, about 500 meters from site 1. It is flanked on both sides by small, one-way residential streets and medium to high-density residential land use (Figure 14.5). The site measures about 600 meters long and ten meters wide. Besides three powerline pylons and a small area with gravel used for community purposes (e.g., festivals, trash collection), the site is divided into dozens of small allotment gardens (Figure 14.5). Plantings include decorative flowerbeds, vegetable patches (e.g., onions, cabbage, radish, carrots), fruit trees (e.g., clementine and peach trees), and ornamental trees (e.g., groomed pine trees). In contrast to site 1, the allotment gardens show a constant, high level of modification and resource investment. Lots have been secured with fences where the power line corridor meets the street, but rarely between two patches. Users have repurposed pots, ski poles, umbrellas, office chairs and other equipment for gardening purposes.

In contrast to the other two sites, use of this informal allotment garden is characterized by long-term stability due to an agreement with the property owner, the local power utility Chubu Electric Power, which is a publicly owned corporation. Although still an informal greenspace in management and use, the agreement formalizes usufruct access. According to one user, this arrangement has allowed residents to garden the land free of charge (personal communication). In return, the residents have agreed to keep vegetation "orderly" and below a specified height to prevent it from reaching the overhead powerline. The agreement is between the utility and the local neighborhood associations (*chōnaikai*), which manage allocation to the local residents. Gardens are generally not protected against theft in any way, a marked difference from the roadside verge gardens. Possibly the semi "official" status of the allotment gardens is enough to deter potential thieves. Our informant also showed clear pride in her garden, vegetables, and flowers. She had none of the insecurity and uncertainty about the future of her garden felt by informants from the other sites, suggesting this case offers a potential model for other cities.

The role of tenure and management

All three of the above sites provided local residents with recreational and economic benefits without producing any obvious signs of environmental gentrification. The small scale of the gardening activities and their informality likely play a role, but

FIGURE 14.5 Photographs of site three, allotment gardens under powerline transmission corridor (Minami Ward, Nagoya): (a) Peach tree in allotment gardens flanked by small, residential one-way roads; (b) Allotment gardens with improvised tools (ski poles, umbrella core); (c) Office chair repurposed as place of rest; (d) Trees and water storage in allotment gardens; (e) Vegetable patches and cooking pot repurposed as water cask; (f) Low height, inter-lot fencing without warning signs or other anti-theft measures

may also limit the benefits for residents. Small lot size, and the residents' knowledge that any investment of time and resources is somewhat precarious, may prevent extensive embellishment – allowing gardeners to exist somewhat "below the radar" of authorities. Here residents have found ways to derive benefits from IGS without financial or organizational assistance from authorities, and have seemingly avoided displacement because the small-scale and informal qualities of their embellishments has not changed neighborhood character or amenity. However, this success comes at the price of long-term stability, limited space, and potential conflict with thieves and/or property owners.

We argue that the crucial difference between these three sites and places where environmental gentrification has occurred, such as the New York High Line in New York, can be understood as a function of design and management. The High Line was completely redesigned from its industrial origin, and is a professionally maintained greenspace, with substantial running costs. It caters to visitors and new residents drawn to its visual appeal and "hipness". Millington (2015) offers a compelling critique of the High Line as "a neoliberal green space, one that traded luxury development for green space provisioning". And he cautions against viewing informal green space as intrinsically opposed to capitalist politics, noting how its "weediness" can be appropriated to undergird a "narrative of ecological sustainability" (Millington 2015, 12), which depoliticizes and dehistoricizes the space, paving the way for investment that masks the violence and marginalization typical of communities battling brownfield redevelopment.

The Japanese sites we have discussed above were not designed by professionals (e.g. landscape architects). They are vernacular spaces, shaped through day-to-day use and by the aesthetic ideals and culinary preferences of their users (Berthelsen 2015). Running costs are modest. For site three, although the neighborhood associations allocate lots, and the residents maintain them, the utility does not charge a fee. Consequently there is no "windfall gain" to property owners. External private capital investment is not required to create an informal greenspace like these. The marginal character of these sites – a road verge, a drainage floodplain and a powerline easement – also renders them less attractive to speculative property development. Environmental gentrification is therefore less likely.

Conclusion: Implications for policy, planning and geography?

In this chapter we have examined how using informal greenspace (IGS) in Japan and Australia to meet residents' needs could function as an anti-gentrification strategy. We found that IGS in Sapporo and Brisbane did not exhibit the patterns of disadvantage common for public parks. Instead, these spaces were co-created by residents as designers, managers and users. This raises important questions for urban policy and planning and private property management.

Many local governments grapple with fiscal constraints in providing greenspace. Research shows that public greenspace provision can displace poorer residents, due to rising property values. Informal greenspaces, characterized in the literature as "liminal", "ambivalent", or "overlooked", have tended to be ignored as an urban greening alternative (Rupprecht and Byrne 2014b; Jorgensen and Tylecote 2007). Planners' and developers' lack of interest in such spaces opens the possibility for residents to appropriate them, with or without the cooperation/consent of their formal owners, and to modify them according to residents' specific needs. This raises the question of whether we could leave some greenspace creation, design, and management fully in the hands of local residents. And if so, what role should be played by planners and private property owners?

Planners might begin by assisting residents to identify and reduce barriers to IGS use, such as removing fences around vacant lots (Hayashi, Tashiro, and Kinoshita 1999) or by cataloguing and making public soil contamination (McClintock 2012). Planners could also provide residents with information about the availability of IGS in their neighborhoods (e.g. via an IGS map or app). For instance, 596 acres, a New York NGO, maps publicly owned vacant land and helps local residents to convert it to community gardens. Some of the money saved by avoiding costly design and maintenance of formal parklands could be redirected to provide residents with resources to start their own community-led projects. Private property owners could follow the example of the Japanese utility and enter into usufruct agreements with local residents, without harming management and occupancy rights.

In this chapter we have offered some insights into the accessibility and use of IGS in Australia and Japan, but more work is required. Quantitative methods should be further applied to investigate the socio-spatial distribution of IGS in different cities, and the socio-demographic profile of IGS users. This would assist in determining if IGS accessibility is correlated with patterns of social (dis)advantage. In-depth interviews, focus groups, participant observation, ethnography, or participant photography should be undertaken, to better understand the motivations driving IGS users (e.g., lack of access to gardens or formal greenspace, use restrictions, proximity), the difficulties they face (e.g., conflict with property owner, theft), and what possibilities exist to employ IGS as an anti-gentrification strategy more widely. Our research suggests that IGS has considerable potential to play a key role in urban greening.

Acknowledgements

An earlier version of this paper was presented at the American Association of Geographers Annual Meeting 2015 in Chicago. We thank the session organizers and participants for their helpful feedback on this paper. We also thank Yumi Nakagawa and Kumiko Nakagawa for their help with fieldwork and data collection, and all respondents for participating in this study. Parts of this work were supported by the Japan Society for the Promotion of Science [grant number 24658023] and by Griffith University.

References

Anguelovski, I. 2016. From toxic sites to parks as (green) LULUs? New challenges of inequity, privilege, gentrification, and exclusion for urban environmental justice. *Journal of Planning Literature* 31(1): 23–36.

Astell-Burt, T., Feng, X., Mavoa, S., Badland, H. M., and Giles-Corti, B. 2014. Do low-income neighbourhoods have the least green space? A cross-sectional study of Australia's most populous cities. *BMC Public Health* 14(1): 292. doi:10.1186/1471-2458-14-292.

Berthelsen, C. 2015. Tokyo's non-intentional landscape. http://non-intentional-landscape. a-small-lab.com/?og=1.

Brink, E., Aalders, T., Ádám, D., Feller, R., Henselek, Y., Hoffman, A., Ibe, K., Matthey-Doret, A., Meyer, M., and Negrut, N.L. 2016. Cascades of green: a review of ecosystem-based adaptation in urban areas. *Global Environmental Change* 36: 111–123.

Byrne, J. 2012. When green is white: the cultural politics of race, nature and social exclusion in a Los Angeles urban national park. *Geoforum* 43(3): 595–611.

Byrne, J., Ambrey, C., Portanger, C., Lo, A., Matthews, T. Baker, D., and Davison, A. 2016. Could urban greening mitigate suburban thermal inequity?: the role of residents' dispositions and household practices. *Environmental Research Letters* 11(9), 095014.

Byrne, J. and Wolch, J. 2009. Nature, race, and parks: past research and future directions for geographic research. *Progress in Human Geography* 33(6): 743–765.

Campo, D. 2013. *The Accidental Playground.* New York: Fordham University Press.

Checker, M. 2011. Wiped out by the "greenwave": environmental gentrification and the paradoxical politics of urban sustainability. *City & Society* 23(2): 210–229.

Curran, W. and Hamilton, T. 2012. Just green enough: contesting environmental gentrification in Greenpoint, Brooklyn. *Local Environment* 17(9): 1027–1042.

Eckerd, A. 2011. Cleaning up without clearing out? A spatial assessment of environmental gentrification. *Urban Affairs Review* 47(1): 31–59.

Fitzgerald, J. and Laufer, J. 2016. Governing green stormwater infrastructure: the Philadelphia experience. *Local Environment.* doi:10.1080/13549839.2016.1191063.

Hayashi, M., Tashiro, Y., and Kinoshita, T., 1999. A study on vacant lots enclosed by fences in relation to urbanization. *Landscape Research Japan* 63: 667–670. doi:10.5632/jila.63.667

Kern, L. 2015. From toxic wreck to crunchy chic: environmental gentrification through the body. *Environment and Planning D: Society and Space* 33(1), 67–83.

Lafontaine-Messier, M., Gélinas, N., and Olivier, A. 2016. Profitability of food trees planted in urban public green areas. *Urban Forestry & Urban Greening* 16: 197–207.

Lin, B., Meyers, J., and Barnett, G. 2015. Understanding the potential loss and inequities of green space distribution with urban densification. *Urban Forestry & Urban Greening* 14(4): 952–958.

Jorgensen, A. and Tylecote, M. 2007. Ambivalent landscapes – wilderness in the urban interstices. *Landscape Research* 32(4): 443–462. doi:10.1080/01426390701449802.

McClintock, N. 2012. Assessing soil lead contamination at multiple scales in Oakland, California: implications for urban agriculture and environmental justice. *Applied Geography* 35(1–2): 460–473. doi:10.1016/j.apgeog.2012.10.001.

Miller, J. T. 2016. Is urban greening for everyone? Social inclusion and exclusion along the Gowanus Canal. *Urban Forestry & Urban Greening* 19(1): 285–294.

Millington, N. 2015. From urban scar to "park in the sky": terrain vague, urban design, and the remaking of New York City's High Line Park. *Environment and Planning A* 47(11): 2324–2338.

Mowen, A. J., Payne, L. L., and Scott, D. 2005. Change and stability in park visitation constraints revisited. *Leisure Sciences* 27(2): 191–204. doi:10.1080/01490400590912088.

Nohl, W. 1990. Gedankenskizze Einer Naturästhetik Der Stadt. [Thought sketch of a natural aesthetic of the city, in German] *Landschaft Und Stadt* 22(2): 57–67.

Pearsall, H. 2010. From brown to green? Assessing social vulnerability to environmental gentrification in New York City. *Environment and Planning C: Government and Policy* 28(5): 872–886.

Pearsall, H. 2012. Moving out or moving in? Resilience to environmental gentrification in New York City. *Local Environment* 17(9): 1013–1026.

Pink, Brian. 2013. Socio-economic indexes for areas (SEIFA) 2011. Australian Bureau of Statistics.

Qviström, M. 2012. Taming the Wild: Gyllin's Garden and the Urbanization of a Wildscape. In *Urban Wildscapes*, edited by A. Jorgensen and R. Keenan, 187–200. Abingdon: Routledge.

Quastel, N. 2009. Political ecologies of gentrification. *Urban Geography* 30(7): 694–725.

Queensland Government, Department of National Parks Recreation Sport and Racing. 2012. QPWS Monitors Fire near Brisbane's D'Aguilar National Park. Department of National Parsk, Recreation, Sport and Racing. http://www.nprsr.qld.gov.au/mediarelea ses/2012-12-qpws-monitors-fire.html.

Rupprecht, C. D. D. and Byrne, J. A. 2014a. Informal urban green-space: comparison of quantity and characteristics in Brisbane, Australia and Sapporo, Japan. *PloS one* 9(6): e99784.

Rupprecht, C. D. D. and Byrne, J. A. 2014b. Informal urban greenspace: a typology and trilingual systematic review of its role for urban residents and trends in the literature. *Urban Forestry & Urban Greening* 13(4): 597–611.

Rupprecht, C. D. D.Byrne, J. A., Garden, J. G., and Hero, J.-M. 2015. Informal urban green space: A trilingual systematic review of its role for biodiversity and trends in the literature. *Urban Forestry & Urban Greening* 14(4): 883–908.

Rupprecht, C. D. D., Byrne, J. A., Ueda, H., and Lo, A. Y., 2015. "It's real, not fake like a park": residents' perception and use of informal urban green-space in Brisbane, Australia and Sapporo, Japan. *Landscape and Urban Planning* 143: 205–218. doi:10.1016/j. landurbplan.2015.07.003.

Rupprecht, C. D. D. Byrne, J. A., and Lo, A. Y. 2016. Memories of vacant lots: how and why residents used informal urban green space as children and teenagers in Brisbane, Australia, and Sapporo, Japan. *Children's Geographies* 14(3): 340–355.

Rutt, R. L. and Gulsrud, N. M. 2016. Green justice in the city: a new agenda for urban green space research in Europe. *Urban Forestry & Urban Greening* 19: 123–127.

Sapporo Kankyōkyoku Midori No Suishinbu. 2013. Bear sighting information [in Japanese]. City of Sapporo. http://www.city.sapporo.jp/kurashi/animal/choju/kuma/syutsubotsu/ index.html.

Shackleton, C. M. and Blair, A. 2013. Perceptions and use of public green space is influenced by its relative abundance in two small towns in South Africa. *Landscape and Urban Planning* 113: 104–112.

Sister, C., Wolch, J., and Wilson, J. P. 2010. Got green? Addressing environmental justice in park provision. *GeoJournal* 75(3): 229–248.

Sproule, W. 2006. Content Analysis. In *Social Research Methods: An Australian Perspective*, edited by Maggie Walter, 114–133. Oxford: Oxford University Press.

Sreetheran, M. and van den Bosch, C. C. K. 2014. A socio-ecological exploration of fear of crime in urban green spaces – A systematic review. *Urban Forestry & Urban Greening* 13(1): 1–18.

Wikipedia, "望月寒川." [motsukisamugawa, in Japanese] 2014. https://ja.wikipedia.org/w/ index.php?title=%E6%9C%9B%E6%9C%88%E5%AF%92%E5%B7%9D&oldid=53380229.

Wolch, J. R., Byrne, J., and Newell, J. P. 2014. Urban green space, public health, and environmental justice: the challenge of making cities "just green enough". *Landscape and Urban Planning* 125: 234–244.

15

PATIENT CAPITAL AND REFRAMING VALUE: MAKING NEW URBANISM JUST GREEN ENOUGH

Dan Trudeau

In theory, sustainable urban development incorporates social equity, but this often fails to materialize in practice. This is evident in many North American cities where urban sustainability projects are only accessible to the affluent. Inclusion of the poor and concerns for their right to the sustainable city are all too frequently ignored (Sarmiento and Sims 2015; Saha and Paterson 2008; Moore 2007). Scholars have critiqued urban sustainability initiatives as promoting "eco-gentrification," wherein a focus on improving environmental amenities and ecological services in a place makes it attractive to capital, ultimately putting that place out of the reach of lower- and even moderate-income groups (Checker 2011; Bunce 2009; Dale and Newman, 2009; Quastel 2009).

Sustainable urban development, however, does not necessarily lead to gentrification. The "just green enough" thesis points to alternative strategies that promote neighborhood greening and improvements to livability for existing residents in ways that do not trigger displacement of vulnerable or otherwise marginalized groups (Wolch, Bryne, and Newell 2014; Curran and Hamilton 2012). This chapter adds to the discussion through a case study of New Urbanism projects in three metropolitan areas in the United States. I use these examples to examine broader questions about how planning for sustainable urban development can promote just green enough strategies.

To address this question, I analyze the institutional contexts that shape New Urbanist projects. The cases I consider are all projects that have been self-described as applying the New Urbanism planning movement's design principles at the neighborhood scale. I draw on 54 semi-structured interviews with development stakeholders involved in the creation of nine New Urbanist neighborhoods located in the Austin, Denver, and Minneapolis-St. Paul metropolitan areas. I focus on the ways that social equity is marginalized and privileged, which I operationalize by examining whether affordable housing is incorporated into New Urbanism projects that have an explicit environmental sustainability agenda.

I find that the privileging of social equity can occur where there is an institutional champion that brings "patient capital" and leadership to promote social equity in development that ultimately aims to generate environmental and economic benefits. I argue that sustainable urban development practitioners can produce places that are just green enough, but this has to be something built-in from the start. This requires leadership and policy mechanisms that hardwire social equity into the design of a project and that are managed in a way to limit speculative investment. Otherwise, efforts to insert social equity into the development conversation once eco-gentrification processes are underway have little chance of success.

Sustainable development as eco-gentrification? The case of New Urbanism

New Urbanism is an urban design and planning movement that has been enrolled in sustainable development efforts. The movement started in the United States during the 1980s and grew out of a critique of suburban sprawl (Hirt 2009; Grant 2006; Falconer Al-Hindi and Till 2001). In response, New Urbanism prescribes compact, pedestrian-oriented, mixed-use development that is accessible to diverse income groups (Talen 2013). In this way, the movement purports to foster development that balances concern for economic growth, environmental protection, and social equity. Advocates formalized the movement in 1993 by founding the Congress for the New Urbanism (CNU) and a few years later codified the movement's ideals in the *Charter of the New Urbanism*, which articulates a set of design and land use principles that proponents claim offer actionable strategies for sustainable development (Leccese and McCormick 2000). CNU has tied New Urbanism to social equity efforts associated with re-inventing public housing through the HOPE VI program (Bohl 2000). However, since 2007, CNU has been more focused on highlighting the environmental sustainability aspects of the movement (Trudeau 2013a; Berke 2008), which is evident in its efforts to establish connections with the green planning movement through programs like LEED-ND and release of the *Cannons of Sustainable Architecture and Urbanism* (CNU et al. 2007). While the New Urbanism may be aligned with the goals and interests of sustainable development, how does it fare in practice?

Research on the implementation of New Urbanism at the neighborhood scale suggests that the movement has made limited progress in advancing social equity dimensions of sustainability, a problem that also plagues other sustainable urban development efforts (Sarmiento and Sims 2015). To be sure, New Urbanism has proved appealing to both consumers (Tu and Eppli 2001) and developers (Kenny and Zimmerman 2004; Veninga 2004), and has thus become a noteworthy strategy for capital accumulation. Mayo and Ellis (2009) note, however, how social equity-oriented elements of New Urbanism are frequently ignored in development practice because they are seen as adding little value to stakeholders that apply a market-based rationality to development. Indeed, New Urbanism has generally struggled to create projects that include affordable housing opportunities (Talen 2010; Garde

2004). This shortcoming has consequently given rise to a number of critiques about New Urbanism as a movement for the affluent (González and Lejano 2009; Grant 2007). Most prominent among these critiques is that New Urbanism promotes gentrification.

One of the enduring critiques of New Urbanism is that it excludes poor people and people of color (Smith 2002; Marcuse 2000). González and Lejano (2009) note, for instance, that New Urbanism was enrolled in a strategy to redevelop downtown Santa Ana, California, a place that had been a Latinx-dominated part of the city, in order to attract national chains, which alienated the Latinx population. This and other cases bolster criticisms that New Urbanism creates places that privilege aesthetics, expectations, and interests of propertied white people at the expense of welcoming more diverse groups (Fraser et al. 2013; González et al. 2012; Hanlon 2012; Day 2003).

As proponents have moved to align New Urbanism with sustainability projects, these efforts have also been critiqued for fostering eco-gentrification. New Urbanist projects often feature landscapes with attractive environmental amenities, including parks and open space for wildlife habitat (Till 2001; Zimmerman 2001). In some other cases, New Urbanism projects are part of a feel-good narrative of urban regeneration in which brownfields are cleaned up and centrally located land is returned to everyday use (Bohl 2000). In both contexts, the marketing of New Urbanist projects discursively constructs these as places that are wedded to the new green economy. Solar panels adorn private homes. LEED certifications mark the landscape with distinction. Streets are designed to promote walking and bicycle use and neighborhoods are platted to generate densities that will make public transit use economically feasible. Proponents frame New Urbanist projects as places where people can live environmentally sustainable lifestyles, perform green subjectivities, and demonstrate cultural distinction (Quastel 2009). Developers and other real estate speculators embrace these qualities of New Urbanism as ways to promote accumulation and pursue a sustainability fix for accumulation crises (Temenos and McCann 2012; Keil 2007; Zimmerman 2001). To the extent that New Urbanism promotes environmental sustainability, it seems to do so at the expense of social equity (Hanlon 2015).

The case for social equity

New Urbanism's relationship with social equity is more complicated than what the literature describes. There are, in fact, examples where New Urbanism projects advance affordable housing outside the context of HOPE VI. In his long-term evaluation of Orenco Station in Portland, Oregon, Podobnik (2011) documents that a mostly white and affluent residential population has actually moved to support the expansion of affordable housing there, reflecting a desire for more ethnic and income diversity. Examining the full spectrum of housing options, Trudeau and Kaplan (2016) find that New Urbanism projects host populations that are as diverse, if not more diverse, than other nearby neighborhoods that were developed at the same time. It is clear that some approaches to the movement perform better than others in creating opportunities for a diverse mix of people to live in the same place. Acknowledging such variation can help explain why some see New Urbanism as providing a development strategy that can, under the right circumstances, promote neighborhood revitalization and resist gentrification (Trudeau and Kaplan 2016; Bohl 2000). To this end, I now turn to discuss the conditions under which New Urbanist neighborhoods incorporate affordable housing in substantive ways and thereby advance social equity.

Analyzing social equity in New Urbanism

Using a typology of New Urbanist neighborhoods that I describe elsewhere (Trudeau 2013b), I explore how the development of different types of New Urbanist neighborhoods relate to the incorporation of affordable housing. The typology identifies three types that are differentiated by their size, density, mix of nonresidential land uses and housing types, and location within metropolitan areas. Moore's (2010) examination of divergent forms of New Urbanism in Toronto shows how an array of actors, including design firms, government planners, public officials, real estate developers, urban development consultants, banks, and philanthropic foundations, among others, come together to form a *development community*. In her work, different forms of New Urbanist neighborhoods emerge through the ways that development communities interpret New Urbanist ideas and translate them into practice in specific regulatory and ideological contexts to achieve particular ends. I therefore use the different types of New Urbanism neighborhoods as a proxy to select differently situated development communities and examine the extent to which they incorporate affordable housing in the development of New Urbanism projects. In defining affordable housing, I follow HUD's (2008) approach, which counts housing as affordable to low-income households if they earn less than 60 percent of the Area Median Income spend no more than 30 percent of their annual income on housing costs.

I selected three metropolitan areas to study because all types of New Urbanism neighborhoods appeared in each of the areas. This allows me to examine variation or consistency in the ways that differently situated development communities operate within a single political economic context of the metropolitan area. While all three metro areas promote sustainable development through policy, it is worth acknowledging some of the differences between them.

Minneapolis-St. Paul has a sophisticated regional planning apparatus that promotes the creation of compact, transit-oriented neighborhoods as well as affordable housing. New Urbanism in this metro area is thus explicitly connected to affordable housing policy through incentives (Trudeau 2016). In Denver, there is greater focus on the compact urban design principles of the movement, while concern about affordable housing has not been tied to New Urbanism in either the discourse or implementation (Ratner and Goetz 2013). Austin stands out because the sustainable development agenda there is explicitly tied to New Urbanism, connecting it with both environmental and social equity concerns. Further, the city government has been active in generating affordable housing generally, and has tied these efforts to the development of New Urbanism neighborhoods (Lopez 2006; McCann 2003).

I conducted interviews with individuals representing different actors in the development communities of each of the nine projects I studied. A list of these projects is provided in Table 15.1, which includes details about affordable housing as well as the distinct type of New Urbanism project it represents. I used the interviews to understand the interests and motivations of different actors and how these shaped and were shaped by the regulatory and ideological contexts in which development communities operated. In each case, I spoke with public and private sector actors who were stakeholders in the project's development process. In several cases, I met with multiple sets of actors in each sector. For instance, in the case of Belmar, I interviewed the planning director and mayor who shepherded the project through the design and development process. I met with representatives from the firm hired as the master developer for the project as well as the project's architect. I also interviewed a resident who participated in the community input processes for the project's vision. In total, I conducted 54 interviews across all nine projects. I also collected planning documents and articles published in the popular press for each project.

I use planning documents and interviews to assemble a narrative about the development of each New Urbanist project. Each narrative speaks to the project's origins and development process, but also the goals of the project, how the development community works to realize them, and how ideological and regulatory contexts matter. The information in Table 15.1 confirms an earlier point: there are New Urbanist projects that incorporate significant amounts of affordable housing as well as projects that exclude this altogether. I focus here on sharing abstractions about how and why projects incorporate affordable housing – a point that is

TABLE 15.1 Projects included in the study

Project name	Metropolitan area	% of total units that are affordable housing	Type of New Urbanism neighborhood
Cedar Park Township	Austin	0	Hybrid
The Triangle Square	Austin	0	Dense
Mueller Redevelopment	Austin	25	Mainstream
Bradburn	Denver	0	Hybrid
Belmar	Denver	0	Dense
Lowry Redevelopment	Denver	11	Mainstream
Heritage Park	Minneapolis	55	Hybrid
Heart of the City	Minneapolis	35	Dense
Clover Ridge	Minneapolis	18	Mainstream

underdeveloped in the literature – and discuss the significance of these for efforts working to resist eco-gentrification. This emphasis is enhanced by consideration of why affordable housing is excluded in the development process.

The exclusion and marginalization of affordable housing

The literature exploring why development of master planned projects fails to include affordable housing has highlighted several explanations. First, real estate developers often balk at incorporating affordable housing into market rate projects because they see these as either too costly to provide or incongruous with the fast-paced rhythm of speculative investment (Talen 2010). Even nonprofit developers note how much time it takes to assemble the necessary capital, through grants and subsidies, to construct affordable housing complexes (Sarmiento and Sims 2015). This underscores how slowly the affordable housing development process unfolds and why there may be a lack of interest from market-oriented developers. Second, outside support or a mandate to include affordable housing may be lacking from the development equation. Planners and other social equity advocates frequently note that affordable housing is absent because of a lack of financial incentives or regulatory allowances that could help developers adjust the costs of land and con-structing housing for lower-income groups (Szibbo 2016; Garde 2006). Without providing a mix of appropriate carrots (e.g., tax credits, development fee-waivers) and sticks (e.g., inclusionary zoning ordinances), developers will not be compelled to incorporate affordable housing (Garde 2016). Finally, public opposition to affordable housing in the form of NIMBYism ("Not In My Backyard") may also affect the calculus of development communities as such efforts can raise the costs – and risks – of incorporating affordable housing into a project (Galster et al. 2003).

The projects in this study that do not incorporate affordable housing can be explained primarily through the second point: a lack of regulatory support. For instance, in suburban Denver, the City of Westminster, Colorado agreed to the development of Bradburn, a New Urbanist neighborhood, primarily because the compact footprint and aesthetically pleasing design would help to maximize the taxable value of developable land, which is limited in the city. The developer likewise sought out the opportunity in order to build commercial property in a high-growth area that would retain value over the long term. In pursuing these goals, neither the city nor the developer took an interest in the affordable housing concerns that are codified in the New Urbanism. Instead, emphasis was on creating a denser landscape that was culturally distinctive for its resonance with a green growth agenda. A subtly different process was at work in another suburban Denver project. The develop-ment of Belmar in Lakewood, Colorado, further illustrates how New Urbanist design was used to assuage the concerns that residents expressed about the density represented in a plan to create a "new downtown." The City of Lakewood and the master developer drew on New Urbanism for the design of Belmar in order to create a new narrative for the suburb as an up-and-coming place that is inviting to environmentally conscious members of the creative class. This focus helped mute

"Not In My Back Yard" (NIMBY) sentiment. It also rationalized the decision to turn down a proposal to locate an affordable housing project in Belmar. Discussing the decision to decline the project, the developer explained, "that would send the message that [Lakewood] is a place that's declined and that this is the kind of housing that you can expect."

These cases illustrate a broader point: in the absence of a policy expectation for incorporating affordable housing, New Urbanism projects do not compel its incorporation, even though it is a tenet of the movement. Mayo and Ellis (2009) offer that a lack of patient capital is one of the primary reasons why equity drops out of the sustainable development picture. Patient capital refers to a type of financial resource in speculative investment that either expects returns to be realized over an extended time frame or looks to generate returns that are not financial in nature. Mayo and Ellis thus theorize that if more patient forms of capital were involved in the development of New Urbanism projects, these would achieve better results in promoting social equity in general, and affordable housing in particular. In this view, the involvement of government and non-profit real estate developers, and use of strategies like community land trusts and density bonuses help because they incorporate measures that reconfigure the calculus of real estate development. They direct development it toward equitable ends or enable equity by freeing development from the short-term expectations of speculative investment. I advance this argument by discussing the development processes that illustrate the importance of patient capital in cultivating a substantive commitment to social equity.

Making space for equity

I identify two generalizations about how sustainable urban development processes work to make space for social equity. First, patient capital is a necessary resource to promote equity in sustainable development. Second, social equity needs to be championed by actors in a given development community. I expand on these points in turn.

Patient capital is a key component in projects that advance equity. Patient capital materializes in a number of forms, but a consistent component across these variations is a capacity to expand the timeframe and/or the expectations of what investment should yield. This appears in some projects through policy requirements, such as inclusionary zoning ordinances (e.g., Lowry), or through market-based inducements, such as fee-waivers and tax credits (e.g., Mueller). Other projects incorporated affordable housing because governments and public housing authorities worked to locate the development of these institutions' investment in affordable housing within New Urbanism projects (e.g., Heart of the City), or worked with nonprofit affordable housing developers to create affordable housing on site (e.g., Clover Ridge). Municipal governments also worked to create community land trusts to provide affordable housing (e.g., Mueller, Clover Ridge). Finally, a patient approach to development emerges when development communities adopt a different relationship with land.

Development communities can elect to hold onto land, letting it remain undeveloped, for relatively long periods of time. For instance, the City of Austin metes out relatively small subdivisions of land to the master developer at Mueller so that it can be developed rapidly and according to plans that call for 25 percent of all units to be affordable housing. While not all development communities are able to use land banking, city governments can play an important role in fostering relationships with land that exceed speculative logics.

The way that development communities frame the goal of developing affordable housing can also contribute to a different way of evaluating return on investment. City government officials in Clover Ridge, for instance, framed affordable housing as "workforce housing," thus making the case that it is necessary to provide housing opportunities for people who are essential for the local economy to function, but unable to afford market-rate housing in the locality. Key to such an approach is that it does not seek immediate and quantifiable financial returns, but instead sees value over the long term in making space for people with lower incomes whose labor is vital to the overall health of a local economy. This approach creates an opening for social equity interests to be seen as necessary for the success of the project.

The presence of patient capital in development may be a necessary resource, but it alone is not sufficient to the task of promoting social equity. Leadership is also necessary to work through NIMBY-like opposition or hesitation from impatient capital interests. Indeed, as Campbell (1996) points out, sustainable development faces multiple tensions by virtue of the potential conflicts involved in balancing economic, environmental, and social interests. This balancing act is frequently performed on just the first two of these pillars. Social equity is often avoided and written off as infeasible or impractical. Consequently, equity needs to be championed by an actor playing a significant part in the visioning and development process.

This can happen in several ways. Planners can fashion a narrative about affordable housing as vital infrastructure. Development communities can also play an influential role in preparing citizens to accept the incorporation of affordable housing in a project. In many cases, however, the barriers to incorporating affordable housing come from capital and not from a resistant citizenry. In such cases, leadership must attend to a different set of concerns.

One of the principal problems that champions for social equity face is reluctance for capital to participate in development. Inasmuch as a steadfast commitment to equity from at least one actor in the development community is a necessary component for the incorporation of affordable housing in a project, the realization of such a commitment is also contingent on cooperation from private developers. In all cases examined, the ability of more patient capital to make space for affordable housing was made possible by the participation of developers. In many cases, developers agreed to participate in building a project because local governments worked with them to find ways in which developers could support equity *and* make a profit. In Mueller, for instance, this occurred through the City of Austin granting specific builders a minimum number of buildings they could construct, which enabled profits to accumulate through an economy of scale. In another case, the City of Burnsville agreed to use Tax Increment Financing to develop amenities, including a central park and a performing arts complex, which served to reduce the level of perceived risk among developers and encouraged them to move ahead with developing according to the mixed-income housing plans for Heart of the City. In several cases, cities and developers also pushed for design standards that regulate the visual and material variation of the built environment in a project such that the affordable and subsidized housing look comparable to (and support the value of) market-rate housing in the project.

These experiences attest to the idea that proponents of social equity labor diligently and deliberately to orchestrate circumstances in which development communities make a substantive commitment to social equity. As Stone (1993, 25) points out, leadership "is about developing a larger view of what might be and then crafting the arrangements that advance that vision." To accomplish this, leaders must "weave material and nonmaterial incentives together and ... combine achievable small purposes in a way that contributes to a large purpose." Thus, while actors who seek to incorporate affordable housing in sustainable urban development will undoubtedly need to marshal material resources and use these to leverage "patience" in the development process, they also need to inspire participation and consent among other participants in the development process. On the one hand, this entails generating a narrative about how affordable housing contributes to a larger vision for well-being. On the other hand, this requires sensitivity for understanding the inhibitions of investors and working carefully to cultivate a different perspective through which development communities can realize the benefits of financial investment. Bringing capital to such a vista may require public investment in amenities. Yet it can also be accomplished through measures that dispel uncertainty in the market, such as building consensus among citizens about the shape that development ought to take.

Conclusion: Planning for equity from the start

This analysis helps to build theory about the processes through which social equity can be incorporated substantively into sustainable urban development projects. Through case study research on the New Urbanism, I find that sustainable urban development communities that make space for social equity are able to do so through three interlocking practices that form a distinct development strategy. First, development communities must generate a vision for development that makes the incorporation of social equity – affordable housing, in this case – a necessary part of realizing success in the project. In the projects that are exemplary on this point, affordable housing was framed as vital infrastructure. Second, citizens and capital must accept this vision, if not support it. The actions of local government agencies are normally pivotal in overcoming NIMBYism and concerns about risk in generating such support and acceptance. Moreover, as Campbell (1996) points out, local governments play an important role in development communities that are able to resolve the potential conflicts that arise in promoting economic, environmental, and social interests. Yet, it is possible that other institutions could play such a role. Third, development communities must also mobilize the participation of patient capital in the development process as it allows a more intentional approach that supports equity interests. Some or all of these practices were notably absent from the projects in which affordable housing was left out or marginalized. Thus, comparison of projects with divergent outcomes lends support to the idea that there is a more general process through which development communities can foster social equity. At the same time, there are place-based contingencies that affect whether such processes would unfold through New Urbanist development in a particular locale.

While this chapter has focused on New Urbanist projects, its conclusions apply more broadly to neighborhood-scale sustainable urban development efforts. This is because New Urbanism does not compel development communities to incorporate social equity into development practice. Rather, New Urbanism merely offers a framework for already-existing aspirations for social equity to connect with green urban design. Indeed, social equity is incorporated into New Urbanist projects because of a constitutive outside where leaders mobilize resources to realize equity goals. This research thus points to the potential of sustainable development initiatives to provide a greening program that also includes lower-income households and others in socially and economically precarious positions. To this end, creating a vision for sustainable communities that includes marginalized populations and gathers patient capital in support of the vision are crucial steps that can help realize the potential of New Urbanism to serve as a resource for just green enough strategies.

References

Berke, P. 2008. The evolution of green community planning, scholarship, and practice. *Journal of the American Planning Association* 74(4): 392–407.

Bohl, C. 2000. New Urbanism and the city: potential applications and implications for distressed inner-city neighborhoods. *Housing Policy Debate* 11(4): 761–801.

Bunce, S. 2009. Developing sustainability: sustainability policy and gentrification on Toronto's waterfront. *Local Environment* 4(7): 651–667.

Campbell, S. 1996. Green cities, growing cities, just cities: urban planning and the contradictions of sustainable development. *Journal of the American Planning Association* 62(3): 296–312.

Congress for the New Urbanism, US Green Building Council, and National Resource Defense Council. 2007. *Pilot version: LEED for neighborhood development rating system.* http://www.cnu.org/leednd.

Checker, M. 2011. Wiped out by the "Greenwave": environmental gentrification and the paradoxical politics of urban sustainability. *City & Society* 23(2): 210–229.

Curran, W. & Hamilton, T. 2012. Just green enough: contesting environmental Gentrification in Greenpoint, Brooklyn. *Local Environment* 17(9): 1027–1042.

Dale, A. & Newman, L. 2009. Sustainable development for some: green urban Development and affordability. *Local Environment* 14(7): 669–681.

Day, K. 2003. New Urbanism and the challenges of designing for diversity. *Journal of Planning Education and Research* 23(1): 83–95.

Falconer Al-Hindi, K. & Till, K. 2001. (Re)placing the New Urbanism debates: toward an interdisciplinary research agenda. *Urban Geography* 22(3): 189–201.

Fraser, J., Burns, A., Bazuin, J., & Oakley, D. 2013. HOPE VI, colonization and the production of difference. *Urban Affairs Review* 49(4): 525–556.

Galster, G., Tatian, P., Santiago, A., Pettit, K., & Smith, R. 2003. *Why not in my backyard?: Neighborhood impacts of deconcentrating assisted housing*, Center for Urban Policy Research, New Brunswick, NJ.

Garde, A. 2004. New Urbanism as sustainable growth? A supply side story and its implications for public policy. *Journal of Planning Education and Research* 24(2): 154–170.

Garde, A. 2006. Designing and developing New Urbanist projects in the United States: insights and implications. *Journal of Urban Design* 11(1): 33–54.

Garde, A. 2016. Affordable by design? Inclusionary housing insights from Southern California. *Journal of Planning Education and Research* 36(1): 16–31.

González, E. & Lejano, R. 2009. New Urbanism and the barrio. *Environment and Planning A* 41(12): 2946–2963.

González, E., Sarmiento, C., Urzua, A., & Luévano, S. 2012. The grassroots and New Urbanism: a case from a Southern California Latino Community. *Journal of Urbanism* 5(2–3): 219–239.

Grant, J. 2006. *Planning the Good Community: New Urbanism in Planning and Practice*, Routledge, London.

Grant, J. 2007. Two sides of the same coin? New Urbanism and gated communities. *Housing Policy Debate* 18(3): 481–501.

Hanlon, J. 2012. Beyond HOPE VI: demolition/disposition and the uncertain future of public housing in the U.S. *Journal of Housing and the Built Environment* 27(3): 373–388.

Hanlon, B. 2015. Beyond sprawl: Social sustainability and reinvestment in Baltimore's Suburbs, in K. Anacker (ed.), *The New American Suburb: Poverty, Race and the Economic Crisis*, pp. 133–152, Ashgate Publishing Company, Burlington, VT.

Hirt, S. 2009. Premodern, modern, postmodern? Placing new urbanism into a historical perspective. *Journal of Planning History* 8(3): 248–273.

Keil, R. 2007. Sustaining modernity, modernizing nature: The environmental crisis and the survival of capitalism, in R. Krueger & D. Gibbs (eds), *The Sustainable Development Paradox: Urban political economy in the US and Europe*, pp. 41–65, Guilford Press, New York.

Kenny, J. & Zimmerman, J. 2004. Constructing the "Genuine American City": neo traditionalism, New Urbanism and neo-liberalism in the remaking of downtown Milwaukee. *Cultural Geographies* 11(1): 74–98.

Leccese, M. & McCormick, K. (eds) 2000. *Charter of the New Urbanism*, McGraw-Hill, New York.

Lopez, S. 2006. Comprehensive planning in Austin, Texas: one neighborhood at a time. *Planning Forum* 12: 52–79.

McCann, E. 2003. Framing space and time in the city: urban policy and the politics of Spatial and temporal scale. *Journal of Urban Affairs* 25(2): 159–178.

Marcuse, P. 2000. The New Urbanism: the dangers so far. *DISP* 36(140): 4–6.

Mayo, J. & Ellis, C. 2009. Capitalist dynamics and New Urbanist principles: junctures And disjunctures in project development. *Journal of Urbanism* 2(3): 237–257.

Moore, S. 2007. *Alternative Routes to the Sustainable City: Austin, Curitiba, and Frankfurt*, Lexington Books, Lanham, MD.

Moore, S. 2010. "More Toronto, naturally" but "too strange for Orangeville": de-universalizing New Urbanism in greater Toronto. *Cities* 27(2): 103–113.

Podobnik, B. 2011. Assessing the social and environmental achievements of new urbanism: evidence from Portland, Oregon. *Journal of Urbanism* 4(2): 105–126.

Quastel, N. 2009. Political ecologies of gentrification. *Urban Geography* 30(7): 694–725.

Ratner, K. & Goetz, A. 2013. The reshaping of land use and urban form in Denver Through transit-oriented development. *Cities* 30(1): 31–46.

Saha, D. & Paterson, R. 2008. Local government efforts to promote the "Three Es" of sustainable development. *Journal of Planning Education and Research* 28(1): 21–37.

Sarmiento, C. & Sims, J. 2015. Facades of equitable development: Santa Ana and the affordable housing complex. *Journal of planning Education and Research* 35(3): 323–336.

Smith, N. 2002. New globalism, New Urbanism: gentrification as global urban strategy. *Antipode* 34(3): 427–450.

Stone, C. 1993. Urban regimes and the capacity to govern: a political economy approach. *Journal of Urban Affairs* 15(1): 1–28.

Szibbo, N. 2016. Lessons for LEED for neighborhood development, social equity, and affordable housing. *Journal of the American Planning Association* 82(1): 37–49.

Talen, E. 2010. Affordability in New Urbanist Development: principle, practice, and strategy. *Journal of Urban Affairs* 32(4): 489–510.

Talen, E. (ed.) 2013. *Charter of the New Urbanism*, McGraw-Hill, New York.

Temenos, C. & McCann, E. 2012. The local politics of policy mobility: learning, persuasion, and the production of a municipal sustainability fix. *Environment and Planning A* 44(6): 1389–1406.

Till, K. 2001. New urbanism and nature: green marketing and the neotraditional community. *Urban Geography* 22(3): 220–248.

Trudeau, D. 2013a. New Urbanism as sustainable development? *Geography Compass* 7(6): 435–448.

Trudeau, D. 2013b. A typology of New Urbanism neighborhoods. *Journal of Urbanism* 6(2): 113–138.

Trudeau, D. 2016. Tracing New Urbanism's suburban intervention. *Journal of Planning and Education Research*. [Published online October 6, 2016.] https://doi.org/10.1177/0739456X16671996

Trudeau, D. & Kaplan, J. 2016. Is there diversity in the New Urbanism? Analyzing the demographic characteristics of New Urbanist neighborhoods in the United States. *Urban Geography* 37(3): 458–482.

Tu, C. & Eppli, M. 2001. An empirical examination of traditional neighborhood development. *Real Estate Economics* 29(3): 485–501.

Veninga, C. 2004. Spatial prescriptions and social realities: New Urbanism and the production of Northwest Landing. *Urban Geography* 25(5): 458–482.

Wolch, J., Byrne, J., & Newell, J. 2014. Urban green space, public health, and Environmental justice: the challenge of making cities 'just green enough'. *Landscape and Urban Planning* 125: 234–244.

Zimmerman, J. 2001. The nature of urbanism and the New Urbanist frontier: sustainable development, or defense of the suburban dream. *Urban Geography* 22(3): 249–267.

INDEX

Note: page numbers in italic type refer to Figures; those in bold type refer to Tables.